"Like the ancient desert monastics whose wisdom tradition is 'a stream that surrounds him on all sides,' Benoît Standaert is a teacher worthy of the spiritual seeker who asks, 'Give me a word.' Each word in his alphabet connotes a world of meaning. There is rich food for the mind and the soul in these pages."

—Rev. Rachel M. Srubas, OblSB
Author of *City of Prayer: Forty Days with Desert Christians* and *The Girl Got Up: A Cruciform Memoir*

"This book is a spiritual gem. Written in the tradition of the Desert Father's transformation into God, Fr. Standaert uses each letter of the alphabet to designate spiritual practices to guide us in the art of living. What is more needed in our society today than such an art? As we make our way through this alphabet from Abba to Zero we find ourselves entering a world created from the wisdom of many ancient and modern traditions. We learn that each letter interacts with the one next to it just as monastics do in community. This type of interaction of word and person is true *lectio divina* and awakens the heart or core of our being where we find silence as the language of heaven."

—Fr. Brendan Freeman
Author of *Come and See: A Guide to Monastic Living*

"Reading Benoît Standaert's new book *Spirituality* is like having coffee with the prophet Isaiah. This longtime monk's 'alphabet of spiritual practices,' as the subtitle has it, welcomes us to the table with saints, desert fathers, ancient rabbis, Zen masters, and Hindu wise men. I have not been so delighted with a conversation in years, nor learned so much from a single book. Highly recommended."

—Paula Huston
Author of *One Ordinary Sunday: A Meditation on the Mystery of the Mass*

Spirituality An Art of Living

A Monk's Alphabet of Spiritual Practices

Benoît Standaert, OSB

Translated from the Dutch by Rudolf V. Van Puymbroeck

LITURGICAL PRESS
Collegeville, Minnesota

www.litpress.org

Cover design by Ann Blattner. Illustration by Frank Kacmarcik, OblSB.

Original title: Spiritualiteit als levenskunst: alfabet van een monnik.

Translated from the Dutch language. www. lannoo.com.

1 2 3 4 5 6 7 8 9

Library of Congress Cataloging-in-Publication Data

Names: Standaert, Benoît, author.
Title: Spirituality : an art of living : a monk's alphabet of spiritual practices / Benoît Standaert ; translated from the Dutch by Rudolf V. Van Puymbroeck.
Other titles: Spiritualiteit als levenskunst. English
Description: Collegeville, Minnesota : Liturgical Press, 2018.
Identifiers: LCCN 2017045164 (print) | LCCN 2017030333 (ebook) | ISBN 9780814645413 (ebook) | ISBN 9780814645178
Subjects: LCSH: Spiritual life—Christianity—Dictionaries.
Classification: LCC BV4501.3 (print) | LCC BV4501.3 .S72813 2018 (ebook) | DDC 248—dc23
LC record available at https://lccn.loc.gov/2017045164

CONTENTS

Translator's Note and Acknowledgments xi

Preface xiii

A

Abba 3

Adoration 5

Anawim: The Poor and the Humble 7

Aspiration 10

B

Beginning 13

Blessing 15

Breathing 17

C

Chastity 23

Confession of Sins 25

Conversation 30

Culture 32

D

Dancing 35

Death 36

Detachment 41

Dhikr 43

Dialogue 45

Dreaming 47

E

Eating 59

Ejaculatory Prayers 62

Emptiness 67

F

Fasting 73
Fear of the Lord 80
Feasting 86
Fight 90
Forgiveness, Reconciliation 93
Forms and Formlessness 101
Friendship 103
Fruitfulness 108

G

God 113
Gratitude 115
Gratuitous 118
Growing 120

H

Hallowing 125
Heart 129
Hospitality 134
Humility 141

I

Icons 149
Intercessory Prayers 152

J

Jesus and the Jesus Prayer 159
Jubilee, Jubilation 164
Judge (Do Not) 169

K

Keeping Silent 175

L

Lament, Lamenting 179
Lectio Divina or Scripture Reading 181
Listening 188

Love for One's Enemies 191

M

Mary, Marian Spirituality 203
Measure and Beyond Measure 205
Meditation 207
Memory 215
Mercy 224
Mindfulness 229
Mourning 231
Music 234

N

Name, To Name 239
Night Vigil 245

O

One, the One 253

P

Paradox 257
Patience 264
Peace 268
Pilgrimage 272
Poustinia 278
Praise, To Praise 281
Profession of Faith 284
Psalmody 287

Q

Quest 293

R

Reciprocity 297
Resurrection 299
Retreat 306
Rituals 308

S

Sabbath 313
Sacrament 317
Salmon, or Mocking Gravity 319
Serving 320
Sexuality 324
Simplicity 326
Sleeping 329
Smiling 333
Solidarity 335
Source 337
Spirit 339
Strategy 342
Sunday 345

T

Tears 353
Time and the Experience of Time 355
Tsimtsum 357

U

Unapparent Virtue 361

V

Visiting 367
Vulnerability 369

W

Walking 373
Weeping 375
Wisdom 377
Wonder 383
Wu Wei 385

X

X 393

Y
Yes-Amen 397
Yin and Yang 399
You as "You" 402

Z
Zero 407

Epilogue 409

TRANSLATOR'S NOTE AND ACKNOWLEDGMENTS

I ask the same indulgence of the reader as the anonymous author of the prologue to the Greek translation of the book of Sirach/Ecclesiasticus, who says,

> You are invited . . . to read [this work] with goodwill and attention, and to be indulgent in cases where, despite our diligent labor in translating, we may seem to have rendered some phrases imperfectly. For what was originally expressed in Hebrew does not have exactly the same sense when translated into another language. Not only this book, but even the Law itself, the Prophesies, and the rest of the books differ not a little when read in the original. (Sir Prol. 2)

While Fr. Standaert wrote in Dutch, he used Scripture and other sources written in Hebrew, Greek, Latin, French, and medieval Dutch. Rendering the author's intent in light of the different languages of his sources while remaining compliant with approved and respected English-language usage proved to be a significant challenge.

This translation uses the New Revised Standard Version of the Holy Bible published by the Division of Christian Education of the National Council of the Churches of Christ in the United States of America (1989). There are some exceptions to the rule indicated by footnote from the New Jerusalem Bible, Reader's Edition (New York: Doubleday, 1990), the Saint Joseph "New Catholic Edition" of the Holy Bible (1962), the Holy Bible in the Original King James Version (Gordonsville, TN: Dugan, 1988), and *The Revised Grail Psalms* (Collegeville, MN: Liturgical Press, 2012).

My source for quotations from the Rule of Benedict is Terrence G. Kardong, *Benedict's Rule: A Translation and Commentary* (Collegeville, MN: Liturgical Press, 1996).

All excerpts of poetry quoted by Fr. Standaert are my original translations.

I owe a great deal of thanks to David Gibson of Reston, Virginia, for reading and correcting the manuscript over the course of the two years it took to complete this project. David was the founding editor of *Origins*, a documentary service of Catholic News Service, and served on the CNS editorial staff for thirty-seven years.

This translation was born out of a desire to help those for whom medicines and medical science fail. Fr. Standaert's work was immensely helpful to Bieke Vandekerckhove, author of *The Taste of Silence: How I Came to Live with Myself*, translated by Rudolf V. Van Puymbroeck (Collegeville, MN: Liturgical Press, 2015). As she battled ALS for more than twenty-six years, the monastic wisdom shared by Fr. Standaert, both in his writings and as a friend, became for her an indispensable source of nourishment and support.

The Spirit-filled life has its own mysterious way of leading us to beauty, kindness, and peace. One does not need to have a terminal medical condition to seek its blessings.

Rudolf V. Van Puymbroeck
January 31, 2017

PREFACE

A Shift

Spirituality exerts a powerful gravitational pull these days: everybody feels its attraction. We are witnessing a marked shift in the landscape of thinking and searching. "Philosophy has become the art of living. Theology is becoming spirituality," as Dutch philosopher Ilse Bulhof put it a few years ago. The philosophical works of the popular German author Wilhelm Schmid have words to the same effect: they constitute a veritable program, as is also true of his *A Philosophy of the Art of Living: The Way to a Beautiful Life.* He argues that this turning of the tide is nothing but a return to what philosophy has always been about, even though we sort of lost sight of it. Leaving Michel Foucault behind, he goes back to Montaigne and Seneca. In our day philosophy is rediscovering its roots in the wisdom traditions of humanity.

We see a similar evolution taking place in theological literature. We may wonder at the early and continuing popularity of people like Anselm Grün, Henri Nouwen, and Thomas Merton, but they all went through a process that led them to a particular kind of wisdom, a wisdom that is close to the heart and the body, close to the original forms of freedom and un-freedom. Indeed, all three men reach back to the wisdom of the Desert Fathers—several hundred monks of the fourth and fifth centuries in Egypt who, in the desert of Scetis, experimented with a way of mastery and passed it on through sayings and aphorisms. In Christian thought they continue the tradition of Seneca and his Stoic colleagues as well as the Epicureans. They ruminate on the words of Jesus and Paul, Ecclesiastes and Solomon, and they forge new proverbs, incisive and liberating, disarmingly human in their kindness and in their finely-honed sense of what may offend or what can be affirmed.[1]

1. It is appropriate to refer here to a kind of interreligious bible of all wisdoms, published by Bayard Presse in 2012, *Le livre des sagesses. L'aventure spirituelle de l'humanité* (*The Book of Wisdoms: Mankind's Spiritual Adventure*). The publication of such a book says a lot about the needs of our generation. For the Desert Fathers, see *Wijsheid uit de Woestijn. 365 dagen met de woestijnvaders* (*Wisdom from the Desert: 365 Days with the Desert Fathers*), collected and introduced by B. Standaert (Tielt: Lannoo, 2005).

Transformation

I myself stand in this tradition. It is a stream that surrounds me on all sides; it permeates me and impregnates me. I keep receiving and cannot but pass it on. In the encounter with other cultures, at first African and in later years those of Eastern origin (Chinese traditions, Buddhism and Taoism), I found affirmation. Interestingly, wisdom turns out to be much more international, and more capable of intercultural identity, than science or technology.

Spirituality blossoms as an art of living, as wisdom to live by. Spirituality is, at least for me, the art of living. More precisely, spirituality is the cultivation of an art of living that through the application of concrete practices gradually works a transforming effect. Spirituality, thus, seeks transformation; we are dealing with a process. The list of these practices is ultimately indefinite, but the direction is constant: the transformative process leads to freedom, to beauty—to "the freedom of the glory of the children of God," in Paul's unforgettable formulation (Rom 8:21).

Doing Something Feasible Well

A Buddhist aphorism may illuminate our perspective. Here is a saying by Rikyu, a Japanese Zen master from the sixteenth century: "Life is impossible. Let's do something feasible well. Maybe then life is possible after all?"

"Life is impossible"—this pronouncement reminds us immediately of the first truth of Gautama, the Buddha. Everything is *dukkha*, he said, "suffering," transitory, inconsistent. Life is not doable. It is impossible.

"Let us do something feasible well"—actually Rikyu was thinking very concretely about the offering of a cup of tea to a guest: let's do it well. Whoever has the good fortune to attend a Japanese tea ceremony—the *cha no yu*—discovers a ritual of perfection, entirely focused on the guest. Everything about it bespeaks harmony, purity, respect, and peace. Rikyu regulated its every aspect, even to the smallest details. After you drink the tea, life is different, although nothing has changed.

Other Japanese arts are based on the same principle, such as the arrangement of flowers in a vase: nothing more, nothing less. You can bend a bow, fit an arrow to the cord, and then cleanly and with detachment swiftly release cord and arrow. Hit the bull's eye: simplicity, concentration of body and mind, creation of force or, better, drawing of force, aim. Everything is folded into oneness, without gimmicks, without words. No prior pretenses, no extra tricks. The movement is pure, as transparent as a ritual. That's the way "to do something feasible well."

Maybe we can take on life, in all its cluttered complexity, if we start with such simple feasible things, executed with perfection. The fundamental questions about life, about the practicality of human existence, the humanity of the person, and the humanization of life on our small blue planet, are still there. But the old wisdom of philosopher Karl Jaspers remains applicable: "This is certain: the world as it is must change. Otherwise we shall all perish. But the premise for this wholesale change is that I—here and now—change. Only then will there be a future: the world will change."

There is a complementary Eastern wisdom saying, in which we have perhaps less confidence: "He who in his room thinks the right thought is heard ten thousand miles away." Both pieces of wisdom are precious. I myself am responsible for the rightness of my life here and now. And if I do it right, I can stop worrying: the whole world will benefit, even the fish in the ocean and the stars in the sky.

Alphabet of Practices

John Climacus, a seventh-century monk who lived high up on Mount Sinai, wrote a book of instruction called *The Ladder.* He gave his ladder thirty steps, the number that in his view corresponded to the thirty years of Jesus' hidden life, and for every step he discussed a virtue, something that accords life depth and freedom. His instruction was aimed at monks and at anybody with an interest in monastic life.

The present work unfolds as a complete alphabet, in which each letter supplies one or more practices. It comprises ninety-nine different practices or entrance gates to the spiritual life—just short of one hundred! The one gate that is missing exists beyond the last page, in life itself, and is different for everybody—unpredictable, a true surprise!

The book is addressed to believers and nonbelievers, the churched and the unchurched. Much comes out of the monastic tradition: this is my life. But is there not a monk in everybody or, in the intuition of Raimon Panikkar, is the monk not an archetype, present everywhere?

Monasteries are going through a deep winter these days: few candidates have shown up at our abbey in the last twenty-five years. But the intense longing for inner calm, mental freedom, artful living, and spirituality is felt by just about everybody, which demonstrates that there is great potential receptivity to the monastic inheritance. At least, that is my conviction. Thus, this book addresses itself to all who recognize that yearning in themselves and who are willing to go looking. Passing on the ancient monastic treasure to lay people is my purpose for this book.

More than half of the entries have been published in a more extensive treatment over the last thirty years in a thematic issue of *Heiliging* (*Hallowing*).[2] Here all materials are merged into a modest handbook that, above all, strives to be of practical use.

Spirituality as Art of Living

By applying ourselves to mastering a set of concrete practices we fashion an art of living. One practice influences another, just like the manner in which we eat affects the way we sleep and vice versa. A person who fasts needs less sleep, which makes it easier to keep an hour's vigil in the night. People trained in silent meditation increase their powers of concentration and waste less energy in carrying out other tasks. Sitting behind the steering wheel of a car for hours on end is experienced differently by somebody who has learned to sit still in meditation, or who regularly reads a Bible passage in the morning, or whose memory is filled with verses from the psalms.

The different letters of the alphabet interact with each other and gradually build up a complete language system. After the discussion of each word, the reader will find references to other words, illustrating how the different practices fit together and form a philosophy of life.

Art of Living as Spirituality

One of the remarkable aspects of the art of living envisioned in this book is that while everything is grace, everything is also discipline—a central paradox. "Give your blood and receive the Spirit." This

2. The periodical review, *Heiliging* (*Hallowing*), was published by the monks of St. Andrew's Abbey (Sint-Andries Abdij) in Zevenkerken, Belgium, from 1950 to 2009. Fr. Benoît Standaert was the editor and a frequent contributor from 1978 to 2003 [translator's note].

aphorism of Abba Longinus summarizes the whole dynamic and the tension. By continually performing certain practices we arrive at a new realization: our practices don't confine us to ourselves. We discover that life is a gift and that it carries us.

For example, people who meditate in silence perceive the workings of the breath. And those who, in all stillness, then pay attention to their breathing notice how this pump is not driven by willpower. The transition from breathing out to breathing in happens automatically, as a vital pulse, a pure gift. Aware of this primordial gift we rejoice in the hidden hand of the Giver. Gratitude surrounds our respiration.

Art of living becomes spirituality: the practices turn into experience of the Spirit, available at every moment. The source of "an Other in me, more myself than I" wells up without interruption from the depths of the awakened heart.

The Empty Bowl

Once upon a time a Zen master received a guest at his monastery. The gentleman came from the city, he was a professor at the university and said he wanted to expand his knowledge of Zen Buddhism. The monk received him and, according to custom, offered tea. He poured hot water over the broken tealeaves in the bowl and filled it to the brim. He kept pouring: the water overflowed. . . . Observing this, the professor exclaimed: "Watch out! Don't you see that the bowl is full already?" "Indeed," said the master, who calmly put the teapot aside and continued: "What are you doing here? Your bowl is full and you ask me to pour you some more. First empty your bowl and then I'll be able to offer you something!"

These pages are written for all who approach life with an empty bowl or who are prepared to put some effort into emptying their head and their bowl.

Gratitude

This book is the fruit of many years: sun, rain, soil, and fertilizer were all necessary to bring it to fruition. Without the abbey of Zevenkerken, in whose soil I have been rooted for over forty years now, this fruit would never have seen the light of day. God only knows all I owe to certain wisdom figures or holy brothers, but also to instances of resistance and conflict: everything contributes to a life.

The final draft came about in the last year, at least in part thanks to the small Laura of Abba Poimen, a modest new monastic group that started a bit over a year ago.[3] Without the friendship and intense labor of the Laura's core leadership this book would still be slumbering in a very embryonic state. With gratitude I entrust this bottle to the ocean. I hope that this small, practical work may inspire many, both inside and outside the network of the Laura.

Where to Start?

With the "A" of "Abba"? With the "B" of "Beginning"? Or, perhaps, would you prefer to start with the "S" of "Strategy"? After all, the disadvantage of an alphabet is that there is no order other than the arbitrary sequence of letters, while experience teaches us that order is a key component in every art of living. So, "Strategy" could be an excellent start.

Regardless, at the end of every word under a letter you will find several references. In this manner our alphabet provides links to other letters and, like a dictionary, constitutes a complete language system. Each letter provides only a door or a window; all letters together give access to the living space of a grand spiritual home, an area with room to breathe and with place for many.

3. The Laura of Abba Poimen is a community of lay people who have introduced contemplative practices (including many described in this book) into their lives. They stay in touch mostly through electronic means but come together periodically for psalm vigils or other communal services. The name is derived from the *laura* (pronounced *lavra* in Greek), the "path" that connected the hermitages of Desert Fathers, of whom the kindly Abba Poimen is one of the best known. The first Laura was established under Fr. Standaert's leadership in Bruges, Belgium, in 2005. As of this writing, Lauras are operating in five cities in Belgium and one city in the Netherlands [translator's note].

A

ABBA

We start with *abba*, one of the most cherished prayer words in the Christian tradition. *Abba* is an Aramaic word. According to the passion narrative of Mark, Jesus used it to address his God and Father ("*Abba*, Father") during his agony in the garden. A few scholars, such as Joachim Jeremias, deem it of equal value to our "dad." Others disagree. In any case, the word reveals a familiarity with God: it indicates an awareness of a filial relationship and the experience of being accepted as a child in his house.

According to Paul, the only other author to use this Aramaic word, the word *abba* was well-known to the Christians in Galatia and Rome. Apparently it had been passed on to them from the beginning of their life in Christ. With that name they received the Spirit and acknowledged they were children of God, co-heirs of Christ (see Gal 4:6 and Rom 8:15). As the ritual of baptism was a death, a perishing in the water, together with Christ, so the new members received from that death a new breath of life, the Holy Spirit. That Spirit cried in them "*Abba!* Father!" and lent them the dignity of being "son" in the Son. That spirit of childhood signified freedom from all other forms of slavish subjugation.

As an invocation, *Abba* is indeed one of our most-beloved mantras or prayer words. A Portuguese nun who lived for twenty years (between 1980 and 2000) in a bricked-in hermitage near Bethlehem in Palestine passed on to her sisters, the nuns of the Emmanuel convent, her heart's prayer. It consisted of four words: "Sim, *Abba*, Jesus, Amor," translated as "Yes-Amen, *Abba*, Jesus, Love." With these four words—names of God—she prayed in her heart. She started with the affirmation, the free acceptance, the Marian moment of assent; then she addressed first the Father, in his bottomless, intimate closeness, then Jesus, who revealed the depths of the Father, and finally the Spirit of love, who connects all people and all things.

Jesus taught that we should not use *abba* or "father" for anybody on earth: "And call no one your father on earth, for you have one Father—the one in heaven" (Matt 23:9) and "you are all brothers" (Matt 23:8). By recognizing God as our Father, we show that we are aware of our common brotherhood. Blessed indeed are they who treat their neighbors, wherever they may come from, out of this singular recognition.

Even though Jesus expressly said "call no one your father on earth" (Matt 23:9) certain Christians addressed their spiritual leader with *Abba* or Father. This phenomenon surfaced with the first monks in Egypt at the end of the third century and beginning of the fourth. The commonly accepted salutation of a master by his student became *Abba* or *Apa* (Coptic).

Why is it that these men, who proudly practiced the gospel as literally as possible, ended up contradicting the letter of Scripture so flagrantly? Or is there, in fact, no contradiction at all? Contemporary masters from the monastic tradition explain that the same Spirit who, after we have been initiated in Christ, makes us exclaim *Abba!* also put the word *Abba* on the lips of the first monks when they engaged with their own spiritual teacher. Looking at the teacher, they recognized Christ, the revealer of the Father. Literally, they did not call any earthly person *Abba*: They greeted the heavenly Father in him who, in God's name, provided them with nourishment and enlightenment in their own search for the One.

To say *Abba* connects us with Jesus and with the deepest connection to Jesus' own source. In his Rule, Benedict pays attention to the title of the superior: "abbot." Benedict sees the prompting of the Spirit in it, the Spirit who moves us to invoke *Abba*. As he notes, there is an act of faith in this. In obedience to a superior and ultimately to each other, monks in community discover that precious milieu of freedom and surrender that Jesus revealed to us all.

See also: Aspirations, Ejaculatory Prayers, God, Jesus and the Jesus Prayer, Name, Spirit

ADORATION

"Just as a shadow is wiped out by the rising sun and disappears, so it is with the soul that reaches in prayer for the presence of the Most High" (after a saying from the Muslim tradition). "Everything becomes gift if we are able to prostrate ourselves" (after a Jewish *midrash*). "They who can adore cease to have worries" (after Francis of Assisi).

Adoration is one of the purest forms of life with the Holy One. Especially at night it comes about in simplicity and with force. In the night's stillness, adoration eventually becomes one continuous, wordless event. Adoration means that you acknowledge the Most High in his untouchable light full of diffidence and love. The soul becomes unified and hears within itself the plea of the poor psalmist: "Give me an undivided heart to revere your name" (Ps 86:11). Elizabeth of the Trinity exclaimed in one of her last notes:

> Adoration, ah! It's a word from heaven. In my view you can describe it as love's rapture: love annihilated by the beauty, by the power of the immeasurable grandeur of the Beloved. Love is overcome by a kind of powerlessness, in a complete, deep silence. It is of this silence that King David spoke when he said: "Silence is your praise." Yes, that is indeed the most beautiful song of praise, because it sings for all eternity in the lap of the tranquil Trinity. It is also "the final effort of the soul that overflows and has nothing more to say."[1]

Nowhere is the distance greater and the contact deeper than in adoration. Just as happened to the woman suffering from hemorrhages who was able, in the midst of the crowd, to touch the hem of his cloak in a gesture of faith and instantly felt in her body that her illness had left her, so the Holy One, the Most High, discerned in awe and trembling, touches the soul in its deepest intimacy.

In the most passionate forms of adoration, awe and love are no longer opposites. Diffidence and fervor are no longer distinguishable. John Cassian (ca. 400) speaks of "the prayer of fire" in which

1. Elizabeth of the Trinity, *La dernière retraite* (1906).

all discernible forms of prayer (grace, petition, intercession, praise) burn together.

To make time for just this one practice—kneeling with your whole being to let God be God—shows an awakened soul. This is the soul that takes to heart the Master's words: "Go into your room. . . . Strive first for the kingdom of God" (Matt 6:6, 33). "It is your face, O Lord, that I seek," prays the heart of the psalmist (Ps 27: 8). Or in the formulation of Bernard of Clairvaux: *facies informata formans*, meaning: God's face is without form, without traits, but those who seek it experience how it molds and reshapes the soul. In that fiery silence the heavenly Blacksmith forges his instruments to accord with his heart into instruments of peace and compassion.

See also: Confession of Faith, Gratitude, Meditation, Night Vigil

ANAWIM: THE POOR AND THE HUMBLE

An understanding of the *anawim* is slowly entering into the mainstream of our language, even into some religious education manuals. The *anawim* form a distinct group of pious individuals (*chassidim*), with their own spirituality, within the people of Israel after the exile. The book of Psalms may be considered as the clearest exponent of this spiritual movement. They call themselves "poor," and "attendants" or "servants of the LORD," and are connected with each other in a worldwide community (see Ps 113:2 and Mal 1:11: "From the rising of the sun to its setting").

They are anything but downcast; on the contrary, they show great fighting spirit. They remember and recognize themselves in Moses and Elijah, in Jeremiah and in the later chapters of Isaiah (40–66). As lovers they constantly speak the Name (Lord, YHWH) and meditate on God day and night: "Merciful, charitable, patient, benevolent, full of compassion" (for Moses as a distant source, see Exod 34:6-7). In their mouths we find "the praise of God," in their hands "a two-edged sword"—the Word of God (see Ps 149:5-6).

What used to be a term of abuse, indicating a humiliating category in the social order, gradually became, under the influence of the great prophets Amos and Jeremiah, and also Zephaniah, a noble title worn with pride. They are poor in everything, except that they know the Lord and are known by Him!

All characters presented by Luke at the start of his gospel come from this milieu: Zacharias and Elisabeth, Joseph and Mary, Simeon and Anna. At the circumcision and naming of his son, Zacharias sings a totally new psalm. While visiting her niece Elisabeth, Mary exults in the *Magnificat*. From her well-furnished memory, she recreates a new song, in line with the psalms (see Pss 112, 103) or the song of Hannah, mother of Samuel (1 Sam 2). Simeon also creates a short hymn in the temple when he is allowed to see the Anointed One with his own eyes and to carry him in his arms. The "poor" know a thing or two about praise!

Jesus, born and raised in that milieu, does not hesitate to refer to himself with the honorable title of "poor": "learn from me," he says in the middle of Matthew's gospel, "for I am gentle and humble in heart" (Matt 11:29). The double expression used by the evangelist intends to explain the rich Hebrew notion of *anaw* in as nuanced a fashion as possible in the Greek. Jesus praises this poverty as blessing: "Blessed are the poor, the meek, the merciful, the peacemakers, those who hunger and thirst for righteousness" (from Matt 5:3-10).

In the Torah we read this about Moses: "Now the man Moses was very humble (*anaw*), more so than anyone else on the face of the earth" (Num 12:3). Jesus as portrayed in Matthew applies this concept to himself. The reference to Moses is clear. With this allusion in mind, we can read Matthew's text as telling us: "Here the new Moses is speaking." Thus we can emphasize the continuity with Moses, but we can also set off the new against the old. The latter is more frequent in the apologetic tradition. But when dealing with poverty or humility, does it make sense to play Moses against Jesus or Jesus against Moses? That would subvert the very idea of humility and, hence, defile the hidden greatness of both.

In the Jewish commentaries we read: "Why can we not find anybody today who talks as frankly with God as Moses? Because neither can we find anybody today who kneels as deeply in humility" (*Midrash Rabba* on Exodus 33).

The tradition of the "poor" has been carried forward in Israel as well as in the Church. In generation after generation poor women and men have applied themselves to all one hundred and fifty psalms, playing with the letters of the alphabet to praise the Lord in everything and to hallow his name until death. In today's interreligious dialogue, it's mainly the poor who find each other, in all openness, regardless of the differences among creeds, theological systems, or religious practices. The Buddhist nun from Nagasaki feels at home with the Trappist sisters of Berkel-Enschot while the Franciscan nun of Malonne near Namur rediscovers with joy the "brilliant poverty" of the Poverello in the Japanese Zen convent near Nagoya.

The Lord God himself pays attention to the *anawah* (poverty) of the *anawim*, as we are taught with great authority in Psalm 22: "For he has never despised nor scorned the poverty of the poor." God can do everything, except this: to despise the poor in their greatest poverty. "A broken and humble heart, O God, you will not spurn," says Psalm 51. Yes, "the LORD takes delight in his people; he crowns the poor (*anawim*) with salvation (*yeshu'ah*)" (Ps 149:4). He crowns them in fact "with Jesus," as Christian commentators have invariably read this verse.

See also: Humility, Jesus and the Jesus Prayer, Mary, Memory, Mercy, Name, Psalmody

ASPIRATION

While the word is now commonly used to denote a goal or a striving toward a desired result, between the thirteenth and seventeenth centuries the term "aspiration" acquired a distinct meaning. Derived from the Greek word *anagô,* aspiration denotes an uplifting, inner movement. As prayers, aspirations resemble what, since St. Augustine, we call "ejaculatory prayers." They can consist of a short, set combination of words, such as "Lord have mercy," or "My Lord and my God," but also of a pure movement, as a sigh or a lament, from the deepest layers of the heart, remaining unpronounced, without need for language.

Authors who have committed themselves to this way of praying say that there is nothing quite as fertile for the spiritual life. The whole ladder of our growth to a life in God receives unexpected momentum through this very simple practice. All steps benefit from it, even the most exalted one of unification with God. Masters such as Hugo of Balma, a thirteenth-century Carthusian monk, John of Jesú Maria (d. 1615), a Spanish Carmelite who worked in Italy, and Jean de Saint-Samson (d. 1636), his blind confrère point out that this practice can be carried out in the midst of any other activity, whether corporal or spiritual. It pays to rediscover this ancient path.

Aspirations received little mention in the nineteenth and twentieth centuries, but at the end of the twentieth and the beginning of this century we again find people paying close attention to what Paul once referred to as "sighs too deep for words" (see Rom 8:26). Fundamentally, through aspirations we attune ourselves directly to God. In the ground of our sighs we perceive God's Spirit at work. The inner movement starts with us, but after some time we realize that the actual subject of the aspiration is God. As the blind Carmelite from Rennes dared to say: "We become God." Francis de Sales, his contemporary, also attached significant importance to this form of prayer. He even wrote that without it nothing was possible, neither the active, charitable life, nor the contemplative!

See also: Breathing, Jesus and the Jesus Prayer, Name, Profession of Faith, Psalmody, Spirit

B

BEGINNING

The spiritual path is one of starting over again and again. Gregory of Nyssa, with his dynamic vision of the spiritual life, put it like this in his *Life of Moses*: "Life is an ascent. Again and again we leave the height we have reached to climb higher. We live from beginning to beginning, in a beginning without end."

Thus, you have never arrived. You learn to disengage at each and every level in a continuous uprooting: life becomes a perpetual pilgrimage. "At the highest point," says Gregory in his commentary on Psalm 150, "when virtuousness has reached its perfection, you arrive at God, because God is perfect virtue."

Begin with the End

This is the important lesson of the liturgy. On the first Sunday of Advent, the beginning of the new liturgical year, we always read a gospel message in which Jesus directs our attention to the final end (Mark 13; Matt 24; Luke 21). It is a healthy reflex. When we want to start something new, let's keep our eye on the ball, on the main goal: What, in the end, is it that we want? It is only in light of the final end that many initiatives find their true content, their real core, their lasting or their passing value.

In the Beginning

Reflecting on the beginning is an exercise in itself. What existed when nothing was all there was? Philosophers and theologians, scientists and poets, all are reduced to mere stammering when it comes to the absolute beginning, the moment just before the moment of the Big Bang. As far as the Bible is concerned, there we see a thinker from the fifth century before Christ who posited that "in the beginning" creation only began when God spoke. And his first word was: "Let there be light!" (Gen 1:1-3). From the start, God is "speaking" and this speaking provides light. Few insights have been as creative and as inexhaustible as this one.

Jewish mystics have described the beginning as follows: originally there was only God, and God was everything. (Meister Eckhart thought a bit further and said: "Since there was no distinction between God and something else, there was also no 'God' worthy of the name.

There was nothing and God was that nothing.") Wanting something other than himself, God thought about creating a being separate from himself. What did He do? Since He occupied everything just by himself, he contracted Himself. He "fasted on himself," did *tsimtsum*, and in this way created room within Himself where the other could be. Thus, in the beginning, there was a fasting by God on Himself so that the other-than-God could exist. If we wish to begin something, the creation of something brand new, let's make sure we don't forget to fast.

See also: Conversation, Emptiness, Fasting, Pilgrimage, *Tsimtsum*

BLESSING

"So God blessed the seventh day and hallowed it" (Gen 2:3). At the end of the creation of heaven and earth, with all they contained, we see God honor the Sabbath. Five actions are involved:

He finishes the work that he had done,
He rests, which we often equate with "relaxing" but which has more to do with doing nothing than with relaxing (*noeah* in Hebrew),
He blesses and
hallows the day, and
takes a new breath.

These five verbs from the biblical text have particular importance for us. What does He do on that particular seventh day? "Blessing" stands at the center. That what God blesses may participate in his favor, in his fullness of life. In the book of Numbers we hear how God speaks to Moses and instructs him on how his brother Aaron and his sons should bless the people and pronounce God's Name over them. The two go together. They shall say: "The Lord bless you and keep you; the Lord make his face to shine upon you, and be gracious to you; the Lord lift up his countenance to you, and give you peace" (Num 6:24-26). Thrice the Name appears in the blessing. Its ultimate goal: peace, shalom, which means fullness of life.

Too often and too readily we think that only a few are chosen and able to bless. Life and blessing go hand-in-hand, as we learn especially in the Jewish tradition. Every action can start with, or be encompassed by, a blessing. In their tradition, pious Jews receive a hundred blessings: They never have to improvise to say or invoke a blessing. The range of existing formulas is so varied that there are no or very few actions that would not fall under one or another customary formulation. In the first place we bless God. At the same time we beseech him for His blessing and His favor for what we are about to begin.

Blessing is reciprocal: If we look at the calling of Abraham, we note that, upon leaving his land, tribe, and family, he is both blessed and called to bless. "I will make of you a great nation, and I will bless you, and make your name great, so that you will be a blessing. I will bless those who bless you, and the one who curses you I will curse; and in you all the families of the earth shall be blessed" (Gen 12:2-3). Upon being blessed, Abraham becomes a blessing to others, without limitation.

See also: Gratitude, Reciprocity, Sabbath

BREATHING

Sunk deeply into the silence—
as a fish
as a fish
breathes in the water
water that is breath and beginning.

—Ida Gerhardt, *To Escape*

Breathing has to do with silence, with inwardness, and with beginning, as the poetess teaches us. Most of us live our lives unaware of our respiration. Being conscious of your breath is a sign that you are still and inwardly focused.

While in the East breathing is considered of prime importance, Western philosophy, even in the hay-day of phenomenology, has never paid similar attention to respiration. At the same time, though, some physicians have come to understand the central importance of the breath. A gynecologist acknowledged that he systematically taught all his patients to become conscious of their breath, except for patients from Singapore or Indonesia: they did it naturally.

A Japanese Zen master who does not speak our Western languages knows right away how his Italian or North American student is doing, simply by paying attention to the student's breath. "Your breath reveals you," he said—you can't hide what's happening. Breathing consciously offers a path to well-being, freedom, and fresh energy.

The art of fully breathing starts with paying attention to the out-breath. According to the masters, we don't need to worry about breathing in, which happens naturally. But emptying the lungs by completely pulling in the lower abdomen against the spine never happens spontaneously. That requires willpower and a little push. The spine then lifts itself up in just the right posture.

Too frequently a person limits the movement of the breath to shoulder level and only takes in air at that height. People often don't realize they can also breathe in and out in breadth. Different effects are obtained by breathing vertically (shoulders), horizontally (between the ribs), or in depth (lower abdomen). If you concentrate on breathing in depth, in the pelvic area, you discover that energy gathers there. By meditating in silence monks in Asia accumulate "chi" (or "qi") energy that way. Meditating is not exhausting, on the contrary: it charges your batteries. This happens in the area of "hara" or "tanden" (between the navel and the sacrum).

When consciously breathing in and breathing out, an interesting meditation point arises in the still moment of transition from one to the other. Something happens then, outside our free will: it's like a carp jumping up in the pond. Life pushes through, with an inner beat, irresistibly free. All who realize this feel a spontaneous gratitude welling up inside. Gratefully breathing in and out belongs to the core of the art of living. Similarly, when we pay attention to the pump of our respiration while taking a quiet and mindful walk, we feel gratitude flowing all the way into the soles of our feet. It is a grace to be here, to stand and to walk on this earth: what a wonder!

Many wise words and short prayer forms can be based on the rhythm of our breath. They support this rhythm and, at the same time, are carried by it. I breathe in, I am. I breathe out, I give thanks. Mindfully and in wonder I do one and experience the other. Ultimately, I no longer know if this is happening actively or passively. I continue to give thanks. Vietnamese monk Thich Nhat Hanh recommends that with each out-breath we smile. "Breathe out and smile at life." When we smile countless small muscles relax in our face. If we quietly take the time each day to breathe and to meditate in this manner we'll see, slowly but surely, the wrinkles in the parchment of our face disappear.

The monks of the Sinai—John Climacus, Hesychius of Batos, and others—passed on the tradition that the breath and the Name of Jesus were destined to become one. Thus it is not enough to become mindful of our breath, sign of an acquired inner silence. In a second phase we have to practice associating that breathing as closely as possible to the murmuring of the sweet name of Jesus. That Name is holy and heals—does "Jesus" not mean in Hebrew "the Lord saves"? In Greek we see even a direct relationship between *Ièsous* and *iâsthai*: "Jesus" and "healing"!

In the Jewish tradition, the Sabbath as empty time at the end of the week is also considered the moment when the Jew receives a *supplément d'âme*, an addition of soul (André Néher). By quietly doing nothing you regain awareness of your soul, which now can also celebrate. The source of this original thought can be found in the Bible.

On the Sabbath God ceases his work and gives himself time to rest and to be refreshed (see Ex 31:17, literally: "he took a new breath"). He commands that people also refrain from working on that day, not just the men but the whole family, even the animals. They also may be refreshed on that day. Living beings, people and animals, have a *nefesh*. Literally the word means "gullet" or "throat", but it refers to the vital energy that passes through the throat with the breath. On the Sabbath people and animals can, in imitation of God, catch a second breath, thanks to the cessation of all slavish occupations. By all means, then, let there be a weekly moment of refreshment with mindful breathing, in gratitude and wonder.

See also: Aspirations, Gratitude, Jesus and the Jesus Prayer, Name, Sabbath, Walking, Wonder

C

CHASTITY

Love and chastity go hand in hand. Woe to chastity that is not practiced out of love. Woe to love that excludes chastity. There are those who are celibate by necessity and are chaste and affectionate, and there are celibates by vocation who are afraid of love or who have cast chastity aside. There are married couples who in their love have developed the most sublime levels of chastity and who, at the end of their life together, still experience their sweet love each and every day with modesty as young lovers do.

If love is a source that never runs dry, it is thanks to chastity. Chastity keeps the heart alert, not to avoid love in fear, but to approach love with greater diffidence. You can never be too chaste in love, you can never overdo love when you have a chaste attitude. Having both go hand in hand is an art and, like every art, requires time and patience.

Chastity is a refined form of love and not its opponent or enemy. In our Western culture a rather odd development has taken place in the last few decades: often even the most elementary forms of chastity are deemed unnecessary or uncalled-for, indeed they are even found laughable. In the encounter with other cultures, for example, African, Indian, or Vietnamese, this creates incomprehension; people from other cultures are frequently offended by the lifestyle of Westerners.

The irony of this development leads to the following observation: where there is a greater practice of chastity there is more beauty ready to be admired, while a clear lack of sexual modesty may actually extinguish life's erotic dimension. In this respect, we from the West can learn a lot from others if, of course, we are still able to be open to it. The experience of chaperones who accompanied students from our Western schools to building camps in Vietnam or Congo shows that our young people have a difficult time appreciating norms that have meaning for others and how little inclined they are to accepting and learning even a little bit from others in this regard.

Chastity adds value to the whole area of how we relate to others. A chaste look is the fruit of a struggle, the sign of a victory, and a blessing for the person who receives it. That struggle is all the harder when popular culture diverges from traditional values. Those who carry out their jobs as nurse or doctor, as pedicurist or physical therapist, or all who simply in their manner of dress, are able to convey gentleness as well as chastity, gain not only the appreciation of others but will themselves find greater satisfaction in the practice.

As the Dutch poetess Ida Gerhardt wrote, "What with timidity was abided, in timidity arrived."[1] A reciprocal chaste attitude graces life with an incomparable glow. No earthly world is more beautiful.

See also: Detachment, Fear of the Lord, Mary, Patience, Reciprocity, Sexuality

1. "*Wat met schromen werd verbeid, is met schroom gekomen,*" from *Green Pastures* in *Het levend Monogram* (1955).

CONFESSION OF SINS

While confession of sins is an age-old practice, very few old practices have experienced as many swings as the confession of sins, the sacrament of penance and reconciliation. When Pope Pius X opened access to the sacrament of the Eucharist to children of six or seven years, all these children were also taught how to confess their sins. In schools and convents there were confessions at regular intervals: monthly or sometimes weekly. Perhaps we have known no century in which people used the sacrament of penance and reconciliation as often as in the previous one. But the last twenty-five years have witnessed a precipitous decline in the practice, certainly in Western Europe. However, if you travel through Poland during Holy Week you see something totally different: people by the tens waiting patiently in line for the opportunity to go to confession. And they are of all ages.

Perhaps the time has come for a revision of the practice. If we are ready for it, let's do it then as adults, spiritually awake and mature.

1) There is no need to condemn myself. Yes, I appear before God as the judge, as the Psalmist prays in Psalm 51, but it's not up to me to pass judgment on myself. In my proceeding I cannot be both accused *and* judge!

2) I come to confess my sins, but also to profess his righteousness and mercy. The first action gains deeper meaning in light of the second. There is an unbroken link between the two. Let us never focus single-mindedly only on the confession of our sins.

3) To confess indeed involves naming and bringing to light what I have done wrong. But in doing so I also discard all of that, I disengage. It serves me well to detach completely from my sins.

4) It is possible to confess without contrition, but this indicates an inner attachment to self-righteousness. It has been said of the famous *Confessions* of Jean-Jacques Rousseau that they were confessions without contrition and without penance! Yes, he recounted his life in detail but there never was a smidgen of contrition, let alone penance. Contrition breaks through to our true condition, there where our heart is open and broken in pieces before God.

Psalm 51 is an excellent confessional mirror; it helps us to appear truthfully before God. Authentic contrition shatters our tendency to keep on justifying ourselves. Also, even if we can repent only in some inadequate manner, there is already true repentance. After all, contrition is not only our work: the person expressing repentance allows God's Spirit to enter, which creates the right condition in the heart. Psalm 51 also deals with that Spirit.

5) The sacrament of penance and reconciliation is a conversation between faith and faith. Penitent and priest speak and listen in faith. With either of them, knowledge of psychology or insight into human nature should not dominate, no matter how finely honed and no matter how welcome, but rather the miracle of a conversation from faith to faith (see Rom 1:17). Here God is speaking. The confessor listens believing in his heart that God is at work in a soul in the process of conversion. And the penitent speaks in faith in order to receive from God the words that will illuminate his life. Confession is an event of gratitude and light. The confessor is often privileged to see how the soul that pours itself out before God already has been touched by grace and completely forgiven. In such a confession, joy predominates—in God, in the priest, and in the penitent's heart.

6) Let confessor and penitent both be ready for the unpredictable and the unplanned: confession is an excellent opportunity for encounter.

7) Since the sins are always the same, does it make sense to go to confession? Thank heavens for the lack of variety! By confessing them again, I acknowledge that I fall and that I pick myself up. Probably there is no end to the falling—let's make sure then there is also no end to picking ourselves up! In what bad shape I would be if I fall and resign myself to it, without the strength to get back up! If I continue to go to confession I keep trusting in God's mercy and that keeps me standing, while I have learned not to take myself too seriously or to judge others as if I were perfect. I know my weakness and in my weakness I have learned how His power accepts me time and again and gets me up. This mature understanding grows with regular confessions, and only that way.

8) How often do we have to confess? No longer are there rules the way there used to be (see the canon law). Sometimes scrupulous people ask if it's alright to go to confession daily. Physicians and psychiatrists know there is little or nothing wrong with that. It is and remains a salutary custom for Christians when preparing for the celebration of a feast first to gather and to ask for forgiveness. To ask God and each other. Along the same line, it is also a healthy habit to prepare for the five or six principal feast days of the liturgical year by making use of the sacrament of penance and reconciliation. We can start on a long voyage or a totally new undertaking by going to confession the day before. If you lead a stable and regular life, it is not necessary to go and confess more than five or six times a year. It is a personal feeling: it has to do with light. After confession you experience light, but after a number of weeks the light wanes and it's well to place your life again in the light of God's mercy. Even involuntarily you get dust on your feet and a full bath is necessary now and then.

9) Our whole Christian life is about forgiving. An Our Father, a Kyrie ("Lord have mercy"), the Eucharist itself: they all offer forgiveness. In addition, confession provides an opportunity for a deeper and more personal encounter with God as the One who reconciles us in a radical way with existence.

Is confession really that important? Charles de Foucauld, now beatified, at first lived a highly irregular life until he hit upon the idea of asking a priest for advice. He was hardly halfway through his statement when the mild and ordinarily nondirective Father Huvelin told him forcefully and in no uncertain terms: "Kneel down and confess!" Then something broke open inside Charles: it was the start of a whole new life. He became a Trappist monk and ended up as a hermit in the Sahara. Now he belongs to the beatified: nobody who knew him before his confession could have surmised such a final destination.

Rarely is the act of confession as staggering and determinative as in the case of the future Brother Charles, but what happened to him shows the positive power contained in a confession. What is important is not the act of confessing, but the forgiveness. In a confession God and human being meet, as for that matter in every sacrament.

That is precisely also the definition of sacrament: a meeting place between God and human being. But far too often we put on blinders and look only at the part of the person.

In the new universal *Catechism of the Catholic Church*, we learn what is the part of the person, and what is the work of God:

> What is the part of the human being? Three things: "be contrite of heart, confess with the lips, and practice complete humility and fruitful satisfaction" and all three under "prompting of the Holy Spirit" (1450 and 1453). All too frequently we only think of the confession, the profession of our sins, and in doing so we most often leave far too little room for the "prompting of the Holy Spirit."
>
> And what is the action of God, in the name of Jesus Christ? He does four things, thus one more than the human person, and what's more, the person does it under the prompting of the Holy Spirit! Through the apostolic work of the Church he forgives sins, determines the manner of satisfaction, and prays and does penitence for the sinner.

Here we taste how deeply the sacrament of penance and reconciliation touches you and reconciles you. In the priest to whom you address yourself you meet somebody who prays for you and with you, and who does penance for you. This is more than merely the reconciliation between individuals and their Creator. A whole gamut of reconciliations opens up in the sacrament. Using a text taken from an earlier document, the Catechism says this about it:

> It must be recalled that . . . this reconciliation with God leads, as it were, to other reconciliations, which repair the other breaches caused by sin. The forgiven penitent is reconciled with himself in his inmost being, where he regains his innermost truth. He is reconciled with his brethren whom he has in some way offended and wounded. He is reconciled with all creation. (1469)

A little further on we read: "In this sacrament, the sinner, placing himself before the merciful judgment of God, *anticipates* in a certain way *the judgment* to which he will be subjected at the end of his earthly life. . . . In converting to Christ through penance and faith, the sinner passes from death to life and 'does not come into judgment' (see John 5:25)" (1470).

We arrive at something we do not find in our usual world: life without being judged. While we normally have to live in a merciless place, a harsh world without forgiveness, the practice of the sacrament ripens our inner being into a mature existence. Then we can put aside the yoke of so many condemnations and, gently reconciled, we can blossom into quiet and forceful peacemakers while we season our milieu and culture with seeds of joyful hope.

See also: Forgiveness, Love for One's Enemies, Mercy, Peace, Profession of Faith, Sacrament, Spirit

CONVERSATION

To maintain a conversation is an art, indeed one of the most difficult ones, and, these days, one of the most imperiled.

Radio and TV play such an important role in some households that there is no time left in the whole day to have a conversation. Some youngsters feel uncomfortable in the presence of a guest, or in a quiet moment in the living room. After a few minutes they excuse themselves, jump up, and disappear behind their computer or music apparatus. The narcissistic person—product of our culture—harbors a destructive proclivity that destroys the art of conversation. In order to carry on a conversation we have to learn to become interested, with an open mind, in the stories of somebody else, whether the subject is football or developments in Central Africa, religion or the recent elections. Those versed in conversation take interest in everything, are able to think along with the person who is talking, and do not have to intervene. They enjoy, quietly and receptively—you can see it in their body language. All this is too much for self-absorbed individuals: they get up suddenly, pull back, think it's all nonsense, believe they have more important things to think about.

It's no small thing to develop a culture of conversation. It requires time, quiet, a clear mind that is humbly receptive, wide-ranging interests, a sharing attitude, and appropriate modesty. Conversely, the archenemies of conversation are haste and busyness, noise, self-importance, rancor and gossip, lack of humor.

All great civilizations have recorded stories of unforgettable conversations, often around a table, where heaven and earth, life and death, war and peace, but also friendship and intimacy, asceticism and mysticism, the names of God, and the powers of herbs, have a place. Among the best known in the West are Plato's dialogues and the table conversations of Plutarch and Erasmus. In India, Hindus and Muslims have preserved brilliant conversations around an enlightened master: poetry, philology, ancient commentaries on the Upanishads, verses from the Koran, or expositions by Sufi masters—everything can find shelter under the wings of a broad, open mind. The dialogue wells up like a source. Thanks to great breadth of knowledge, the master does not dominate but confirms and elicits, suggests, and engages in free association.

Monastic literature used to speak of *colloquium* or *colllatio* (meeting for discussion). In Egypt *colloquium* was already practiced at the end of the third and beginning of the fourth century: Abba Ammonas received the brothers as evening fell. They discussed what had transpired during a day of solitude and silence, whether good or bad, humbly and sincerely. They shared the light they may have walked in that day. The *abba* summarized the experiences and put difficulties or possibilities in a larger context. Fortified, they returned to their cells until the following evening. In the company of people who equally searched for God in the purest way, they fed on each other and grew in a shared light. In many of the recorded conversations, two *abbas* sit together while hardly a word is exchanged. Sometimes the dialogue grows toward a pure silence, because all words fail: a fiery glow consumes any verbal communication. In wonder, they keep a silent vigil with the grandeur that arose in their midst.

Clearly, we are in the process of rediscovering the art of conversation. In the same way that book clubs are created for the silent reading of great literature, it should not surprise us if, by extension, discussion evenings are organized so friends can rediscover the delightful art of the open and sustained conversation.

See also: Dialogue, Friendship, Judge (Do Not), *Lectio Divina*, Wonder

CULTURE

It is only by leaving home and traveling to a foreign country that you understand where home is. At the outset we are all culture-blind within the culture that surrounds us. Only by getting to know other cultures do we realize how embedded we are in our own, and do we begin to understand and to distinguish it.

The realization of our cultural definition is both sobering and liberating. Many theological differences of opinion of the past can be traced to different cultural backgrounds: is there anything more culturally defined than the differences in Marian teachings? Depending on whether somebody lives in the East or was born in the West, whether in Northern Europe or in the south of the same continent, their speaking and thinking about Mary will vary. To appreciate the differences regarding Mary between Ephesus and Rome, or between Calvin and Newman, a proper insight into the cultural differences is indispensable.

Aculturation, Inculturation, Interculturality

Nothing is as vague as a given culture: after all, cultures are continually influenced by other cultures, they evolve constantly. Every culture is a never-completed process. The relationship between different cultures can be stormy, crushing, murderous. Conversation between cultures is extremely desirable, but few people receive sufficient open-mindedness in their education to see the inherent relativity of their own culture and, hence, to be able to choose dialogue in their encounter with the other.

I once heard Abbot Michel Van Parijs (Abbey of Chevetogne) talk about how the question of faith and inculturation, or of monastic life and inculturation, always came up during the congresses of abbots that are held in Rome every four years. He believes that inculturation comes about by *lectio*, the reading of God's word. Ruminating with full attention on, and fully assimilating, God's word accomplish true in-depth inculturation. Superficial inculturation is an all too frequent mistake: we are content with cutting and pasting, and with easy imitations by facile borrowing from local religious or social traditions.

See also: Dialogue, *Lectio Divina,* Mary

D

DANCING

Dance Your Life!

The poignant moment stays with me: Nelson Mandela at advanced age in the midst of a crowd, laughing and dancing, cautiously but with elation. In Africa I was taught: "Dancing knows no age! Once you've learned it, you'll still do it when you're old." Mandela was living proof! I had the opportunity myself, in Africa, to approach the altar dancing, with gravity and carried by the music.

There are many ways of dancing without motion. When you admire a sculpture, you first walk around it in circles, then you allow the rhythm of the form to continue vibrating in your own body in a motionless dance. Also a liturgy in which we sing while standing up, almost immobile, is not far from the art of dance. We breathe together, attuned to each other aurally, at times even with the timbre of our voices, and singing we make an almost imperceptible dance pass, led by the elegant hand movement of the choirmaster.

You can dance the moment you are imbued with "life within your life," a "spirit" that propels you forward, or even simply with a silence that fills you with awe in the face of all that surrounds you. "We played the flute for you, and you did not dance" (Matt 11:17). With this a disappointed Jesus revealed the song: his gospel was an invitation to the dance! But who answered it? And if you listened intently to his flute-playing, why would you not dance? The gospel compels us to dance! Who can stay in their chair? Dancing has become a must.

See also: Breathing, Source, Walking

DEATH

In his Rule, Benedict admonishes monks, "Keep your eye on death every day" (RB 4:47). This is an exercise, supported by memory. It helps the monk to reflect continuously on his end, as said by the wise Ben Sirach: "In all you do, remember the end of your life, and then you will never sin" (Sir 7:36). By reflecting on his death, the monk also thinks about the day of judgment, about heaven and hell:

> Fear Judgment Day.
> Have a healthy fear of hell.
> Long for eternal life with the desire of the Spirit.
> Keep your eye on death every day. (RB 4:44-47)

This creates a vigilant heart and adds depth and realism to life: where do I allow my thoughts and desires to lead?

Similarly, at the first step of humility on the majestic ladder established by Benedict in the seventh chapter of his Rule, we find the same points of focus: we must keep God constantly before our eyes and must always be mindful of the fire of hell as well as life eternal. Benedict is not saying anything new here, he is passing on the tradition of the Desert Fathers.

In Evagrius (fourth century) we find a relatively long proverb in which he works out a systematic meditation on death and the hereafter. Step by step we are led to the hour of our death and everything that follows: the decomposition of the body, the activity of microorganisms, the life of the underworld, the inexorable confrontation with the Judge, and the final destination, be it with the damned or the blessed. Soberly and powerfully, everything is summoned. It is unquestionably purifying and not necessarily depressing.

Buddhists also practice such spiritual exercises. The two traditions agree completely on this point. Life and death belong together: "No life without death, no death without life," they say. And indeed, when a child is born, from the start it is considered a mortal being. We can try to forget this notion or to push it aside, but sooner or later it returns, stronger than ever. The monk chooses to internalize that thought and never to be surprised when death arrives, not his own or that of others, even the death of those most dear to him.

In addition, Macarius, the teacher of Evagrius, taught that we should live as if we were to die tonight *and* as if we had another hundred years left. This offers us a powerful, double horizon in the experience of time: on the one hand, extremely short and serious and, on the other, strikingly open and wide. The wise abbot then added that as far as our body is concerned, we should treat it as if we were to live another hundred years. Thus, biting asceticism and self-destructive deprivation are out! We have another one hundred years to go with the body we have!

On the other hand, he taught that we have to prepare ourselves, in all our innermost thoughts, affections, and worries, to meet our death tonight. This is also instructive because if I am going to die tonight, why should I get excited about what I don't have, or about an argument, a vendetta, an insult? If I have to appear before the great Judge tonight, why would I be so foolish as to want to claim things as my own, to insist on getting even, to need to be proven right in squabbles? At the thought of dying this very evening a great gravity and deep peace enter the heart and defeat all those picayune worries and cares.

As a general proposition we could say that it's a good thing to die before meeting our death. Halfway through life the question of our mortality rises up with renewed force. Inevitably, there will come that certain day when we observe that we are declining physically. The athlete in us has to admit: I will never be able to break my previous records. Physically we remain mortal, transitory. We may forget it, but our body reminds us. Many refuse to accept this and attempt to remain, as our culture trumpets it, fit and young, vital and sporty. Dad wants to beat his son in tennis one more time.

People doggedly cling to life, and most end up approaching death backwards. It would appear to be more intelligent if we mustered the courage halfway through life to make an about-face and to carry on with our eyes fixed on death. A lady once told me how she decided on her fiftieth birthday to give away something precious on every future birthday as a way of preparing for her approaching demise.

The theme of death, particularly the good death as a free and compassionate act, is high on the current social and political agenda.

The Greek word *euthanasia* means nothing else: we even want death (*thanatos*) to occur in a good (*eu*) way. New problems have arisen because, among other reasons, medicine has become so astonishingly omnipotent. These days we can use mechanical devices and medicines to support most vital functions of the body to such an extent that the Grim Reaper is kept waiting at the door.

Moreover, physicians are duty-bound to support life to the very end. The debate starts when we as a society and a culture have to attempt to discern what makes for "life" and "a life of human dignity." Today even scientists are no longer able to define "life," and that incapacity throws a shadow over the process of the end of life or death.

To prepare oneself for death remains a major challenge, especially since it is a medical certainty that there is no way out. In Plato's *The State*, Socrates meets a friend of very advanced age who looks calm and radiant. This surprises Socrates and he asks for an explanation. After all, old people have plenty of reason to be grumpy, bitter, unhappy or even fearful and melancholy. The wise man answers: Two things are essential. In the first place, I have absolutely no remorse. When I look back on my past, I don't experience any gnawing pains of unreconciled situations. It's been good. Second, I have been able to organize my life in such a way that now I don't need to worry about material concerns.

A few years ago, somebody came to us at the abbey with the question: "What should I do? The university hospital in Leuven sent me home. There is nothing more they can do for me. I am going to die, and I wish to prepare myself." At the question, "What should I do?" the above fragment from Plato came suddenly to mind. I told him what Socrates had learned from his old friend and said "Two things are important now: First of all, reconciliation, so that you can walk the last straight line in peace with yourself, with your neighbors, and with God, and without remorse. Second, arrange your material, financial, and testamentary matters so that you can face the end without these kinds of concerns." The latter had already been taken care of. The former resulted in a general confession and the sacrament for the sick the following day. Less than six months later I saw him on one last occasion, this time in the hospital. With his wife and son we told him: "George, it's been good. You may go now, toward the great Light." He passed away that same night, quietly, in peace.

People who feel fully reconciled as they approach their end are often the ones who help others, who carry them, and send them back home with renewed meaning. The others come to console them, but they themselves speak the most meaningful words about what really matters, how life can be accepted with gratitude and how we can also see it pass us by. Those who consciously face death turn their dying process into something surprising: Every gesture becomes a testamentary disposition, each encounter an affirmation of the other. For themselves, they seek peace. What is left is the desire to spread the precious gift of friendship widely, without any restraints whatever. As little Thérèse of Lisieux reasoned with utmost confidence: "I do not die. I enter into life. I shall pass my time in heaven by doing good on earth" (*Je ne meurs pas. J'entre dans la vie. Je passerai mon ciel à faire du bien sur la terre*).[1]

Dying remains a mystery. The best preparation does not mean that fear of death cannot strike unexpectedly, fiercely, bitingly, absurdly. A confrère and philosopher, Fr. Raymond, said when he was close to the end, "Even though I have given much thought to the concept of death my whole life long, now I am eye to eye with *my* death, and that is something else altogether!" In his *Dialogues of the Carmelites (Dialogues des Carmélites)*, George Bernanos ventured to show that a person dies not necessarily his or her own death, but that certain people through some strange substitution experience the death of others in their own final agony. Each person's dying process remains mysterious; it is grand if we, as fellow human beings and as a society, with all our science, no matter how advanced it may be, can truly respect this process to its final conclusion.

Some people, no matter how learned and how well versed in theology, reach their death naked, with hardly anything. "I have no particular expectation," said the great exegete Fr. Jacques Dupont repeatedly on his deathbed over a nine-month-long process. At most he hoped to encounter "Somebody," the one to whom he, when he was eleven years old, had said "Yes" from the bottom of his heart one late evening in November. About that affirmation he had no doubt. The rest of his life he deemed a lot less convincing.

1. Thérèse de Lisieux, *Derniers Entretiens* (Paris: Desclée de Brouwer/Cerf, 1971) and *J'entre dans la vie. Derniers Entretiens* (Paris: Cerf, 2015).

To die means, at least for me, to go toward the light, the great, undying Light. All that was light in us cannot be touched by death, but all that was greedy, nontransparent, and self-important will perish into nothingness. Dying is difficult because we experience in mind and body all these self-centered preoccupations that we need to let go. The light we are now shall not fade in death.

I experienced the life of certain confrères as pure, radiant light, muted as in an alabaster vase. What can death do? To be sure, it can break the vase, but the light remains free, untouched. In death it only shines with greater freedom. I saw one of my confrères, Fr. Dominique Van Rolleghem, just a couple of hours before his death. He was covered with a blanket up to his chin, so I was unable even to touch his hand, nothing. Standing at his bedside I looked at him. He returned my gaze with strength and happiness. His face was radiant. We said nothing, but everything in that room lit up. I persevered in not saying a word for a long time. Then I bowed deeply, saw him close his eyes, and left the room. That same day I took the train to Italy. The next day I received a fax from the abbot: "Fr. Dominique died last evening." The great light that he had striven for his whole life as a monk and a hermit had caught up with him even before his death. In his dying, death was absolutely powerless.

See also: Confession of Sins, Memory, Mourning, Night Vigil, Time and the Experience of Time, Yes-Amen

DETACHMENT

To detach ourselves from worldly goods, or to forsake things, or to deny ourselves, are concepts that in our day and age go against the grain. They evoke suspicion, and not wholly without reason. They could lead all too easily to a crippled and immature life, creating a negative attitude that damages the very sources of a grateful existence.

At the same time it is also true that we cannot imagine a spiritually complete life without detachment, without forsaking, without honoring the gospel mandate to "deny [ourselves] and take up [our] cross" (Mark 8:34 *inter alia*). As part of our basic structure, human beings must abstain from indiscriminate behavior that would partake of everything without inhibition.

"Of all the trees in the garden you may freely eat, except from that one." This prohibition from the story in the beginning of the book of Genesis (see Gen 2:16-17) lays out a fundamental order. Not devouring everything, not giving in to unlimited greed: these are part of the initial steps toward a dignified life.

According to psychoanalyst Marie Balmary, this biblical prohibition is of the highest importance if we are to have a healthy society. Ecologically, we, here in the West, live as if we can exploit our earth's narrow ribbon of biosphere at will and without restraint. The harmful consequences of this behavior are felt more pressingly each year. Whether that damage will be able to bring about a change in our individual and collective conduct is very much the question, witness the manner in which some of the great powers continue to violate the Kyoto agreements.[1]

A second step in detachment deals with foregoing things that we could lay claim to with some legitimacy. To be content with less, to be satisfied with little, or even at appropriate times to do without our daily bread and fast. All kinds of motivations may play a role in this, for example eating less so as to be able to share with those who

1. The Kyoto Protocol to the United Nations Framework Convention on Climate Change sets limits on overall emissions of carbon dioxide and other greenhouse gases by the industrialized countries. It was adopted in Kyoto, Japan, in December 1997 and entered into force on February 16, 2005 [translator's note].

do not have enough. Detachment can be an exercise in methodically freeing ourselves from small idolatries that have acquired a grip on our inner freedom. Not turning on the TV one evening, not going online one Sunday, bicycling to the bakery instead of taking the car, abstaining from alcohol for a somewhat longer period, passing a day without arguing with anybody: none of these is absolutely necessary. You don't need to do any one of them, but those who are able to will discover secret sources of an expanding freedom.

The third step in detachment is, in the felicitous phrase of Junayd, one of the most original Muslim mystics of the ninth century: to be detached from detachment itself. Virtue ignores its own virtuousness. A detachment that is too deliberate can become a subtle new form of attachment. Go take a hike then with your observations and noble gestures of detachment! Break your fast and receive the unexpected guest with generosity.

Small forms of detachment, practiced daily, create a freedom that prepares the heart for the day of the great detachment. Small forms of attachment—constantly giving in to comfort, nibbling on everything that comes along, whether with the eyes, mouth, or ears—undermine systematically our inner defenses: the person who cannot say "no" to anything becomes a stranger in his own house, an addict to unbridled caprices, the plaything of a degenerate child.

See also: Emptiness, Fasting, Feasting, Sabbath

DHIKR

Dhikr is the name of a Muslim prayer practice. The word itself means mentioning, recalling, remembering, and making present. In the Qur'an we read: "Remember Me, then, and I will remember you. Give thanks to Me and never deny Me" (2:152). A mysterious reciprocity appears to be present in the remembrance of Allah.

In practice this remembrance consists in the mentioning of God's name. The one Name—Allah—can be repeated by itself, or it can take a number of different forms. "His are the most gracious names," says the Qur'an (59:22-24) and in mystical circles long sequences of names have been collected from the Qur'an, even up to a string of ninety-nine. The hundredth name remains inexpressible, or no single name expresses Him completely.

A tradition exists around the highest or the supreme Name. The person who knows it will always be heard. Prayer strands with ninety-nine beads support the *dhikr* practice. Thus He is called, among other things, the King, the All-powerful, the Creator, the Exalted, the Wise One, the Merciful. We can make God present by softly mentioning the ninety-nine names for ourselves.[1] In the Qur'an *dhikr* also stands for what we call prayer (24:37).

Dhikr can be practiced in a group, with simple formulas (for example, "There is no god but Allah") that are repeated with raised voice, often accompanied by certain rhythmic movements of the body or the head. The purpose of such a litany is to become conscious of the presence of God in your heart. *Dhikr* can also be practiced by just one person alone in meditation. According to the tradition of the prophet Mohammed both are possible: "God says, 'I am with My servant: if he remembers Me in himself, then I shall remember him in Myself, and if he remembers Me in a group, then I shall remember him in a group, better than his own.'"[2]

Three levels may be distinguished in the practice of *dhikr*: there is the *dhikr* of the tongue, the *dhikr* of the heart, and the *dhikr* of intimacy

1. Gé Speelman, ed., *Bidden in het meervoud* (*To Pray in the Plural*) (Kampen: Kok, 1994), 138–39 and 143–44.

2. Ibid.

or *sirr.* In Al Ghazali we read about the difference between the first and the second stage: "The Sufi reaches a point in practice at which he has erased the source of the word from his tongue and experiences the heart continually engaged with *dhikr*." In the ultimate stage, the presence of God is indistinguishable from the one who invokes Him and calls Him by name: all has become one. This can be accompanied by ecstatic experiences.[3]

This practice has indisputable similarities with practices from other religious traditions, such as the Jesus Prayer of Christians or Japa yoga in India.

See also: Aspiration, Ejaculatory Prayers, Jesus and the Jesus Prayer, Memory, Name, Profession of Faith

3. See also Gé Speelman, ibid., M.-M. Anawati and L. Gardet, *Mystique musulmane* (Paris: Cerf, 1961), 185–258; and D. Gimaret, *Les noms divins en Islam. Exégèse lexicographique et théologique* (Paris: Cerf, 1988).

DIALOGUE

This word, derived from the Greek *dialogos*, has over the ages come to be associated with a successful literary genre, which at times was purely didactic, at other times apologetic or polemical: Plato, Cicero, Justinus, Gregory the Great, Erasmus, Sartre, and Jean Guitton all used it, and we should not forget to mention the classic Chinese debates in dialogue format. Pope Paul VI introduced the concept in his first encyclical, which was devoted to the Church (*Ecclesiam suam*). Christians are called to dialogue, he wrote, and to do so in all directions, including Muslims and nonbelievers. Since then the concept has achieved ever deeper penetration. In 1965, on Pentecost, the Vatican established a secretariat that later became known as the "Pontifical Council for Interreligious Dialogue." The periodical linked to this secretariat is called *Pro dialogo*, a brilliant idea. A choice had to made, and the choice was distinctly "pro."

Nevertheless, true dialogues are rare. All too often a symposium billed as "dialogue" becomes a set of parallel monologues: a rabbi, a mufti, and a bishop take their turns speaking and they talk past each other. Fortunately there is usually a journalist who, at the end of the event, poses the somewhat mischievous question, "Your colleague just said such and such: what do you make of that?" Then the true dialogue starts, after the official speeches.

To maintain a true dialectic posture is hard for us. Every *logos* contains an *apologia*, as the philosopher Levinas once said: all speech contains a veiled self-defense. We find it difficult completely to give up a defensive stance. How can you enter into conversation with another without implicitly desiring to defend something? Most of our religious sources were developed outside a sphere of dialogue. We direct ourselves to like-minded people and speak from the obviousness offered by the revelation of the absolute. Dialogue with those who think differently falls outside our perspective. However, a new space was opened up by Vatican II, which posited that the one who believes differently, even the one who does not believe at all, has the freedom and the right to be different, yes, even the right to be mistaken.

A true dialogue presupposes that you take the time to get to know the other and to understand them the way they understand themselves. You don't talk "about" the other in terms that the other would be unable to affirm. That requires patience, love, knowledge, and a real initiation into the world of the other. Sooner or later this leads to self-questioning, an inward dialogue, the famous "intra-dialogue" of the Indian-Catalan thinker Raimon Pannikkar. We no longer speak from our stronghold to theirs, but gradually partake of spaces that expand and enrich each other, sometimes by posing new challenges, past the point where initially we had stopped questioning ourselves.

Dialogue is a practice that starts with the inner debate of self-criticism. Desert Father Abba Poemen (fifth century) thought self-criticism essential to all spiritual work: " 'All the virtues come to this house except one and without that virtue it is hard for a man to stand.' Then they asked him what virtue was, and he said, 'For a man to blame himself.' "[1] In our day we find ourselves challenged to question even our most cherished sources—the gospels of the New Testament—with respect to their veracity or argument. When Paul warns his beloved Philippians against "the dogs" and means fellow Christians, or when Jesus, in John, during a discussion with "the Jews" refers to them as Satan's children, then we are rightfully surprised and we have to question ourselves critically.

Dialogue forms only part of a wider kind of encounter. Some participants in interreligious dialogue prefer to speak of "hospitality" rather than "dialogue." In the dynamic of receiving the other and treating the guest and stranger in your own home, a lot more happens than in mere dialogue, in which, for that matter, *logos* still plays too central a part. Especially in the East, where built-in doubt about the word is far stronger than in the West, the concept of hospitality captures the encounter far better than the notion of dialogue.

See also: Conversation, Hospitality, Love for One's Enemies, Peace, Serving, Visiting

1. *The Sayings of the Desert Fathers*, rev. ed. (Poemen 134), trans. Benedicta Ward (Trappist, KY: Cistercian Publications, 1984), 186.

DREAMING

We all dream, whether we remember our dreams or not. But what do we do with them? And do they have any significance for a mature art of living as human beings and as Christians? Dream without worries and say in advance with little Samuel who slept in the temple: "Speak, LORD, for your servant is listening" (1 Sam 3:10). After all, the dream can be a place of encounter with God!

Pray and dream. Do both. In the Bible, both have to do with angels. You can also pray for a dream, and you can doze off in the middle of a liturgy and receive a vision, just like the young Bernard of Clairvaux who, listening to Psalm 19 on Christmas night, saw the Word come out of God's lap: "It comes forth like a bridegroom coming from his tent, rejoices like a champion to run his course" (Ps 19:5).[1] The poet teaches:

And don't go with fury
into the night
let peace like a sentry
to your sleep provide light.
In your dream
angels do the rounds. (*Tom Naastenpad*, Liturgical hymn)

Let's hear it for the dream. To dream is healthy. Dreaming fits in a fully human life. And, the other way around, those who confidently announce, "I never dream," might well ask themselves, "Is everything okay with me?" Even our everyday expressions about dreams are full of wisdom.

The Wisdom of Our Language

Do we not talk often about "dreams" and "dreaming," mostly in a metaphorical sense? Ordinary life is peppered with "dreams" and "visions." Our language is rich, but also ambivalent: "dream" can mean illusion or the starkest reality. "Dream" is used to denote relief,

1. This translation is from *The Revised Grail Psalms* (Collegeville, MN: Liturgical Press, 2012) [translator's note].

an unexpected alternative, a broadening of the mind, and sometimes something quite unreal and yet present! A glance at a few dictionaries yields a number of interesting expressions:

> "I can recite that in my dreams": that's how well I know it!
>
> "A dream of a dress," "a dream of a man," but also: "the girl of my dreams."
>
> "Life is a dream" (cf. "*La vida es sueño,*" Calderon).
>
> But also "stop dreaming" or "dream on!" to correct somebody's mistaken notion.
>
> "Dream world" is the world of dreams, or a world that could be conjured up in a dream, an unreal world ("the dream world of fairy tales; the masks come from the dream world, represented by a Jeroen Bosch and a Grünewald," G. van der Leeuw).
>
> The definition of the verb "to dream" in Van Dale (a prominent Dutch dictionary) is not without interest: "Strange activity of the mind while asleep, through which lively series of images, most in arbitrary alternation, are fashioned in such a way that people believe they are experiencing them."

From the daily experience of dreaming:

> The young child laughs and cries in her dream, and talks about it as soon as she can: "Mom, there are chickens in my bed!"
>
> My husband/wife laughs, talks, gets up . . . does all kinds of things in his/her sleep.

You can ask yourself, what do I read before going to bed, what do I pray? What is it that I want? You can ask for a dream, you can prepare for it. Dreams on demand? Why not? Try it! It's useful to have some writing instrument handy to jot down a dream or nocturnal insight. If not, experience will show how quickly precious things can be lost.

The Scientific Approach to Dreams

Acceptance of the reality of dreams received a new start with Sigmund Freud.[2] Not that it was totally novel! Freud himself refers to the Bible (think Joseph, Daniel, Pharaoh, Balaam, and other prophets, e.g., Num 12:6, Jer 23) as well as to handbooks for the interpretation of dreams from antiquity (Aristotle, Macrobius, and Artemidorus). In addition, as a Jew he was steeped in a tradition that deals intelligently with this material (ever since Joseph and Daniel!) and that has mastered the art of dream interpretation. There is a discussion of dreams in the Talmud, in the writings of Maimonides, and even in the works of later mystics. Two recent Jewish encyclopedias (Louis Jacobs and Werblovsky-Wigoder) feature an extensive article about dreams. Thus I was amazed to learn that one of the longest digressions in the whole of the Babylonian Talmud is devoted to dreams (see Berachot 55a–57b, six full folio pages, which corresponds to 23 pages in the Italian translation). Here are some sayings from this Talmudic instruction:

> Every dream has meaning, except the one you dream on an empty stomach (R. Hisda).
>
> An unexplained dream is like an unread letter.
>
> A dream is always only partial, even if it comes true. How do we know that? Joseph dreamt about the sun and the moon (which is to say, his father and mother), but when the dream came true, his mother was already dead (R. Berekja).
>
> In a dream nothing is revealed but the thoughts harbored in your heart during the day (see Dan 2:29-30) (Rabbi Samuel).
>
> What does it mean if in your dream you see a camel, a white horse, whether or not galloping, or a donkey? In every instance there is an indication, sometimes positive, sometimes negative. For example, with respect to the donkey: When you see a donkey

2. See S. Freud, *Die Traumdeuting*; C. G. Jung and his analyses of dreams in *Symbols of Transformation (Symbolen van de omvorming)*; E.Äppli, *Der Traum und seine Deutung* (Zürich, 1973).

> in your dream you should prepare for good things to come, for it has been said: "Lo, your king comes to you; triumphant and victorious is he, humble and riding on a donkey, on a colt, the foal of a donkey" (Zech 9:9).

> Five things have one-sixtieth of another thing in them: fire, honey, Sabbath, sleep, and dream. Fire contains one-sixtieth of hell, honey one-sixtieth of manna, Sabbath one-sixtieth of the world to come, sleep one-sixtieth of death, and *dream one-sixtieth of prophesy.*

Dreams are texts that have to be read and interpreted. They are not nonsense, no idle tomfoolery. They are language and carry meaning. To a certain extent they respond to your most intimate nature, but frequently they show a mirror image and thus the opposite of who you are in your conscious daily life.

For Freud dreams are related to libido, sexual urge, unfulfilled desires, or feelings of fear and conjecture about the future. One of his definitions says: "The dream is a (disguised) fulfillment of a (repressed, displaced) desire." That desire is, according to Freud, sexual in nature. His study, completed just before the year 1900, has been reprinted endlessly; interestingly, most buyers have been the general, interested public, and not professionals in psychiatry for whom the book was originally intended! It still is worthwhile reading, with dozens of dreams and their original interpretation. The principal purpose was to give psychiatrists an instrument for the analysis of neuroses. Reactions to the book led Freud to new insights, especially regarding the symbolism inherent in dreams. Starting with the third printing (1911), Otto Rank complemented the study with his own contributions and a rich bibliography. When Freud met Jung they told each other their dreams. Their ways parted because of, among other reasons, a difference of opinion about dream interpretation.

While Freud recognized the importance of dreams, although with rather one-sided bias, Carl Gustav Jung assigns to dreams also the role of the voice of the collective unconscious. Jung often listened to the dreams of very disturbed patients as expressions of the collective unconscious. He found confirmation of his interpretations in myths and esoteric works that developed constructs similar to those found in certain dreams. Here are a few insights gleaned from the Swiss psychiatrist:

> He calls the dream "the old man" whom we must question about the direction of our life, how our development, individually and collectively, is progressing. By learning to listen to our dreams we can resolve the impasses of life.
>
> As shown by research, a child's ego is undetermined when awake but is well structured in its dreams. Jung then poses the question: Where does the structured ego in its dreams come from? And where does it go when the person dies?
>
> In his own life he had dreams that recurred as often as three times and that, among other things, foreshadowed World War I (all of Europe covered by a flood, only Switzerland was saved; he sits by himself high on a mountaintop; the water looks like blood; etc.). At first he feared he was becoming schizophrenic, until the war broke out a few weeks later.

Dreams have to do with your shadow side. A dream provides indirect information about it, which you need if you are going to be able to integrate your shadow steadily into your life and to develop maturity. You also need that information to take ownership of your shadow so as not to reject it or to project it onto others. As in the crossing of two circles, an aura must be formed. This kind of integration allows you to hold on to the paradox of faith and doubt, weak and strong, conscious and unconscious, the crossing of the field of your own ego with the field of the unconscious, of what you desire and what you detest. A dream is one of many ways to access your shadow side. God loves your shadow more than your ego. The important thing is that little by little you start uniting what you originally saw as opposing poles of what is acceptable to your ego and what is unacceptable to it, and that you allow them to co-exist in a paradox within yourself. This requires patience and time. Dreams play an essential role in the process.

Biblical Dreams

In the Bible dreams show up here and there, and a biblical dream is of course not different from any other dream although it may have a literary flourish, including occasional allusions to dreams dreamt by others.

One of the very first dreams recounted in the Bible is the one of Jacob in Genesis 28. Jacob is fleeing from his brother and on his mother Rebekah's advice he sets out for Haran where his uncle Laban lives. Along the way, between Beer-sheva and Haran, he spends the night in a lonely place in open air. "And he dreamed that there was a ladder set up on the earth, the top of it reaching to heaven; and the angels of God were ascending and descending on it" (Gen 28:12). The God of his forefathers speaks and promises him a blessed future. Awakened, Jacob realizes what happened. He takes the stone that he had placed under his head as a pillow, pours oil on top of it, and names the place "house of God" (Bethel).

This dream has something archetypical: in the midst of the greatest desolation, the lonely Jacob experiences the nearness of God, represented here by the ladder with the ascending and descending movement of the angels. The words and promises tell in time what the strong image of the ladder already communicated in the field of space. Past and present come together in this place of extreme poverty and loneliness. He is no longer alone, he is no longer lost. Nowhere at home, he now erects in this place the foundation of the house of God.

A person who dreams and, once awakened, searches for the dream's meaning, would do well always to remember the dream of Jacob's ladder. Benedict put that ladder at the beginning of the longest chapter of his Rule, the one that deals with humility. That ladder is the inspirational symbol of the monk's spiritual path. In John, Jesus already makes an allusion to this dream image at the end of his first gathering. He says to Nathanael, who senses that Jesus sees through him: "You will see greater things than these," and He adds "Very truly, I tell you, you will see heaven opened and the angels of God ascending and descending upon the Son of Man" (John 1:51). To see and to dream, but especially to understand fully what the patriarch dreamt for us: that is what matters in life.

While he is with Laban, Jacob receives another dream in which one of God's angels teaches him how to outsmart his uncle. He recounts the dream to his two wives when he decides to leave his uncle and to return to the land of his birth (Gen 31:11-13). On the way back, all alone at the bank of the river Jabbok, he lives through another extraordinary night. The question whether Jacob had a dream there or went through an actual experience truly is no longer important. No matter how, he encountered God.

According to Jewish tradition as systematized by Maimonides in the Middle Ages, the Lord reveals himself sometimes in the clear light of day and sometimes in the twilight of evening or in the dark of night; at times He comes himself, at other times in the form of an angel; He can appear in a vision or He can talk in a dream, in which He may speak in a highly personal manner or by means of a messenger, an angel. These are all gradations within a self-same communication. God's speaking through an angel in a dream is, then, the lowest step in a series of forms available to the Lord to make Himself known, while God's visit to Abraham under the tree at Mamre constitutes the highest revelation of God's self-representation. While Jacob is an impressive figure with his dreams, the most important dreamer in the cycle of patriarchs is Joseph, Jacob's favorite son. He dreams and, in addition, explains the dreams of others.

The whole story starts with him dreaming, not once but twice. In the prologue of the long story about Joseph and his brothers these dreams serve as disguised predictions containing the whole drama. "The sun, the moon, and eleven stars were bowing down to me" (Gen 37:9). The entire cosmos bows to him: what kind of king, then, is he to become? The young man is clearly naïve: by relating his dreams to his brothers they begin hating him even more. Is it possible that the one who will later explain the dreams of others does not understand what he is telling his brothers, while they appear to get the gist quite well. "Are you indeed to reign over us? Are you indeed to have dominion over us?" (Gen 37:8). Or is it impossible for him to stay quiet about his dreams, like a prophet who cannot refrain from prophesying: "The lion has roared; who will not fear? The Lord God has spoken; who can but prophesy?" (Amos 3:8). If the dream is a hidden language in which God communicates about Himself, how can you hush it up? The dream will come true anyway, whether or not smothered, with or without hatred.

In any event, Joseph pays the price of that hatred and, reduced to a slave in Egypt, is eventually thrown into jail. There he shows himself to be an accurate interpreter of dreams. The dreams of two other prisoners turn out just as Joseph had said they would. Years later, when Egypt's pharaoh receives a double dream that mystifies him and that nobody is able to explain, one of the former fellow prisoners remembers Joseph's mastery in the interpretation of dreams. Joseph then explains his art: "It is not I," but "God will give Pharaoh a favorable answer" (Gen 41:16). To his fellow prisoners, depressed because of the dreams they failed to understand, Joseph had taught: "Do not interpretations belong to God?" (Gen 40:8).

What this old tale teaches us is that God sends dreams and that God Himself explains them best. Joseph is communicating with God and when, close to the end of the story, after the father's death, his brothers still do not wholly trust him, he explicates: "Even though you intended to do harm to me, God intended it for good, in order to preserve a numerous people, as he is doing today. So have no fear; I myself will provide for you and your little ones" (Gen 50:20, 21).

Daniel, in literary form presented as another Joseph, also became proficient in the interpretation of dreams. He too finds himself in exile and ends up being thrown into prison. Life at the margin favors dream activity. In Daniel 2 the challenge is unimaginably great. Daniel has to deal with all the wise men and magicians of the whole empire of Nebuchadnezzar! Not only did they have to explain a dream, they had to be able to recount the dream themselves. Failing that, capital punishment awaited them all! In fact, the death sentence had already been pronounced, "The king flew into a violent rage and commanded that all the wise men of Babylon be destroyed" (Dan 2:12). The drama is brought to a head. Right at that time Daniel acts.

As Daniel explains, "No wise men, enchanters, magicians or diviners can show the king the mystery that the king is asking, but there is a God in heaven who reveals mysteries, and he has disclosed to King Nebuchadnezzar what will happen at the end of days. . . . But as for me, this mystery has not been revealed to me because of any wisdom that I have more than any other living being, but in order that the interpretation may be known to the king and that you may understand the thoughts of your mind" (Dan 2:27-30).

It is on the basis of this text that rabbinical teaching holds that dreams have to do with the thoughts we nourish in our hearts. Daniel and Joseph are the only two biblical figures who excel as visionaries able to interpret the dreams of others.

The prophets also have "visions and dreams" in the Bible. See, for example, the primary text in Numbers: "When there are prophets among you, I the LORD make myself known to them in visions; I speak to them in dreams" (Num 12:6, cf. Jer 23:28). "What has straw in common with wheat?" which in the Talmud is explained as the sense and nonsense present in every dream. Further, the heathen prophet Balaam is a man filled with visions and ecstatic revelations but also with dream images and angelic appearances (in which, ironically, his donkey recognizes the angel before he does) (Num 22:22-24).

There is sufficient ground in these texts for the idea from the rabbinical tradition that the dream is one-sixtieth of prophecy. Dreams belong to the same field as prophecy, albeit in attenuated form.

In the New Testament it is especially the other Joseph who is, just as his forefather, the patriarch, "a man of dreams" (in the first two chapters of Matthew he dreams no less than four times! Also the wise men from the East are warned in a dream not to return to Herod). It is notable that while Joseph accepts his dreams as sources of information and orientation, he certainly does not sleepwalk through life. He looks and listens and acts according to what he hears and sees, and when gripped by doubts or fears a new dream shows the appropriate course of action (see Matt 2:19-22). In his dreams "angels do the rounds," just as the poet wrote.

In Acts, Peter dreams more than once, including in jail. Visions repeat themselves and hint clearly for him to change the way in which he deals with gentiles who wish to participate in the Christian life. So in Acts 10:11 he thrice receives the vision of unclean animals that are lowered from heaven in a large sheet, and then the story is retold another three times. Peter is being spurred on to break the food taboo. He only understands the meaning of this vision when the Spirit moves him to depart for the house of Cornelius, the Roman centurion, without resisting. In fact, it is thanks to this dream that early Christianity's great breakthrough to the gentiles is realized.

In somewhat analogous fashion we see how Paul finds his way to Europe by thrice receiving a sign. First, the Spirit stops him from turning left, the direction of Asia; then "the Spirit of Jesus" does not allow him to turn right to Bithynia. During the night Paul receives a vision in which a man pleads with him to cross straight over to Europe. As soon as he awakes, he acts accordingly. Now he knows unmistakably what God wants him to do (see Acts 16:6-10). The passage is informative: God speaks in three different ways, but the dream or the vision is as authoritative as the Holy Spirit or the Spirit of Jesus. After the third sign, a vision in a dream, the matter is decided: God has called us to go and preach there! Let's cross!

God, either Himself or His angel, speaks in nighttime visions. He brings illumination, expands the field in which we move, unblocks a situation, and sometimes shows the way very concretely while, at the same time, we must exercise our common sense and confront the dream message with the actual situation. This is what Joseph did in returning from Egypt, Peter in receiving the messengers of Cornelius, Paul with his crossing to Macedonia.

Dreams are of vital importance. We do well to adopt an open attitude toward them. They usher us into a creative, wider world in which we become receptive to the unexpected, yes, even to what God wants to communicate to us. When the time is ripe they can throw light on the manner in which we are dealing with an evolving situation. The Bible teaches how dreams can have to do with God. They are a medium for His word. As shown by Joseph and Daniel, God is the sender of the dream and also its best interpreter. In crisis situations, in exile, in jail or in any other form of marginalization we often receive dream images: the Bible teaches us how to decipher their message. Of course, others can be helpful by attentive listening to your dream. But in the final analysis, you yourself are always the best interpreter of what you dreamt: the dream always has to do with you, and with the thoughts of your heart (cf. Dan 2:30).[3]

See also: Humility, *Lectio Divina*, Night Vigil, Paradox, Sleeping

3. This section is a shortened version of what I published in *Heiliging* (*Hallowing*) 51, no. 1 (2001): 22–34. See also A. Grün, *Dreams of the Spiritual Journey* (Schuyler Spiritual Series, 1993). Two of the studies referred to by Grün talk about dreams as God's "forgotten language." See J. A. Sanford, *Gottes vergessene Sprache* (Zürich, 1966), and H. Hark, *Der Traum als Gottes vergessene Sprache* (Olten, 1984). Isn't this sufficient reason to treat dreams with respect and confidence?

E

EATING

There are only two ways to eat: to feast or to fast.

—Venerable Fulton Sheen

This is Jesus' own philosophy in the Gospel, but it is also the way of the poor anywhere in the world: when they eat, it's a feast, widely shared with their kin, and otherwise they eat little or nothing, they "fast."

"Your feasts are too sober and your daily fare is too rich," an African woman observed after a longish stay in Europe. It makes one think. In the heart of Africa a wedding feast can last for days, and sometimes it may take a bride and groom years to pay off the debt for the lavish party. And the matter-of-fact North European then thinks to himself: is all this really necessary?

For many, what we may call the culture of eating has been lost. When does a family sit down to eat together nowadays? We get our food from vending machines, we dig into snacks and fast food. We hardly eat, but we munch on candy all day. Some confess to overeating while others suffer from anorexia. A few even switch between these two extremes.

At the same time, everything can be cooked in an instant, just look at the precooked meals aisle of the supermarket: the vegetables are ready to be popped into the microwave. We can buy the healthiest foods (organic and similar) as well as the strangest dishes from every corner of the earth.

For all too many, enjoying a repast in a healthy, slow, convivial way has become a rarity, an inconceivable luxury. We rush through daily life, and time has become our veritable king, yes, our "god," to whom we apparently owe a heck of a lot.

The art of living has to do with table manners: to be able to wait for each other, to pay attention to the youngest, the weakest, the oldest, the most clumsy of the group, to notice what is lacking, and to look out for the special needs of a particular tablemate. Exceptions are part and parcel of life and thus also at the table: no salt for this one, no sugar or fat for that one.

On the other side, what will "heaven" be like other than having to do with eating? At least that's what stories from just about all traditions tell us. There will be eating and drinking!

Once upon a time, in a rapture a Jewish rabbi was allowed to see the other side. First he arrived in hell and to his astonishment saw that everybody was sitting at table and that the tables were set with abundant quantities of the most delicious apples, pears, berries, strawberries, grapefruits, and pumpkins. He discerned more exotic fruits than he had seen in his whole life as a poor itinerant rabbi. And this in hell!

Looking a bit closer, he observed that all those present had a noticeable handicap: the forearm of all table companions was very, very long. That surprised him but, worse, whenever anybody picked up an exquisite something, they were unable to put it in their mouth. The longer he looked, the more horrible it seemed to him. There was much moaning and groaning around that table: everybody wanted to eat but nobody could place anything in their mouth. The rabbi closed his eyes: this was more than he could take.

When he opened his eyes again, an angel had come and had carried him to heaven. And what did he see there? Tables and more tables, all set with precisely the same abundance and variety of fruits as he had seen in hell! Nothing less and, as far as he could tell, nothing more! Continuing to gaze, he realized that in heaven too all table companions had a noticeable handicap: their forearms were unusually long as well. He held his breath, but it did not take long for him to realize that the atmosphere here was completely different than in the previous hall. Here everybody's face was radiant! Indeed, one asked another "What would you like? What do you prefer to taste now? What can I help you with?" And then one would bring the selected prune to the mouth of the other, and all ate in mutual helpfulness. And, to boot, thanks to their long forearms they could serve from dishes much farther away than normally would be the case!

So, the art with which we consume our meals in this world apparently has repercussions in the next! We find many amusing observations and practical recommendations for serving at table in the oldest rules for monks. Even though food is taken in silence, the nonverbal system has been so fine-tuned that everybody is immediately aware of how the monk at his elbow is doing. In principle you're not supposed to ask anything for yourself, but you can always ask a server to bring something for the person next to you. Once a brother ladled out his soup and to his surprise found a mouse in his plate. He passed the pot of soup to his fellow brother who, deep in thought, had noticed nothing amiss with his neighbor. The first brother waited a moment and then signaled the server to approach. Pointing to his plate and the one of his brother, he said, "My brother does *not* have a mouse in his soup."

John Cassian (fifth century) provides three rules in his wise advice on gluttony, one of the first "demons" or vices that a brother has to learn to overcome during his training:

1) Never eat prior to the ordained time.
2) Eat with moderation, and never until you're full, always leave some room.
3) Gradually become insensitive to the quality of what is put on the table.

Eating prior to the ordained time was a particular temptation for hermits. An aphorism on a related subject is: Never eat between meals. To which a wise guy replied, "Indeed, I never eat between meals. Whenever I eat, it's a meal."

The Danish writer Karen Blixen once wrote such a successful short story that years later it was made into a movie: *Babette's Feast*. All the action takes place in a small, confined village in Norway, in the Berlewaage fjord, in an austere Protestant community. The dénouement defies the imagination: Babette, of Parisian provenance and now a domestic servant with a prominent family in the north, succeeds in making a seven-star dinner! That meal brings about genuine change in the village: All relationships are transformed and everybody is gushing with gratitude and happiness! Never did people feel such connection with each other and so pleased with themselves as on the occasion of this festive dinner, prepared and served up in accordance with the best rules of one of the most famous restaurants in Paris.

In the Christian tradition every meal refers to a coming feast. During the Last Supper with his disciples, when Jesus broke bread and gave it to them as a sign of his irrevocable passing, he also looked toward that other, greater feast that is to come: "Truly I tell you, I will never again drink of the fruit of the vine until that day when I drink it new in the kingdom of God" (Mark 14:25).

See also: Fasting, Feasting, Serving, Solidarity

EJACULATORY PRAYERS

The thoughts so dear and good
they come to me in Mass;
the thoughts so dear and good,
they're Jesus' words to me:
the thoughts so dear and good
sweet balms they are to me
His thoughts so dear and good!

—Guido Gezelle[1]

In the Latin expression *oratio iaculatoria* (ejaculatory prayer) we detect the original image of *iaculum*, an object that is shot, like an arrow.[2] Augustine appears to be the oldest source we have to discuss this type of prayer, even though he makes reference to others before him who used the term. He discusses it in his famous letter addressed to the widow Proba. As a matter of fact, this letter contains a complete treatise on prayer (Letter 130). Although he does not say from whom he learned of this ancient tradition, Augustine, asserts that the Desert Fathers in Egypt practiced this particular form of prayer and passed it on to each other.

> The brethren in Egypt are reported to have very frequent prayers, but these very brief, and, as it were, sudden and ejaculatory,[3] lest the wakeful and aroused attention which is indispensable in prayer should by protracted exercises vanish or lose its keenness. And in this they themselves show plainly enough, that just as this attention is not to be allowed to become exhausted if it

1. Guido Gezelle (1830–1899) was a Flemish Catholic priest and poet who wrote in the vernacular of West Flanders, Belgium. With respect to this short poem's theme "thoughts so dear and good," cf. "Aspirations, Ejaculatory Prayers, and Good Thoughts," the title of chap. 13 of Part II of *Introduction to the Devout Life*, n. 9 [translator's note].

2. The French translation (*oraison jaculatoire*) clings closely to the Latin, but the Dutch term (*schietgebeden*) is quaint and intriguing: it literally suggests prayers that one shoots (*schiet*) like an arrow, flying fast. While the English term *ejaculatory prayers* may be used only rarely today, in Dutch the expression *schietgebeden* is still current and quite popular [translator's note].

3. In the Latin text: *orationes . . . raptim quodammodo jaculatae.* Information provided by Fr. Standaert in the Dutch translation of Letter 130 [translator's note].

> cannot continue long, so it is not to be suddenly suspended if it is sustained. Far be it from us either to use "much speaking" in prayer, or to refrain from prolonged prayer, if fervent attention of the soul continue.[4]

It is interesting to note that the form of these prayers has to do with the issue of attention span.

John Cassian, who devoted two of his twenty-four conferences to prayer, provides a discourse on that short, frequently repeated prayer of the Desert Fathers. It is the subject of just about the whole tenth conference. On the basis of one verse from a psalm, "O God, come to my assistance; O LORD, make haste to help me" (Ps 70:1, in Cassian's text), he sets out a complete methodology to enable one to remain in prayer in any circumstances, whether favorable or unfavorable ones. It suffices to memorize the short formula and to repeat it, not mechanically but, rather, creatively interiorizing it to accord with the mood of the moment.

In this manner one stays constantly in prayer and in relationship with the living, saving God. At the end of the conference, Cassian admits, "[We] wished to follow [the method] very closely, as we fancied that it would be a short and easy method; but we have found it even harder to observe than that system of ours by which we used formerly to wander here and there in varied meditations through the whole body of the Scriptures without being tied by any chains of perseverance."[5]

Elsewhere in his work Cassian describes how the monks in Egypt would lie flat on the ground after a psalm and then pray in that position. You heard nothing ("not as here in Gaul," he added, with some shame, "where there is coughing and sneezing and spitting, the louder the better!"), he wrote, "except somebody who, driven by God's grace, pours his heart out in unspeakable sighs."[6]

4. Augustine, *Letter 130* (chap. 10), available at http://www.newadvent.org/fathers/1102130.htm (accessed November 8, 2016) [translator's note].

5. "Conference 10, The Second Conference of Abbot Isaac: On Prayer," available at www.osb.org/lectio/cassian/conf/book1/conf10.html#10.14 (accessed November 8, 2016) [translator's note].

6. The quotation is translated from the Dutch text used by Fr. Standaert. See also *The Twelve Books of John Cassian on the Institutes of the Coenobia and the Remedies for the Eight Principal Faults* (II:20), available at www.osb.org/lectio/cassian/inst/inst2.html#2.10 [translator's note].

Here we hear another precious expression from the oldest prayer tradition: the sighs of the Spirit in the praying heart. Paul talks about it in the eighth chapter of his letter to the Romans. The citation fits perfectly with a catechesis of prayer: "Likewise the Spirit helps us in our weakness; for we do not know how to pray as we ought, but that very Spirit intercedes with sighs too deep for words" (Rom 8:26). These kinds of sighs are preverbal: they occur at a deeper level than the properly formed word. That longing reaches for what is good, for what pleases God, for God as the highest good.

Later traditions will speak of "aspirations," "lifting up of the soul," and "anagogic" (ascending) movements of the heart.

Benedict mentions prayer repeatedly in his Rule. He expects his monks to pray often and to bow or to kneel frequently, all the while noting that prayer must be "short" and "pure," especially when performed in community. It must arise from the heart, intense, burning, tearfully. Only when somebody is overcome by God's grace may the prayer be prolonged and not be curtailed. Here he is clearly passing on the teachings of Augustine and Cassian.

In the works of other authors we read how the short, pure, and passionate prayer is part of a strategy to deal with the devil. Satan tries to divert us from our path with all kinds of propositions, images, and distractions. The ejaculatory prayer is so fast that even the devil himself cannot stop it. As Cardinal Giovanni Bona (seventeenth century) taught us, it reaches its goal, namely, "the heart of God," unhindered.

In this approach, any attempt to reach God through a lengthy discourse is cut off at the pass. John Climacus finds that a prayer must always be short: nobody's prayers are heard just because they are loquacious. He cites many examples from the Bible in which prayers of little more than a single word were heard:

> The whole fabric of your prayer must be simple, because through a single word the tax collector and the prodigal son reconciled with God (see Luke 18: 13; 15: 21).
>
> Try to refrain from loquaciousness so that your spirit is not distracted with the search for words. One word from the tax collector sufficed to obtain God's merciful attention, and one believing word saved the good thief. The use of oratory in prayer has frequently misled the spirit with propositions and distractions, but the repetition of one word usually promotes concentration of the spirit.

> A person is at the beginning of prayer when he succeeds in removing distractions which at the beginning beset him. He is at the middle of the prayer when the mind concentrates only on what he is meditating on and contemplating. He reaches the end when, with the Lord, the prayer enraptures him.[7]

In these three paragraphs we find the full movement of prayer from many words (*polylogia, multiloquia*) to one word (*monologistos*), let alone one Name. In the famous catechesis of Abba Macarius we note how the prayer becomes ever shorter, but also more intense:

> Abba Macarius was asked, "How should one pray?" The old man said, "There is no need at all to make long discourses; it is enough to stretch out one's hands and say, 'Lord, as you will, and as you know, have mercy.' And if the conflict grows fiercer say, 'Lord, help!' " He knows very well what we need and he shews us his mercy.[8]

The anonymous writer of the treatise *The Cloud of Unknowing* (England, fourteenth century) recommends that we limit ourselves to one-syllable words repeated constantly: two of his examples are "sin" and "God." "Sin" summons up the sense of our insignificance, impotence, and unworthiness vis-à-vis God, who enfolds you in his holy and saving embrace of mercy. One of the sayings of the fathers tells of how one person, after having committed a terrible act of violence against a pregnant woman, retreated to the desert and repeated till his death, "I am a human being and I have sinned. You are God, please forgive me."

There are plenty of examples of ejaculatory prayers. St. Francis liked to pray, "My God, my All." Others, including Blessed Charles de Foucauld, cry out with the Gospel's doubting Thomas, "My Lord and my God,"—the highest profession of faith in the New Testament. Dom Marmion liked to repeat, with the disciple whom Jesus loved, "*Dominus est!*" ("It is the Lord!" John 21:7). Augustine found he could say everything with "*Deo gratias!*" ("Thanks be to God!"),

7. John Climacus, *Ladder of Divine Ascent 28:4.9.20* as quoted by Jean M. Heimann at http://catholicfire.blogspot.com/2009/03/st-john-climacus-my-favorite-quotes.html (accessed November 9, 2016) [translator's note].

8. *Sayings of the Desert Fathers* (Macarius the Great 19), 131.

and that it fit all circumstances (Letter 41). From one of the Desert Fathers we learn the following: A brother visited an old man who lived on Mount Sinai and he asked him, "Father, tell me how to pray, because I have incurred the wrath of God." The old man answered, "Child, when I pray, I say this: 'Lord, make me worthy to serve you the same way I served Satan, and make me worthy to love you the way I loved the sin.'" Francis de Sales noted in his book about the devout life, addressed to his dear Philothea, that

> Many people have made collections of vocal ejaculations and they can be very useful. However, my advice is not to restrict yourself to a set form of words but to pronounce either within your heart or with your lips such words as love suggests to you at the time. It will supply you with as many as you wish. . . . Such are the aspirations strewn so thickly throughout the psalms of David, various invocations of the name of Jesus, and the loving thoughts uttered in the Canticle of Canticles.[9]

The whole of chapter 13 of book 2 of Francis de Sales' *Introduction to the Devout Life* could be quoted on this topic. St. Francis de Sales has a brilliant memory and remembers countless examples from the lives of the saints. All of creation and every occurrence lead his soul to partake of that upward movement and to nestle in God as the highest good.

At the end of this discourse he adds that ejaculatory prayers are indispensable for the spiritual life. Those who use them will soon reach the highest peaks of spiritual freedom, even if they are not highly educated, while those who neglect them will get nowhere. For such persons, neither the active nor the contemplative life will lead to anything! "Without [spiritual recollection and ejaculatory prayers] rest is mere idleness, and labor is drudgery. Hence I exhort you to take up this practice with all your heart and never give it up."[10]

See also: Aspirations, *Dhikr*, Jesus and the Jesus Prayer, Name, Psalmody

9. St. Francis de Sales, *Introduction to the Devout Life*, trans. John K. Ryan (New York: Doubleday, 1989), 99.

10. St. Francis de Sales, *Introduction to the Devout Life*, 103.

EMPTINESS

"The quality of a bouquet in a vase depends on the manner in which the emptiness between branches and flowers is arranged," a Japanese woman once said.

However, emptiness invariably creates fear. According to a learned physicist, *horror vacui* appears to be a law of nature: nature abhors a vacuum. And indeed, we have to admit that we fill up empty spaces real quickly. An attic that is cleaned out begets company within the shortest time: discarded dolls or three-legged chairs soon fill the emptiness again.

But nature itself is conspicuously empty: it's hard to describe it any other way than "empty." Look at the firmament: together with a handful of planets we revolve around the sun at a distance of millions of kilometers and the sun itself revolves around an essentially empty Milky Way, which revolves within an exploding cosmos that primarily consists of emptiness. If we observe the smallest particle that can be seen under a powerful microscope, we must conclude that our world of atoms is made up of almost nothing in, proportionally, an enormously large, empty space. Microcosmos and macrocosmos: everything is empty, but we hardly realize it.

Those who have learned to build emptiness into their time schedules or even into the spaces of their lives, have discovered an inner treasure.

Our abbey is built around a large vacant square. The center of our building complex is unoccupied. Not the church, not the dining hall, not the community hall, not the library, but an empty courtyard stands at the center of the whole undertaking. Every day we take the cloister walk around the square of that garden. In this center, nothing happens. It is our lung. When we move on to another activity, we necessarily have to walk along this inner court—and we rearrange our energies. We let go of the bad ones. We breathe, think about nothing, and proceed with a broadened heart.

How much room is there for emptiness in my calendar? And do I possess something like a storm-free zone on the inside, a small square like that abbey's courtyard, that I can fall back on in-between two activities, a still point that cannot be threatened or overtaken by busyness, by criticism, or by flattery. A wheel turns around an axle that does not turn. How come? Thanks to the emptiness around the axle. A vase or a ladle can only add to its usefulness to the extent that the receiving emptiness of the object is expanded.

Where the culture of fullness reigns, there we now hear the cry for a culture of emptiness. Fullness collides with everything: a billiard ball, a bullet, a bomb. Chock-full, as the expression goes. Full, even explosively so, loud and obtrusive because it cannot help itself: this is the final thrust of a culture dominated by fullness—our current culture in the West.

The culture of emptiness creates room, enables new relationships, learns to fast without fear, and avoids neither silence nor slowness nor pleasant idleness. All the great traditions speak extremely positively about emptiness or in powerful paradoxes.

Judaism teaches how God created the world by practicing a contraction on himself. He did *tsimtsum,* which literally means He fasted on himself and so created an emptiness within himself. A space opened up: otherness was allowed to exist. The relationship was born.

In Christianity we know, with Paul, the act of "self-emptying" through which God revealed himself in Christ. This *kenosis,* or emptying, shows how Christ loved to the extreme. "[He] emptied himself, taking the form of a slave, being born in human likeness. And being found in human form, he humbled himself and became obedient to the point of death—even death on a cross" (Phil 2:7-8). That is the concrete meaning of the self-emptying or *kenosis* of Jesus. Paul asks his dear Philippians to nourish in their hearts exactly the same feelings Christ showed in his self-emptying. Also we should "Do nothing from selfish ambition or conceit" but, rather, have a higher regard for others than for ourselves, and we are to place the interests of others above our own (see Phil 2:1-4).

In Buddhism "emptiness" (*shunyata*) is a central concept. It reverberates in the famous Heart Sutra: "Form is emptiness, and the very emptiness is form; emptiness does not differ from form, form does not differ from emptiness." No form exists that does not at the same time contain emptiness and vice versa. The systematic hollowing out of thinking in terms of substance and of things existing with a certain density and independence, does not lead to nihilism in Buddhism but to the rewarding intuition that everything stands in relationship to everything else and is connected. Everything is interrelated, and nothing exists on its own. Also here we find that consideration of emptiness creates a space in which the experience of relationships is possible. While the fullness perspective kills relationship, attention to emptiness allows the potential for life in relationship to flourish.

To cultivate emptiness means to become poor. To become poor leads to seeing the whole clearly, in mutual interdependence. Purity opens the eye and reveals God. Clarity, transparency, and emptiness work together and, in the end, correspond to the greatest mystery. The following appears in passing in the unpublished writings of French philosopher Louis Lavelle: "Ne rien avoir pour voir Dieu qui n'a rien et est tout" (To own nothing in order to see God, who has nothing, but is everything).

See also: Breathing, Culture, Memory, Pilgrimage, Psalmody

F

FASTING

Of all the useful instruments in our arsenal for a spiritually liberated life, fasting is, nowadays, one of the most forgotten. We, Christians in the West, are the only ones among all religions of the world who no longer realize what fasting can mean.[1] In the East, Christians still know its meaning very well. And it is the Muslims in our midst who are the ones who now show us that there is joy in fasting for a whole month in global solidarity at Ramadan.

To argue for the re-introduction of an authentic practice of fasting is an uphill battle. Talk about fasting scares many people off. Actually, there are only two kinds of people: those who fast and everybody else. Bringing up the subject of fasting in a conversation tends to strike terror in the listener; and those who have no experience with fasting but would like to make counterarguments are quickly disarmed by the authority that comes from experience.

A few aphorisms and proverbs from various traditions may shake us awake and call our attention to the fact that fasting has to do with wisdom and joy:

> "Love fasting" (*ieiunium amare*), Rule of Benedict (RB 4:13).
>
> "Be cheerful in fasting" (*in ieiuniis hilares*) (Rule of Macarius).
>
> "Fasting, the soul's joy" (Abba Helladius).
>
> "Fasting is a check against sin for the monk. He who discards it is like a rampaging stallion."
> "It is better to eat meat and drink wine and not eat the flesh of one's brethren through slander" (Abba Hyperechius).

1. The new *Catechism of the Catholic Church* says nothing meaningful about the practice of fasting and refers to canon law, which itself is quite limited on the subject. Fasting is recommended on only two days: Ash Wednesday and Good Friday. People older than sixty are no longer required to fast. And it is not supposed that during a day of fasting one should not eat anything at all.

"Fasting humbles the body, and keeping vigil purifies the spirit" (Abba Longinus).

"Hunger and keeping vigil cleanse the heart of impure thoughts and the body of the urges of the enemy, so as to make a dwelling for the Holy Spirit" (Anonymous saying of one of the Fathers).

"The whole body is transformed by fasting, keeping vigil, and repentance, and thus it may be led again by the Spirit. . . . In this manner, I believe, it already receives 'the spiritual body' that it will have at the resurrection of the just" (Abba Anthony the Great, first letter).

"Abba Joseph asked Abba Poemen, 'How should one fast?' Abba Poemen said to him, 'For my part, I think it better that one should eat every day, but only a little, so as not to be satisfied.' Abba Joseph said to him, 'When you were younger, did you not fast two days at a time, abba?' The old man said, 'Yes, even for three days and four and the whole week. The Fathers tried all this out as they were able and they found it preferable to eat every day, but just a small amount. They have left us this royal way, which is light.' "[2]

"If you want to win the battle with the first demon, the one of gluttony, and muzzle him, keep to these three rules: 1) never eat prior to the ordained time; 2) never eat till you are full; 3) gradually become indifferent to the quality of the food that is served" (John Cassian).

"A stomach that is always full cannot see secrets" (Zulu saying).

"Eat when you are hungry and drink when you are thirsty. And know this: all that is too much is detrimental" (Lao Tsu, Chinese sage).

"Most people eat too much. They live on one-fourth of what they eat. The rest serves to feed physicians" (found on Egyptian papyrus, third millennium BCE).

2. This and the previous sayings are from *Sayings of the Desert Fathers.*

> "Fasting is something between God and me. Feeling powerless, I rested my head on God's knees, and I fasted" (Mahatma Gandhi).
>
> "I only know two philosophies of life: the first begins with fasting and ends with a feast; the second starts with a feast and ends with a blasting headache" (Venerable Fulton Sheen).
>
> "You must fast on Fridays. Fasting does not mean to eat something in lieu of something else, but means not eating at all. Those who fast make themselves transparent. Others become transparent to them. The pain of others enters them and they are defenseless. Thus, those who do not wish to be consumed by love, let them fill up their senses and eat heartily" (Lanza del Vasto).
>
> "Prayer and fasting give us a pure heart. A pure heart can see God. When we see God in our neighbor we will know peace, love, unity, and joy" (Saint Teresa of Calcutta).

Let us fast joyously, for example on Fridays. In the ancient monastic tradition meals were taken twice a day: around noon and around three in the afternoon. A small fast meant skipping the first meal and eating for the first time around 3:00 p.m. Those who wanted a major fast moved the first meal to the evening. Benedict wanted his monks to take their last meal prior to sunset. Other fathers said the sun never had seen them eat: they ate after sundown. The fast practiced by Muslims follows this venerable tradition. This is perhaps something we all could do: waiting to eat till evening on Fridays and, thus, not to eat anything from Thursday evening to Friday evening.

In the middle of the Sermon on the Mount, Jesus discusses three practices much beloved by the Pharisees: almsgiving, prayer, and fasting. The three go hand in hand. They support each other. They encompass the three possible relationships: *to the other* through alms, *to God* through prayer, and *to yourself and the universe* through fasting. Relating to the other receives emphasis in the Bible's prophetic tradition; relating to God occupies the center of attention in the priestly tradition; and the third relationship is analyzed with discernment by the sages and expressed in their proverbs. To neglect any one of these three relationships works to our detriment. When the third pole—relation to oneself and the cosmos—is neglected, self-knowledge and proper relationship to the universe are lost. What room, then, is there for wisdom?

Jesus knew how to fast. Some people think he abolished the tradition. But the opposites of fasting and feasting are part and parcel of his life. Let's not forget that he started his public ministry with a long fast of forty days. There is little reason to believe that this was purely symbolic. At other times he praises fasting, albeit in a discrete, unassuming manner: "when you fast, put oil on your head" (Matt 6:16). This is not just a paradox. In fasting toxins are excreted through perspiration and the body starts to smell. Anointing or perfuming not only masks the smell but the body is cleansed, inside and out.

Just once do we see Jesus react negatively to the practices of the Pharisees and the disciples of John the Baptist. He introduces a new norm that will become a sign for the Christian movement: "The wedding guests cannot mourn as long as the bridegroom is with them, can they? The days will come when the bridegroom is taken away from them, and then they will fast" (Matt 8:15; cf. Isa 53:8 on the Suffering Servant). The feast is defined by the presence of the Bridegroom; fasting signifies mourning his absence. As a result, for Christians the practice of fasting acquires a clear Christological reference point; it is not just something that is determined by the calendar. Whenever we learn about somebody's suffering we can show our solidarity by a fast, and whenever there is a feast we can freely break our fast because of the nearness of the bridegroom. Occasionally fasting with a person from another religious tradition creates an enormous interreligious bond.

Some of the church fathers transmit a word of Jesus that is not found in the gospels but that comes very close to other sayings of the Lord. Jesus would not only have said that we have to bless those who curse us, or to love those who hate us, or to pray for those who persecute us, he would also have said that it is well to "fast for those that persecute you."[3] Fasting and praying go hand in hand, the former reinforces the latter. That is why it is truly vile if we fast in form while at the same time we spread slander, or if we ostentatiously sit in sackcloth and ashes but go on extorting the poor. That kind of

3. *The Didache Online* 1:3, Paraclete Press, reproduced under Creative Commons license (accessed January 20, 2016) [translator's note].

conceit was already exposed in Isaiah's great chapter 58, which we hear each year at the beginning of Lent and which comes to us as a stern warning. Church father Basil the Great wrote indignantly, "To fast means to become a stranger to all vices. You don't eat meat but devour your brother! You abstain from wine but don't moderate your curses in the slightest! You wait till evening to eat your food but spend the whole day at the tribunal! Woe to those 'who are drunk, but not with wine' (Isa 51:21)."

Eating and fasting touch our humanness in a most vital aspect: every child struggles with it in the oral phase, which is so fundamental to the further development and structuring of life. Thus, we are dealing with something that is absolutely elementary and essential. The first sin in Genesis has to do with the mouth, just as the first temptation of Jesus in the desert ("command these stones to become loaves of bread" Matt 4:3). For that matter, life in the desert is marked by especially this kind of trial, as shown in the meditation in Deuteronomy 8, referenced by Jesus: "One does not live by bread alone, but by every word that comes from the mouth of God" (Matt 4:4).

In her psychoanalytic study of Bible texts, Marie Balmary points out the foundational role of the primary command and prohibition: don't just devour everything (*ne pas dévorer*). What is out of the question is excessive, unlimited consumption. That is prohibited. You may eat from every tree except that one (see Gen 2:16-17). How wise is that command! And it can be found in just about all cultures. It establishes a framework against unbridled gluttony. In Africa there is a traditional rule of foregoing one's own food for the guest who passes by.

The question arises: as a culture, what are we doing today? Aren't we plundering the biosphere, devouring it, ruining it, despite all the promises made at Kyoto?[4] The great powers were the first to shirk their obligations. And they do it with impunity. How much longer?

A culture of fullness is afraid of emptiness, silence, slowness, fasting, openness, everything other than itself. The person who never fasts seeks to negate the other. Do we actually realize how serious this is?

4. See Detachment, n. 1.

The mystical side of fasting is fully elucidated in Jewish teaching, which deals with a fast that precedes creation, a fast in God. In the beginning God created heaven and earth by effectuating a contraction on himself. God did *tsimtsum*. He fasted (*tsom*) on himself! And thanks to the thus-created emptiness, otherness could be born.

Three centuries ago a great rabbi by the name of Judah Loew, also called the Maharal of Prague, lived in the city of Prague. He studied the teaching of God's contraction on himself and said,

> God does it in order not to be everything. This makes it possible for the human person with his innate freedom to arrive on the scene. But if from his side the human being cannot bring himself to fear God, then he will completely fill up that emptiness, worse: he becomes everything, in a totalitarian fashion. Then there is no more world, no more creation, and no more God. . . . Thus, for the world to be world depends completely on the human person! He also must fast on himself and needs to fear God.[5]

Fasting gives expression to my fear of the Lord. This creates a proper relationship in all directions and with everything that is different. Through fasting I create an emptiness for the otherness that exists outside myself. The person who never fasts lives out of an abundance that sooner or later chases everybody else away, that steamrolls along and reduces everything to itself, until only one world remains, ours, the same, and nothing different is left, or simply nothing is left at all.

So, good fasting is an act of wisdom, of balance, of immense respect. Fasting is even a political and a cosmic deed, a deed that engages the world's salvation.

How to put this into action? Try to eat nothing for a twenty-four period (see Lanzo del Vasto). Have no fear: the puny ego, just like a spoiled child, will manifest itself soon enough and whisper all manner of things in your ear. Be a wise mother for that child. Don't spoil it! The child will calm down after less than ten fasts. The more difficult thing after a somewhat longer fast is how to resume eating. Especially, do not hurry! Start with little and chew your food well. Do it for God and nothing else; do it on account of the Bridegroom,

5. André Neher, *Le puits de l'exil. Tradition et modernité: la pensée du Maharal de Prague* (Paris: Cerf, 1991), 175–77.

the reference point used by Jesus in the Gospel. Maintain silence during the day of the fast. Search for God in his word. Fill the time gained with quietude, mindfulness, and prayer. Pay attention to all the needs you know of. Put things in order. Seek peace and experience the poorest in your own body. Bless them and do not fail to attend to those hidden deeds of which the left hand does not need to know what the right hand does. Fast with a joyful spirit and end your fast as if it were a quiet feast. Everything becomes communion and your thanksgiving knows no end.

See also: Eating, Emptiness, Feasting, Gratitude, Night Vigil, Solidarity, *Tsimtsum*

FEAR OF THE LORD

If our art of living is to have depth, we must devote ourselves to that distinctive attitude that the Bible calls "fear of the Lord."[1] Contrariwise, a world that lacks this dimension of awe before God is truly a terrible world. The paradox is this: those who, in contemplation of the Lord, allow awe into their hearts gradually lose their fear of anything. But those who live their lives denying that awe soon make fools of themselves or turn dangerous.

We must admit that the culture that surrounds us and that we breathe in every single day has lost all familiarity with the expression "fear of God." Even the very term is unattractive: we find it rather repulsive, and we spontaneously shrink from it. But it was not always so.

Whoever opens the Bible's Wisdom Books (Proverbs, Ecclesiastes, Sirach, but also the Psalms) discovers passionate praise for that "fear of the Lord" as a source of happiness, a way forward in life, the beginning and end of all life in wisdom.

Ecclesiastes concludes with this statement: "Fear God . . . for that is the whole duty of everyone" (Eccl 12:13). And the wisdom traditions repeat over and over: "The fear of the LORD is the beginning of wisdom" (Ps 111:10 *inter alia*). Another psalmist implores fervently: "give me an undivided heart to revere your name" (Ps 86:11; in *The Revised Grail Psalms* rendered as "single-hearted to fear your name.") This is at the same time the only and the loftiest essence of his searching desire for God. "Happy is everyone who fears the LORD," his whole life becomes blessed into the next generation, and Jerusalem and Israel shall know peace. God's blessing appears without limit as soon as we make room in ourselves for that holy reverence (see Ps 128).

In Isaiah we read that Jesse's offspring, a personification of the coming Messiah, receives the spirit of the Lord in abundance. The

1. A more extensive treatment of this topic can be found in Benoît Standaert, *De schat van God. Over de vreze des Heren. Een zoektocht door 25 eeuwen spiritualitei* (*God's Treasure: On Fear of the Lord: An Inquiry through 25 Centuries of Spirituality*) (Tielt: Lannoo, 2005). Published in French as *La Crainte de Dieu*, ed. Anne Sigier (Quebec, 2006).

Spirit is manifested in a series of seven gifts, in descending order. The first and highest gift is that of wisdom, the seventh and the last is that of the fear of the Lord, which is often equated with piety. Of this figure it is also said: "His delight shall be in the fear of the LORD" (Isa 11:3).

The Desert Fathers distill the same delight in their Proverbs: "Our breath and fear before the LORD must become one. We cannot but live by breathing that fear in and out."

Abba Poemen said: "The fear of God is simultaneously the beginning and the end. Because it is written: 'The beginning of wisdom is fear of the Lord.' On the other hand, when Abraham had finished preparing the altar for the offering of his son Isaac, God said to him: 'Now I know that you fear God.' " Abba Poemen also said: "As the breath which comes out of his nostrils, so does a man need humility and the fear of God."[2]

In the correspondence of John and Barsanufius, the wise hermits from Gaza (fifth to sixth centuries), we read how they often summarized the spiritual life in just two verbs: *to fear* God and *to thank* him in everything. They breathe in fear and breathe out thanks. In this manner their whole respiration is accomplished.

In various chapters of his Rule, Benedict sketches a portrait of the brother tasked with a specific function, such as infirmarian, guest master, cellarer, or prior. He always notes this one characteristic: he must be "*timens Dominum*, one who fears the Lord." We note that right away this opens an inner space. This person has an inner attitude of openness, accessibility; this person is not just occupied with himself. In one of these portraits Benedict amplifies that he has to be "a brother who is full of the fear of God" (*cuius animam timor Domini possidet*, RB 53:21). Awe of the Lord has conquered the man's inner castle and taken possession of it (*possidet*). Henceforth the brother belongs to the Lord and acts in Him.

When someone has acquired a holy reverence for the Lord, she gradually becomes possessed of a desire for God. Her life becomes unthinkable without Him. Once this basic attitude is acquired, everything receives depth. It qualifies even one's love of God—there is no contradiction between love and awe. In light of this, many of the masters made the following distinction. Beginners have a fear:

2. *Sayings of the Desert Fathers* (Poemen 49), 173.

they are afraid of the day of judgment, punishment, and hell. But, according to the great teachers, also the perfect ones know fear: awe, timidity, and immense respect are part and parcel of the holy life of those who come closest to God.

Many writers have discussed the relationship between love and fear; Julian, the anchoress from Norwich (early fifteenth century), penned perhaps the most lucid clarification. She distinguishes several forms of fear and, in its most authentic form, finds it a "brother" of love. It is worthwhile to read the whole discussion:

> For I recognize four kinds of fear. One is the fear of attack which suddenly comes to a man through weakness. This fear does good, for it helps to purify people, just like bodily sickness or other sufferings which are not sinful; for all such suffering helps people if it is endured patiently.
>
> The second fear is that of punishment, whereby someone is stirred and woken from the deep sleep of sin; for those who are deep in the sleep of sin are for the time being unable to perceive the gentle comfort of the Holy Ghost, until they have experienced this fear of punishment, of bodily death and of spiritual enemies. And this fear moves us to seek the comfort and mercy of God; and so it helps us and enables us to be contrite through the blessed touch of the Holy Ghost.
>
> The third is doubtful fear. Since it leads us on to despair, God wants us to turn doubtful fear into love through the knowledge of love; that is to say, the bitterness of doubt is to be turned into the sweetness of tender love through grace. For it can never please our Lord that his servants doubt his goodness.
>
> The fourth is reverent fear; the only fear that we can have which thoroughly pleases God is reverent fear; and it is very gentle; the more we have it, the less we feel it because of the sweetness of love. Love and fear are brothers; and they are rooted in us by the goodness of our Maker, and they will never be taken from us for all eternity. To love is granted to us by nature, and to love is granted to us by grace; and to fear is granted to us by nature, and to fear is granted to us by grace. It is fitting that God's lordship and fatherhood should be feared, as it is fitting for his goodness to be loved; and it is fitting for us who are his servants and his children to fear him as lord and as father, as it is fitting for us to love him for his goodness. And though this

> reverent fear and love are not separable, yet they are not one and the same. They are two in their nature and their way of working, yet neither of them may be had without the other. Therefore I am certain that those who love also fear, though they may only feel it a little.
>
> Even though they may appear to be holy, all the fears which face us, apart from reverent fear, are not truly so; and this is how they may be told apart. The fear that makes us quickly flee from all that is not good and fall upon our Lord's breast like a child upon its mother's bosom, which makes us do this with all our mind and all our willpower, knowing our feebleness and our great need, knowing God's everlasting goodness and his blessed love, seeking salvation only in him and clinging to him with sure trust—the fear which makes us do this is natural, gracious, good and true. And everything contrary to this is either completely wrong or partly wrong.
>
> This is the remedy, then: to recognize them both and refuse the wrong one. For the same natural profit which we gain from fear in this life through the gracious working of the Holy Ghost, shall in heaven be gracious, courteous and delightful in God's sight. And so in love we should be familiar and close to God, and in fear we should be gracious and courteous to God, and both equally.[3]

And she ends her reflections with a supplication:

> Let us ask God that we may fear him reverently and love him humbly and trust him strongly; for when we fear him reverently and love him humbly, our trust is never in vain; the greater and stronger our trust in God, the more we please and honour the Lord we trust. And if we fail in this reverent fear and meek love (which God forbid we should), our trust will soon slacken for the time being. And therefore we have a great need to pray to God that by his grace we may have this reverent fear and meek love, as his gift, in our hearts and in our deeds; for without this, no one can please God.[4]

3. Julian of Norwich, *Revelations of Divine Love,* trans. Elizabeth Spearing (London: Penguin Classics, 1998), 162–64.

4. Julian of Norwich, *Revelations of Divine Love*, 164.

When, a century and a half earlier, Francis of Assisi discusses fear of the Lord, he spontaneously experiences a surprising and revelatory fullness in the expression: in the fear of God it is Jesus himself who fears, who restrains himself, and who does not wish to overpower the human person as he draws near. The Lord approaches our freedom only with timidity, with apprehension:

> What with timidity was abided
> in timidity arrived. (Ida Gerhardt, from *Green Pastures*)

By experiencing awe before the Lord we are able, sooner or later, to detect this mysterious reciprocity. It is a source of enormous joy and inexhaustible bliss. Who would not want this kind of fear?

Toward the end of the last century Jewish thinker and philosopher André Neher drew attention to the original thought of Rabbi Judah Loew of Prague (ca. 1700). Rabbi Loew reminded everybody that, according to Talmudic wisdom, God had created the world for only one purpose: to have reverence for the Lord. He also noted that God could do anything, except this: to experience that awe. This depends solely on the human person. Well, if God withdrew an instant to make room for otherness and to create the world, then it is imperative that, reciprocally, we humans show awe before God. If we are incapable of that, then soon there will be no more world, no more human being, and no more God.[5]

The warning of the eighteenth-century master from Prague sounds even sharper now that we witness a built-up world without any trace of true awe before God. If we wish to live in a world fit for humanity, we can only make it come about by continuing to reserve the deepest respect for God.

In the Catholic liturgy we pray Psalm 67 on New Year's Day as a response to the ancient priestly blessing in Numbers:

> The Lord bless you and keep you;
> the Lord make his face to shine upon you,
> and be gracious to you;
> the Lord lift up his countenance upon you,
> and give you peace. (Num 6:22)

5. See Neher, *Le puits de l'exil*, 175–77.

This great blessing descends on the new year, and the psalm directs it to all peoples:

> May God be gracious to us and bless us
> and make his face to shine upon us,
> that your way may be known upon earth
> your saving power among all nations. (Ps 67:1-3)

The psalm then ends with: "Let all the ends of the earth revere him" (Ps 67:7). This reverence by all on earth is at the same time the fruit of God's blessing and its silent, indispensable precondition. Let us hope that over the years we may experience this blessing and reverence again and again, to the salvation of the farthest ends of the earth.

See also: Friendship, Hallowing, Hospitality, Mercy, Name

FEASTING

"But we had to celebrate and rejoice, because this brother of yours was dead and has come to life; he was lost and has been found" (Luke 15:32). These are Jesus' words in the story of the prodigal son, one of his most famous parables. There has to be a feast. It is a *must*. This is how Jesus thinks and how he talks to the Pharisees, who think likewise. The feast is a biblical duty and the Pharisees are sensitive to that. Their rules specify how it is to be conducted by the observant Jew. The center of gravity of a religious celebration is that the feast belongs to God. During the feast men and women share in God's joy. So let men and women rejoice. The joy becomes a duty: to share in the joy of God, and nothing else. Thus, you have to be able to go outside yourself and enter into the joy of our Lord. People with too narcissistic an orientation find such a vision nearly insupportable. Celebrating is then labeled "difficult."

Upon the return from exile, Ezra convokes a mass gathering at Jerusalem's temple square. The whole morning long the Law of Moses is read to the crowd and commented on. People are broken-hearted and weep, deeply moved. Priests, scribes, and Levites say to them:

> "This day is holy to the LORD your God; do not mourn or weep." For all the people wept when they heard the words of the law. Then he said to them, "Go your way, eat the fat and drink sweet wine and send portions of them to those for whom nothing is prepared, for this day is holy to our LORD; and do not be grieved, for the joy of the LORD is your strength." So the Levites stilled all the people, saying "Be quiet, for this day is holy; do not be grieved." And all the people went their way to eat and drink and to send portions and to make great rejoicing, because they had understood the words that were declared to them. (Neh 8:9-12)

The feast is a *must*. "For the joy of the Lord is our strength" (Neh 8:10). In this text from the fifth or fourth century before Christ we see the clear outlines of a truly Jewish philosophy of the feast. And the Sabbath became the feast par excellence. Even though one is mourning, the joy of the Sabbath is greater than our grieving heart. It is said of a rabbi in the fourth century CE that he did not tell his wife that two of their children had died until the Sabbath was over. A few days after the start of the Yom Kippur War (1973), Jews celebrated Sukkoth, which is the greatest of all pilgrimage celebrations. The evening before, Golda Meir, dressed in white, appeared on television and wished the viewers "the joy of the feast" (*Hag sameach*). This was in the midst of war, with many young people killed on the Egyptian and Syrian fronts. But the first thing she communicated was joy, as if it were self-evident, because of the feast.

The feast provides a horizon for all we do. We are always in-between two feasts, and we go from feast to feast in a cycle that does not simply go round and round but that ascends. Because, of course, the greatest feast is still to come. The end of all time is a feast, as we learn from the Bible and liturgical tradition. Our time on earth is a preparation for that feast. So, we comport ourselves as invitees. You don't enter the banquet hall in just any outfit: you are expected to dress appropriately. The metaphor teaches us that even in the present our conduct has to demonstrate that we are worthy of the feast.

Whatever we may go through, let us never lose sight of the coming banquet. When Jesus reclined at table with his disciples for the last time, he passed the cup around and said, "I will never again drink of this fruit of the vine until that day when I drink it new with you in my Father's kingdom" (Matt 26:29). To give up drink means to fast, symbolic of death. Thus, he announces his death. But his regard remains steadfastly fixed on the feast: in the kingdom of God there will be drinking, festively! Even in this painful hour he keeps looking forward to God's feast!

We must handle our quarrels on this side of life in such a way that we remain worthy of the coming feast. The person I would now like to go fly a kite is perhaps the one I will later meet at the heavenly banquet. And if that is precisely what I do not want, chances are high that I will be excluded from the table myself! The perspective of the coming feast takes the air out of all our personal feuds.

When Thomas More faced the executioner who was about to behead him on orders of King Henry VIII, he said that he prayed to God for the king to see the error of his ways. He hoped that they would meet on the other side just as Stephen once had prayed in the hour of his death for Saul, his persecutor. Now they lie at the same table and share in the same joy, Stephen and Paul, both received into the one community of saints. So let us properly assess our most painful conflicts in the light of that festive future and generously share with all the time we have left.

Jews live "from Sabbath to Sabbath" and each Friday evening a second marriage ceremony takes place: Queen Sabbath enters, greeted as a bride. And each Saturday evening (as late as possible) a small rite of divorce (*havdalah*) takes place, because the queen again leaves the community. However, in order not to forget the Sabbath's sweet scent, a fragrant herb is passed around: everybody breathes in the smell of the Sabbath, smell being the strongest faculty for memorization that we have. So, see you next week Friday!

Godfried Bomans[1] once said that the Flemish live "from feast to feast." A trait inherited from our erstwhile Burgundian rulers, perhaps? A deeply Christian reflex? Both? Any person who spends time as a guest in a Benedictine abbey may be surprised: there's a celebration at the drop of a hat! Besides the liturgical feast days, there are birthdays and feast days of saints and patrons, or just the singular pleasure of a guest's visit. The simplest occasion suffices for its specialness to be marked: a pint of beer is poured or a bottle of wine is uncorked, a bunch of flowers decorates the table of the person whose birthday is being celebrated, chocolates are served with the coffee, etc.

A feast breaks through the everyday routine. "There are only two ways to eat: to feast or to fast," said Venerable Fulton Sheen. This is how Jesus lived. This is how the poor live. In principle monks should not live any differently. One cannot "feast sumptuously every day," as the parable of the rich man and poor Lazarus tells us. Similarly, in the beginning of the book of Job, we see that Job's sons and daughters have the same strange habit of feasting every day of the week. The ordinary has become the exception, while the festive is reduced to a banality. The contradiction is abundantly clear. Stories like that end up in catastrophe, guaranteed. But how do the well-to-do citizens of the West live today? Where does their story end, sooner or later? Is a culture that no longer fasts and that only has an eye for fun and parties not a culture in peril, for itself and for others?

The phenomenologist Fr. Libert Vander Kerken once wrote, in the 1950s, a pithy article about feasting. In the last sentence he noted that in the Christian perspective it must be possible to taste the exceptional

1. Dutch Catholic writer (1913–71) [translator's note].

even in the ordinary. Indeed, something like a "daily feast" must exist. For the person who lives a quiet and subdued life, the simple feast of grace is revealed in everything. "All is grace." "We live from grace to grace." God's smile permeates a child's life and that of anybody who in child-like manner "tunes in to his grace" (Dom André Louf). The feast is drawing near, already now.

See also: Eating, Fasting, Gratitude, Jubilee

FIGHT

"I fought the good fight."

—Paul to Timothy

Fight, agony, mortal combat: a ubiquitous theme in the oldest accounts of the spiritual life. You have to arm yourself. You have to take the fight to the enemy. You have to fight against thoughts. "For our struggle is not against enemies of blood and flesh, but against the rulers . . . against the spiritual forces of evil in the heavenly places," writes Paul in his letter to the Ephesians by way of introduction to a recommended list (not less than ten verses long) of appropriate armor (see Eph 6:10-20). This text is repeatedly cited in the monastic literature of the early centuries, including by John Cassian in his *Institutes.* He describes a fight on eight fronts, against the eight demons that coincide with what later will be called the eight capital sins: three at the level of the flesh (gluttony, lust, and avarice), three at the level of heart and character (anger, sadness, and listlessness), and two at the highest level, that of the spirit (vanity and pride).

Benedict starts his Rule by addressing the candidate-monks as future soldiers ready to take up "the powerful and shining weapons of obedience" in order "to fight for the Lord Christ, the true king" (RB Prol. 3).

The later monastic Rule of Carmel (early thirteenth century), directed at hermits wishing to live in community, is a relatively short text. Yet it quotes in full the above-referenced examples of armor in Ephesians 6 and then explains them: the monk shall only persevere in the battle if he indeed has put on helmet, breastplate, and proper shoes, has armed himself with sword and shield, and has learned to use them. To the fight, then.

Anselm Grün imbues that old fight with new, contemporary relevance by interpreting the old texts in light of the dynamics of spiritual growth as described by Carl Gustav Jung.[1] Thus, to fight the good fight remains as relevant today as it was in the time of Paul or Benedict.

1. See, e.g., Anselm Grün, *Het omgaan met de Boze: de strijd van de oude monniken tegen de demonen*, Cahiers van Bonheiden 27 (Bonheiden: Abdij Bonheiden, 1984).

What is it really all about? Christ, with his great peace, lives deep inside of me. He resides there, living, radiating. He is working, a source. He wells up continually. He is firm as a rock. Thanks to a well-lived solitude, the monk can build his dwelling on that rock anytime. Peace does not enter it from outside; the monk has learned not to build on sand, not to count on this or that relationship, not to expect another's approval and validation. The masters he does consult invariably point him to that inner Rock, to that wisdom in Christ—that first light, the morning light that precedes our every thought and that illuminates it even before sunrise brightens the sky.

If a troublesome thought arises from without, perhaps a devastating word that hits smack in the face, or a gesture that unmistakably demonstrates complete disregard, then it is important to fight that thought. If I allow that thought to enter my innermost self it can cause great damage, even destroy my whole inner courtyard. It resembles those advanced bombs used by the United States and its allies on large Iraqi buildings: the bomb enters through a window and annihilates everything inside while the outer structure remains more or less intact. The good fight requires sentries that guard my inner sanctuary day and night. The guard questions the thought, as in Joshua, "Are you one of us, or one of our adversaries?" (Josh 5:13). He only allows the friend to enter.

The harmful thought has its attraction and can exert a seductive influence on the guard. Because even if it hurts me, I feel alive, which is better than chilly indifference: I find myself important, even if I'm the victim. But at the same time, then, I recognize that my inner self is being wrecked, that my hope is vanishing, that my courage is deserting me. I am left defenseless and, in particular, without wherewithal to find shelter on the Rock, to find refuge in Christ.

The inner fight means that we have to be systematic about locking out certain harmful influences and ignoring them, that we have to throw them away and forget them. Every individual has to develop such a strategy for him- or herself. Just as nobody can show me how to use my eyes in order to appreciate a beautiful landscape, so must I learn on my own how best to develop this strategy within the vigil of my heart. Psalms play an important role in the process: they regularly express a fight. It's up to me to recognize the harmful foe and then to pray for the foe to be vanquished by the power of God.

In the great fight, our small ego and numerous narcissistic tendencies, singularly or as a group, are our most common opponents. The end goal is an inalienable freedom, an unshakeable peace, a joy that nobody can take away.

The essence of living the good fight consists in returning, again and again, to the center: there where Christ reigns and radiates. "I have said this to you, so that in me you may have peace. In the world you face persecution. But take courage: I have conquered the world!" (John 16:33). These were Jesus' last words to his disciples after the Last Supper. They say all that needs to be said. In him we receive victory. He is our peace.

See also: Chastity, Ejaculatory Prayers, Fasting, Heart, Judge (Do Not), Peace, Psalmody, Source, Strategy

FORGIVENESS, RECONCILIATION

The New Testament, with its twenty-seven Scriptures, always surprises: on the first page of nearly every one of these twenty-seven letters or texts we are hit with the expression "for the forgiveness of sins." So we read, for example, in the first sentence of the oldest Gospel that John the Baptist offered a baptism "for the forgiveness of sins" (Mark 1:4). In these words we hear not just the purpose of the baptism of repentance proclaimed by John the Baptist: the whole Gospel of Mark is geared to accomplishing nothing else but this forgiveness in the reader.

Thus, we can say that Christian thought is grounded from the very start in a teaching about the forgiveness of sins. The liturgy and sacraments confirm this: all who enter into Christendom and accept baptism are immersed in Christ, with the consequence that all is forgiven and that from then on they are fully reconciled with God. Their existence is "justified by faith," as Paul put it in his letter to the Romans (Rom 5:1). No more condemnation (Rom 8:1). From now on the initiated will have "peace with God" (Rom 5:1).

We start every Eucharist by repenting and praying for the Lord's mercy. This is followed by the presider's words, confirming that God indeed bestows his mercy on us, forgives us our sins, and leads us to eternal life. In the signature Christian prayer, the Our Father, forgiveness comes through loud and clear and is reciprocal: "Forgive us . . . as we forgive those who have sinned against us." A Christian's self-image is thus stamped with the concept of the forgiveness of sins.

A World Silent about Reconciliation

What happens when a culture systematically bans talk of reconciliation and the words "you are forgiven" are no longer heard? A world devoid of reconciliation is a harsh world: all people stand condemned, surrounded by fear and a strange sense of suspicion. Nobody can trust anybody. After all, you are already judged, sized up, weighed, and found wanting.

Judgment is carried over from person to person. Parents judge their children, children their parents; teachers criticize students, who in turn do the same on the playground, behind the backs of educators and parents. Unrest strikes, and so do fear, self-pity, self-doubt, and the feeling of constantly being in another's debt. "Again, it's not good enough."

Judging others also affects you inwardly: you end up criticizing yourself, your education, your growth, and all authority figures along your life's path: parents, superiors, God himself, as well as the language of the Bible or the liturgy and all who have said anything about God. Because what would they say other than that I always fail and that I am irremediably condemned?

Judgment makes us bashful and fearful, and even somebody who has learned more or less to deal with it does not for that reason go through life happily. Our world becomes cynical. We carry on, but it doesn't really matter. There is a growing sense of isolation, there is nobody to talk to, we even cease really hearing anything because nothing gets through to us anymore. Not one person comes and sits next to me and weeps quietly with me—I, the one who can't go on.

When you open the paper or watch the news, you only see or hear stories of corruption, betrayal, war or bombings, now here then there, hitting adults and children. Entire societies are bankrupted; young people, even ever increasingly younger people, give up and put an end to their lives. Nobody goes unpunished, the word "forgiveness"—let alone "reconciliation"—does not cross anybody's lips.

We cannot deny that such a world exists. At times mistrust and suspicion assume pathological proportions, as in some Eastern European countries or in the Great Lakes region of Africa. Those who come from a totalitarian regime (think Poland, Rumania, or Hungary) often no longer know how to trust anybody, even if the regime fell more than twenty years ago.

The demand for forgiveness is immense. In at least five of the great novels of the Russian writer Leon Tolstoy, one of the main characters expresses this yearning. The question, directed to a life partner, is always: "Can you forgive me?" Usually the other person in the story does not know how to handle the request so that the plea needs to be repeated: "Can you forgive me?" Was Tolstoy prophetic when he wrote about this with such insistence over a century ago? Without a doubt the same question resonates in the heart of innumerable people, albeit muffled, hardly uttered, barely audible.

To Awake and to Distinguish

A world that has closed itself to the possibility of reconciliation exists, but it is not all of reality. We must muster the courage to continue to make distinctions: good and evil, real and fake, truth and lies should not be confused.

This is a fight, and sometimes a tough one. But it brings us back to the center of our inner authenticity where we find rest because of the truth that is recovered. Each well-formed individual can determine for him- or herself: yes, this is true, or no, that cannot be. When Jesus addresses his contemporaries, he assumes that they can make up their own minds: "What do you think? If a shepherd has a hundred sheep, and one of them has gone astray?" (Matt 12:18). "What is your opinion? A man had two sons" (Matt 21:28).[1] To the young man who somewhat impulsively runs up with the greeting "Good Teacher," Jesus does not respond immediately but slows him down ("Why do you call me good? No one is good but God alone.") and first lays out the wise structure of the covenant with God: "You know the commandments: 'You shall not commit adultery; You shall not murder; You shall not steal; You shall not bear false witness; Honor your father and mother'" (Luke 18:18-20; Matt 19:16-20). Only then comes a new, revelatory, and challenging discourse.

This stage of truth requires patience and exercise in self-knowledge. The result is true adulthood. Before a person is ready for forgiveness, he or she must be able to enter into truth in their own mind, despite all complexity.

What Is New with Jesus

The core of Jesus' message lies in his different treatment of God's judgment.

According to Jesus, God recognizes sin as sin. But God does not charge us with sin. He forgives, gratis, even without regard to all my virtuous efforts or good intentions. God anticipates in a radical way, he absolves everything, even beyond what we could ever repay.

In Matthew 18, Jesus tells Peter the great parable on forgiveness after the latter asked how often he had to forgive his brother—as

1. Translation from the New Jerusalem Bible, Reader's Edition (New York: Doubleday, 1990) [translator's note].

many as seven times? Jesus shows how God operates: when the lord in the parable hears the supplication of his slave, he is moved with compassion. He forgives "from [his] heart" (Matt 18:35) and absolves the debt completely. That debt was enormous: billions of euros. Thus acts our heavenly Father, says Jesus. And if *we* have to absolve our neighbors of something, how then should we do it, in light of all that God has forgiven us?

Jesus demonstrates the reciprocity that is involved in the experience of forgiveness. Nobody who shows himself incapable of forgiveness will himself be forgiven and, the other way round, somebody who stops making judgments and who understands and forgives, that person appears acceptable to God and is forgiven. At the same time, Jesus underlines the unimaginable disproportion between God's freely absolving an immeasurable debt and our forgiving of piddling claims (a few hundred euros, in the parable's language, compared to many billions!).

We encounter the same contrast in the parable of the mote and the beam. There we deal with the opposite of forgiving: judging. Actually, we ourselves are to be judged by God, and not just for a little bit. Nevertheless, we have the nerve to judge others. We have a beam in our eye, which separates us from God and prevents us from seeing clearly, but dare to suggest that we need to take the mote out of the other's eye. "First take the log out of your own eye" (Matt 7:5; Luke 6:42).

The teaching of the reciprocity of forgiveness is present even in the prayer formula—the Our Father—that Matthew passes on to us in the true center of the Sermon on the Mount as a synopsis of the sermon and, ultimately, of the whole Gospel. We ask for forgiveness but oblige ourselves at the same time to forgive others. Otherwise we are not worthy of that great forgiveness, as the evangelist relates in the second half of the parable of the unforgiving debtor (Matt 18:28-35).

The Desert Fathers, who were masters in dealing with their own weaknesses and those of others, had a keen eye for the inherent reciprocity:

> A brother questioned Abba Poemen saying, "If I see my brother committing a sin, is it right to conceal it?" The old man said to him, "At the very moment when we hide our brother's fault, God

> hides our own and at the moment when we reveal our brother's fault, God reveals ours too."[2]

> A brother asked Abba Poemen, "If a brother is involved in a sin and is converted, will God forgive him?" The old man said to him, "Will not God, who has commanded men to act thus, do as much himself and even more? For God commanded Peter to forgive till seventy times seven" (Matt 18:22).[3]

Thus nobody enters the Kingdom of forgiveness if they have not broken through their own judgmental disposition. Those who close themselves off from this reciprocity risk remaining outside the salvation and reconciliation of God. For this is the one sin that is unforgiveable: callousness that shuts out the Holy Spirit. Because receiving forgiveness or allowing the Holy Spirit into your life are two sides of the same reality. "Give your blood and receive the Spirit," as the Desert Fathers used to say. To give your blood is not different from giving up your own self and your own righteousness. Then God's Spirit can come over you and anchor your life anew in the living covenant with him.

In Practice

We enter into the world of God's free forgiveness by faith. Indeed, in the proclamation of the gospel we hear, just like the paralytic who was lowered to Jesus' feet through the roof: "Son, your sins are forgiven" (Mark 2:5). That first word resounds over each child receiving baptism: "From now on you are reconciled with God." Or as with the woman caught in adultery: "Neither do I condemn you. Go your way, and from now on do not sin again" (John 8:11). Through our baptism a new beginning opens up.

From that moment on we lead a life continually surrounded by forgiveness. All seven sacraments and nearly every prayer remind us that our sins have been forgiven and that we can live from forgiveness to forgiveness, from grace to grace. A *Kyrie* ("Lord, have mercy"), an Our Father, a *Gloria* ("Glory to God in the highest") prayed with faith bestows on us eternal reconciliation with God. As a general rule, this

2. *Sayings of the Desert Fathers* (Poemen 64), 175.
3. *Sayings of the Desert Fathers* (Poemen 86), 179.

is insufficiently emphasized. Praying in faith to our forgiving God accomplishes what we pronounce.

In a Christian life, almost everything works forgiveness, including the Eucharist: receiving communion accomplishes for us, sinners, the healing and forgiveness of sins because, as expressly stated in Matthew's account, he poured out his blood "for the forgiveness of sins" (Matt 26:28). Confession offers a very personal way to remain anchored in that same forgiveness: also in a confession the point of gravity does not so much lie in the recital of concrete sins as in the saving event of God's actual forgiveness of the person with a contrite heart.

All this does not mean that we don't continue to fall and get up. In this, the wise Abba Sisoes gives comfort:

> A brother asked Abba Sisoes, "What shall I do, abba, for I have fallen?" The old man said to him, "Get up again." The brother said, "I have got up again, but I have fallen again." The old man said, "Get up again and again." So then the brother said, "How many times?" The old man said, "Until you are taken up either in virtue or in sin. For a man presents himself to judgment in the state in which he is found."[4]

To Forgive and Forget

Life can hurt terribly, even from the very start in a mother's lap or in tender infancy. A young girl abused by her dad, while mother turns a blind eye: how can the girl carry on? And what does "forgiveness" mean in such a context? Can you forgive when the person who insulted you or took advantage of you is now in old age and no longer remembers, or disputes the facts? How can you live in a climate of reconciliation after the collapse of a totalitarian regime when collaborators who were long-time informers now participate in your church community? What does the kiss of peace mean in this context? Or think for a moment of the genocide on the high plateau of Rwanda and Kivu. How can you look people in the eye who did this to members of your family?

In these kinds of situations, it does not make a lot of sense to talk of forgiveness too quickly. The better way is to advance in small and

4. *Sayings of the Desert Fathers* (Sisoes 38), 219–20.

clear steps under the guidance of a third party who did not have direct involvement in the conflict. It is smart to work with appropriate "ladders." A number of cultures developed a step-by-step approach to arrive at real reconciliation. In Rwanda, in the post-1994 years, a ten-step scheme was widely used in order to reach "the hut of reconciliation," where the parties drank beer, through three straws, from the same gourd. In Buddhist tradition, according to Thich Nhat Hanh, there are seven separate steps. The community gathers and proceeds according to the following scheme:

1) sitting face to face;
2) recollecting;
3) avoiding stubbornness;
4) covering mud with straw;
5) confessing voluntarily;
6) deciding unanimously;
7) accepting the verdict. [5]

Start by Not Keeping Score

The expression "I forgive you" often comes across as too high-flown or even offensive. It's good to respect the folk wisdom of letting bygones be bygones. Start by not keeping score in your heart of the wrong that was done to you. This is frequently a more realistic stance than to talk about "forgiving." Those who no longer register the wrong in their heart eventually demonstrate so in their deeds: through symbolic gestures they are able to show that they wish the other well. Then, after greater ripening, the heart can regain magnanimity: we remember the words of Jesus when he referred to his Father as the one who "makes his sun rise on the evil and on the good and sends rain on the righteous and on the unrighteous" (Matt 5:45).

We are all called to that height, not on our own but supported by the powerful insight that God dealt with us in the same way through

5. Thich Nhat Hanh, *La paix, un art, une pratique. Approche bouddhiste* (Paris, 1991), 67 v.

Jesus Christ. In its complete form, reconciliation always bears the mark of the person *and* of God: complete reconciliation cannot come about without our full accord and, once achieved, we cannot but thank God without end. We see with our own eyes how his deepest will is done, "on earth as it is in heaven."

See also: Confession of Sins, Love for One's Enemies, Mercy, Patience, Peace, Reciprocity, Spirit

FORM AND FORMLESSNESS

Complete bliss cannot increase or decrease.
The greatest joy is without joy,
the highest glory is without glory.
The greatest form has no form.

—Taoist saying

We apply ourselves to concrete forms, but we search for that which has no form. Everything that has form is destined to perish. Only that which is without form is without end, because it is without beginning. According to Ruusbroec, a spirituality that pays attention to "forms that transform" ends up in something *wieseloos*, or *sine modo* in the expression of St. Bernard: without measure, without method, without form.

The paradox is that all who apply themselves to silence gradually come upon a far side where word and silence are one, as is the case with God. Those who make a practice of sitting still will, little by little, perceive in themselves the source that is without beginning or end. The person who devotes herself to any kind of pursuit with discipline and effort will sooner or later discover a spiritual state where all is grace, even the effort.

The heart unhitched from the world of forms,
the heart detached from all the changing forms,
that is the empty heart.
Just like the great blue sky,
the empty heart has no frontier, no end,
does not expand, does not contract.
Because it's free from
all that perishes in this world,
this heart is unafraid to live its life
without regard to fear of failure.
It is a thousand miles removed from all fears.
As sundrops rest on new leaves
and embrace and feed the whole wide world,
so the empty heart forgives
and nourishes all beings of the world.
This is a light without limits

a pleasure without end
a happiness without self.
Oh simple heart so full of joy,
Oh simple heart with fiery glow. (Hidemi Ogasawara)

See also: Detachment, Emptiness, Heart, Meditation, Paradox, Silence, Source, X

FRIENDSHIP

No, not the parents who lost us soon;
nor love and sweet love's swoon.
It's friendship that sets us free,
Free as we are meant to be.

—Ida Gerhardt

Whichever way you look at it, we in our Western world count friendship among the highest values in life. The roots of this particular appreciation go deep: they are of Doric origin and fed ancient Greek culture. All great thinkers of antiquity sang songs of praise to friendship: Pythagoras, Plato, Aristotle, the Stoics, Epicurus, and Cicero. Here is Cicero's definition of friendship, which has been continually studied and expounded in the West: "a complete accord on all subjects human and divine, joined with mutual goodwill and affection." He adds, as the highest imaginable praise of friendship: "And with the exception of wisdom, I am inclined to think nothing better than this has been given to man by the immortal gods."[1]

Of all the values offered by Greco-Roman culture, none was adopted as quickly by the early Christian movement as friendship. Already in the New Testament, thinkers like Paul, Luke, and John took great pains to commend the ancient value of friendship as they extolled the virtues of their new life ideal. This thought continues with the first church fathers. Even before he converted to Christianity, Augustine had already mastered everything about this ideal form of friendship through his contacts with philosophers influenced by Pythagoras. Also the Cappadocians Basil the Great and Gregory of Nazianzus gave friendship a central place. In the monastic tradition, the key concept of *koinônia* (which refers to the practice of owning and sharing everything in community) is embedded in all its rules, starting with Pachomius (fourth century), the true founder of the monastic communal way of living.

1. *Ancient History Sourcebook: Cicero: On Friendship, or Laelius*, part 1, para. 6 (New York: Fordham University, Paul Halsall, 1998), available at www.legacy.fordham.edu/halsall/ancient/cicero.friendship.asp (accessed January 25, 2015).

Whenever in the course of history a renaissance of spiritual thought breaks through, we see a rejuvenation of the experience of, and reflection on, friendship. Bernard of Clairvaux and the first Cistercians, such as Aelred de Rievaulx and William of Saint Thierry, are the best examples. In the school of Dominic we see a flourishing of friendship with new accents, notably with Jordan of Saxony and Diana. In our day, the novel experiment in monastic living among Protestants, inspired by Roger Schutz in Taizé, was in fact a rediscovery of friendship.[2] Even more recently, with Jacques Derrida we see a renewed search for the origins of friendship, socially as well as politically, in the discipline of philosophy.[3]

What, then, marks friendship as part of the art of living? Many short proverbs point to what is key:

> Friends share and share alike. They possess everything in common. They also endeavor to share their spiritual gifts, as noted in the Rule of Taizé. Thus it appears that the sharing of material things alone is not enough.
>
> Friends are "of one heart and of one soul." They possess one soul in two bodies. The friend is "the second half of my soul" (*dimidium animae meae*) (Horace). They "want the same thing and refuse the same thing" (*idem velle, idem nolle*) (Caius Sallustius Crispus).
>
> Friends are prepared to sacrifice everything for each other, even their life. "No one has greater love than this, to lay down one's life for one's friends" (John 15:13). Thus, together they stare death in the face, and "neither death nor life can separate them" (Lucian).
>
> Certain proverbs underline the uniqueness of the friend and hence the impossibility of having many: "The person who has many friends has none" (Aristotle). At the same time, both the Stoics and the Epicureans held that every human being is a po-

2. See Fr. John, *Une multitude d'amis. Réimaginer l'Eglise chrétienne à l'heure de la mondialisation* (Taizé: Presses de Taizé, 2011).

3. See Derrida, *Politiques de l'amitié* (Paris: éd. Galilée, 1994).

tential friend.[4] There is a selective dimension to friendship, and so only a couple of people, and often just one person, can truly be one's "friend" for life. Yet friendship also has a universal dimension: every person, also a stranger and even an enemy, is a potential friend. Friendship, then, becomes a political virtue.

Friendship is only possible between two or among several people who practice virtue. "Only among those practicing virtue can friendship reign." True friendship is demanding: the one expects of the other what is highest, most attractive, most noble, and most magnanimous.

Friends are not simply allies with a common plan or agreement, outside of which they carry on in their own way, sometimes licentiously, sometimes more or less principled. Already Aristotle distinguished between the establishment of a group, with internally agreed upon rules but without the highest ethical requirements, and the creation of a true friendship. Crooks can create a gang, but please don't call that friendship.

Within a friendship the greatest freedom can be found. There is no place for mandatory rules of conduct. Thus, friendships can thrive regardless of distance in time or space—good conversation and the exchange of letters have traditionally played a large role in maintaining them.

Augustine has no peer when it comes to friendship. He saw the growth of friendship as a steady search for Beauty. In his Christian vision, Beauty is the personification of the very Wisdom that is Christ. True friendship lasts if God is its purpose and instrument. His vision of being Church or of the formation of a (cenobitic) community is soundly based on his philosophy of friendship, which he had already formulated prior to his baptism.

In one of his earliest works about the soul and its possibilities for growth (*De quantitate animae*), he delineates the four highest steps of the spiritual ladder as follows: first come the two steps of a moral life in which the soul submits to precepts or rules (*praecepta*)—she applies herself to the virtuous life, and she seeks to become rooted in it. These

4. See also, Louis Lavelle, *Conduite à l'égard d'autrui* (Paris: Albin Michel, 1957).

two stages have to do with the soul itself: first *in relation to* itself, and then *in* itself (*ad seipsam, in seipsa*). The two highest steps concern the witnessing or contemplative life—access to God, and reposing in God. Thus these two stages have to do with God, no longer with the soul herself: *toward* God and finally *with* God (*ad deum, apud deum*).

"Honoring the precepts lends the soul its beauty, in harmony with the beauty that she is herself. Thereafter the soul is as it were immersed in the beauty that she is; this leads her to enter the Highest Beauty itself and prepares her to take repose in that divine Beauty" (*De quantitate animae*). Augustine summarized the whole action and transformation in these four formulas:

1) *Pulchre ad pulchrum* (from beauty to beauty);
2) *Pulchre in pulchro* (beauty from beauty);
3) *Pulchre ad pulchritudinem* (from beauty to Highest Beauty);
4) *Pulchre apud pulchritudinem* (from beauty until dwelling in Highest Beauty).

Augustine formulates this purpose in an original fashion in the very last paragraph of his Rule for cenobites: "May the Lord grant that you, seized by desire for spiritual Beauty, observe all this in love" (8.2).

Keeping the precepts of the Rule leads to contemplation of the divine Beauty. Elsewhere he explains: "We shall become beautiful people by loving Him who will always remain beautiful. As love grows in you, so will beauty. Because love is the beauty of the soul" (Commentary on the First Letter of John 9:9). We are one because we all are in love with the Beauty present in our midst that is Christ himself. Love for that Beauty makes us beautiful and at the same time that increasing beauty in us unites us in love.

In the meantime we have rediscovered the simplicity and the great freedom offered by friendship. In a recent interview, Jewish literature critic George Steiner speaks from the bottom of his heart: he is convinced, just like Ida Gerhardt, that the highest form of relationship, even within marriage, is nothing else but the holiness of friendship.

> Among the quotes that are guiding principles for my life is one from Rilke: "In a deep, felicitous love between two people you

> eventually become the loving protectors of each other's solitude." A very profound insight. Eros does not live forever; passion comes to an end sooner or later. I am convinced that, again gainsaying those dull-witted Freudian exaggerations, sexuality is only one of the many fundamental human motivators (and for many people not the most important one), no matter how powerful, beautiful, and wondrous it may be. If you become the loving protectors of each other's solitude, love gradually changes into friendship. And as Montaigne already has said, in the end friendship may be more important than love. That is one of the great taboos in our culture. The Greeks knew it and Keats mentions it here and there in his letters. But for the rest, there are very few people who dare to say it. The holiness of friendship. . . . About his friendship with La Boétie, Montaigne says: "It is because he is he and I am I." There is no explanation. But that definition is equally valid for the love between a man and a woman. If a marriage progressively turns into a friendship, you are blessed. Then the epiphanies of youth have blossomed and ripened into something lasting.[5]

Let us, perhaps against the pull of the culture that surrounds us, seek friendship in a shared love for that which is more beautiful than anything until we live in its blessing.

See also: Fear of the Lord, Love for One's Enemies, One, Reciprocity, Salmon or Mocking Gravity, Wonder

5. George Steiner, *La question à laquelle ne vint aucune réponse,* in Wim Kayzer, *Het boek van de schoonheid en de troost* (Amsterdam: Contact, 2000), 55.

FRUITFULNESS

Great fruitfulness springs from a life that maintains access to the Source. Without a sense of our origin, sterility sticks to everything we do, no matter how hard we try. So, if we wish to be fruitful, let us never force ourselves. The key thing is to safeguard the true source of vitality, and we do that by a slight shift in the center of our existence. "And it is no longer I who live, but it is Christ who lives in me" (Gal 2:20). This sentence of Paul provides us with the grammar for a full-fledged spiritual life. As he writes elsewhere: "I can do all things through him who strengthens me" (Phil 4:13).

In God we can do everything; left to our own devices we may do too much and lead a rather busy and exhausting life. But as Jesus says in the parable of the vine and the branches in the Fourth Gospel: "apart from me you can do nothing" (John 15:5). "Apart" we remain sterile: the transmission of life does not take place.

On the other hand, Paul understands his apostolate as entirely paradoxical: he dies and Jesus' life springs up everywhere. However, Paul himself cannot be destroyed: the Source renews his life from day to day; even if the external nature dies, the inner nature lives and undergoes a transformative process "from one degree of glory to another" (2 Cor 3:18; see, generally, 2 Cor 3, 4). Second Isaiah expresses the experience in a poem as follows:

> Even youths will faint and be weary;
>   and the young will fall exhausted;
> but those who wait for the Lord shall
>   renew their strength,
> they shall mount up with wings like eagles,
> they shall run and not be weary,
>   they shall walk and not faint. (Is 40:30-31)

There are interesting correspondences here with Taoist wisdom. As opposed to people who put their store in rules and laws, structures and systems, the Taoist masters give centrality to non-action (*wu wei*) and spontaneity. The great fruitfulness reaches to the stars and brings harmony to the deepest seams of yellow clay. Attuned to the Tao that cannot be named, the holy one keeps contact with the source. He knows how to cautiously allow the interplay of the two principles—yin and yang—and in this manner to bring harmony to the ten thousand sentient beings.

This means that we need to go about our business mindfully and, paradoxically, carefully and carefree, effectively and spontaneously. Blessed are those who have learned to follow this unique path. Even death is no longer to be feared: the fruit is life eternal.

> Happy are those
>   who do not follow the advice of the wicked,
> or take the path that sinners thread,
>   or sit in the seat of scoffers;
> but their delight is in the law of the LORD,
>   and on his law they meditate day and night.
> They are like trees
>   planted by streams of water,
> which yield their fruit in its season,
>   and their leaves do not wither.
> In all that they do, they prosper. (Ps 1:1-3)

See also: Paradox, Source, *Wu Wei*, Yin and Yang

G

GOD

"God" is and is not a name. As a name, it is proper and improper. To name God reaches too far: indeed He remains the Unnamable. So we keep on searching for God, but not as object, because He can never be that; the first thing we have to unlearn in dealing with God is precisely that, making him into an object. He is subject, more subject than my own subjectivity. As soon as we realize this in ourselves, a totally new perspective emerges in our search. I am known, loved, sought out, even before I myself start out on my search. "Where did you get to know me?" asks Nathanael in John's Gospel. "I saw you under the fig tree *before* Philip called you," Jesus responds (John 1:48, emphasis added).

God is "Act," according to a tradition in philosophy that goes back to Aristotle and that flourished with Thomas Aquinas—the bubbling source which is forever new Act, omnipresent and unnoticed. Just as we, sitting in our chair, fail to realize how fast the earth is spinning around its axis while simultaneously drawing a large ellipse around the sun, all within a Milky Way that itself rushes through space at enormous speed, so can we go on missing the godly primal act that maintains everything in balance. Yet, the person in meditation is able to come ever closer to the Source. The angels closest to God, yes, those who "continually see the face of my Father in heaven," as Jesus himself says in the Gospel, are also the beings that share most perfectly in the pure "Act." Their existence is uninterrupted "deed." The search for God as the subject within my own subjectivity signifies an increasing participation in the pure "Act" that He is.

"God" is a projection of the human person, an idea, a human creation in our image and likeness. At least that is what some thinkers say. The Bible tells us on the first page that God created humankind in his image and likeness (Gen 1:26). The church fathers say in unison: we personify his image and we are called to be his likeness, meaning that we are as free and as responsible as He is. Louis Lavelle, in one of his unpublished notes, wrote: "God is not an idea of the human person. It is much more the other way around." We are carried in God's thought. Whoever, in wonder, accepts this insight will continue to discover new meanings in it and has a new future.

Discover God via the trail of all that in our experience can be called "godlike": the freely given, the sublime, an act of forgiveness, beauty and graciousness, pure patience. Marvel about, and stay close to, these kinds of acts and the people who perform them. Look for the source or possible origin of such delightful phenomena. Maybe you'll discover, sooner or later, how what is undeniably godlike does not come out of thin air, but presupposes in one way or another a Subject. May this realization then fill you with reverence and unspeakable joy.

See also: Adoration, Fear of the Lord, Gratuitous, Gratitude, Memory, Name, Source, Spirit

GRATITUDE

"At the top of your prayer scroll, write: gratitude," exhorts John Climacus in the chapter on prayer in one of the last steps of his famous *Ladder*.

Gratitude at the start and gratitude at the end. In his letters, Paul twice offers a list of four ways of addressing God: praying, requesting (or seeking intercession), supplicating, and thanksgiving (Phil 4:6; cf. 1 Tim 2:1). In both cases, gratitude comes at or near the end of the list. On the basis of these two examples in Paul, the classic treatises on prayer by the church fathers (beginning with the Alexandrians Clement and Origen, ca. 200) time and again emphasize thanksgiving as the highest form of prayer.

Moreover, in John Cassian we encounter again the idea that the highest form of thanksgiving also encompasses the future: already now we can give thanks for what is still to come but is already prepared by God. Cassian explains that this prayer of gratitude can lead us straight to the "prayer of fire": a remarkable transformation is in store for the person who in advance gives thanks for what "no eye has seen, nor ear heard, nor the human heart conceived, what God has prepared for those who love him" (1 Cor 2:9). His prayer begins to blaze with fire. All forms of prayer burn in one conflagration. At times the fire's flare is so intense that the person praying cannot hold on to what is happening and afterward is unable to recount exactly what he experienced. To thank God for what he has made ready, though it is yet to come: focus on this future from time to time in your meditation, and praise God for it. You will find it amply worthwhile.

We learn in indirect ways that there is more to gratitude than the appropriate response of a well-educated child who has learned to say "thank you" for a present. It is well to start the day with a prayer of thanksgiving. Even if you know that the day ahead will be difficult and overflowing with tasks, you can address God about it right now and thank him in advance. It increases your readiness and fuels your courage to get started. Note the precious formula that we find in the preface of the Eucharistic liturgy: "In hope of health and wellbeing, and paying . . . homage to you." Note that we literally pay homage and thanks *before* obtaining "health and wellbeing." And we hear Jesus say "my yoke is easy and my burden is light" (Matt

11:30). Somebody who gives thanks in advance discovers how true this statement can be. Who knows, perhaps Jesus' "yoke" is nothing other than the Holy Spirit, whom we give room to work within us when we give praise and thanks.

To thank and to think: these two verbs are linked not just phonetically but semantically as well. Heidegger, the philosopher, perceived the substance hidden in their relationship. In order to profess gratitude we have to be able to think and to commemorate. But the reverse is also true: the grateful person is easily moved to reflection. She sees new connections, detects in everything in creation and in any "given" object a gift, a present, in which she believes she can discern the presence of a Giver. Any "given" is not just a bare fact, it is what the word says: given, and thus it must be received, with wonder and gratitude. Ever since Plato, wonder has been considered an entryway to thought, but gratitude is a sister of wonder, and when these two walk hand in hand, nobody knows who exactly is guiding the other.

In Greek, "thanksgiving" is also the word that means "Eucharist." Eucharistic prayer is the richest and most synthetic form of all prayers. A Lord's Supper or Eucharist or holy Mass—three terms that refer to the same symbolic act—is one great thanksgiving, the response of a community that lets itself be formed by God's message in the liturgy of the Word.

"Be thankful"—be *eucharistoi*, we read literally in Paul's letter to the Colossians (Col 3:15). Actually, the whole letter is rife with calls for, and allusions to, gratitude (Col 1:3; 1:12; 2:6-7; 3:15; 4:2). In Paul's way of seeing things, it is possible to speak of a "eucharistic person," for whom all of existence becomes one act of thanksgiving. We are all called to this. "It is truly right and just, our duty and our salvation, always and everywhere to give you thanks, Father most holy, through your beloved Son, Jesus Christ," these are the opening words of the preface to the second Eucharistic Prayer. Independently from each other, the Orthodox thinker Olivier Clément and the French poet Patrice de la Tour de la Pin both consider the eucharistic person (*l'homme eucharistique*) as the most perfect human being. This is clearly the way of Paul's life. In the midst of trials, he continues to offer thanksgiving, again and again, and he sees his fellow Christians do the same thing. "Rejoice always, pray without ceasing, give thanks in all circumstances, for this is the will of God in Christ Jesus for you" (1 Thess 5:16-18).

The monastic tradition is fond of this summons. In the famous correspondence between the hermits Barsanufius and John the Prophet, in a monastery near Gaza (early sixth century), we find a truly remarkable association: they are always asking their followers "to fear God in everything and to thank Him continually." These attitudes follow each other as an in-breath and an out-breath: first have holy reverence, then say thanks. Their entire correspondence shows that those who live this way radiate peace and joy!

There are not many yardsticks in the spiritual life and, according to the Egyptian desert fathers, it is not at all right to take your own measure. But if you absolutely want to know how far you have come, it is sufficient to ask: how thankful am I in all my doings, right here and now? Gratitude is the great indicator (cf. Ps 50:14-23: "Offer to God a sacrifice of thanksgiving"). I do not know a better one.

See also: *Dhikr*, Fear of the Lord, Memory, Mindfulness, Peace, Psalmody

GRATUITOUS

Whether the totally gratuitous gift actually exists is impossible to prove. Indeed, every attempt at conclusive proof ruins gratuitousness: the very attempt implies a denial of the purely gratuitous. Only the person who herself is predisposed to give without recompense may encounter something of the truly gratuitous. Hence, doubting the gratuitous gift is always possible: whoever allows ambivalence to creep in will quickly be overcome by unbelief. The evidence insinuated by doubt is too strong. To believe in what is gratuitous is purely a matter of faith, based in nothing but faith.

So we find here both an attractive reciprocity between object and subject and a questionable, circuitous reasoning. The freely given is only known by those who share in it. Each gracious dance step is a victory over gravity. But you must dance to experience that wondrous victory.

We may profess the gratuitous and bear witness to it, but it is an open question whether we can demonstrate it. What is truly attractive about gratuitousness is that it reveals itself as the purest core of everything: free, gratis, a sheer melody that transcends everything that exists.

Prophets, apostles, and poets regularly mock anything that is deemed essential or necessary in order to try to show some aspect of the truly gratuitous. The person who is geared to what is freely given and who applies herself to it may at times succeed in seeing it in everything. Because inside all reality hides a godlike child, playful, omnipresent and happy in the company of those who resemble that child. In the biblical book Proverbs, this child is called wisdom from "before the beginning of the earth" (Prov 8:23). That wisdom was coursing in Jesus and he relied on it. And even though nobody in the market square wanted to dance to the melody that flowed from his flute, he went ahead because, as He said, "Wisdom is vindicated by all her children."

What is gratuitous, no matter how much it is denied or mocked, is often shunned. It is viewed as a threat, because it introduces an element of play and freedom within the realm of the essential. "Weighed and found wanting," say the scoffers. If the gratuitous is too light for one, it is too heavy for another, a real danger. The closed loop of the logic of revenge—also in the cunning and balanced forms of "an eye for an eye" that attempt to moderate excessive revenge—trembles before the one who announces forgiveness freely.

To forgive freely has something shocking about it. The God of Jesus forgives debts purely out of compassion. Jesus sees how his Father "makes the sun rise on the evil and on the good" (Matt 5:45), without distinction. These kinds of considerations fascinate one person but irritate another. Every unconverted Jonah is scandalized by such freely given benevolence.

It should be noted that the religious person is not *per se* receptive to the gratuitous. The exemplary Pharisee Saul of Tarsus could at first not deal with it, not until he faced the radiant countenance of Stephen being stoned. Stephen prayed for forgiveness of the ones who were stoning him to death. Saul reeled from that incomprehensible fundamental attitude of gratuitousness, and it opened room in him for the way of Christ's grace.

To discern the gratuitous is an art of mindfulness and wonder. Even in the inevitable and the necessary—such as the sequence of the seasons, the arrival of a new sunrise, the opening up of a flower, or the spreading perfume of a rose—the enlightened person discerns the wonder: "This is the new sunrise"; "This is the full moon!" Once discerned, the gratuitous becomes a source of limitless gratitude and boundless wonder. Arranging a flower in a vase in the early morning is part of the art of perceiving that all is grace, pure gratuitousness.

See also: Dance, Forgiveness, Gratitude, Mindfulness, Reciprocity, Source, Wonder

GROWING

To live is to grow. To live a spiritual life means to make progress, without interruption (Cassian). "Forgetting what lies behind and straining forward to what lies ahead," wrote Paul to his beloved Philippians (Phil 3:13). For, as he noted, "I press on hoping that I may lay hold of that for which Christ Jesus has laid hold of me" (Phil 3:12). We are continually en route, always pulling against the temptation to stay put. Because, of course, staying in one place signifies a dying.

Day after day we leave the barracks to renew the good fight, living "from beginning to beginning, in a beginning without end," as Gregory of Nyssa said, and he used the above pronouncements of Paul as his motto when he wrote his *Life of Moses*. In this work, Gregory sketches every person's, every Christian's, prime potential for growth into perfection. This presupposes an inner resilience, with nothing forced or done in a fit of nervous temper and with the encroachments of middle-class comforts always fended off, like a snake that sheds its old skin: young wine in new wineskins.

The growing process cannot be forced. The Chinese learned this lesson with a bit of humor: "Pulling on blades of grass does not make them grow any faster," according to an old Taoist saying. In monastic literature, young monks are cautioned not to skip any stages on the path of spiritual growth. Paying attention in a practical everyday way to the common virtues lays the basis for the contemplative life. The person who wishes to engage in contemplation without first having conquered purity of heart and freedom from the passions is skipping a number of stages, and this is not recommended by anybody in the monastic tradition. On the contrary, the masters would say: "Early ripe, early rotten." Or to put it another way: It is important first to have a properly formed ego, free from the super ego, and to be delivered from all passions and instinct. Only then does it become possible to break the ego in a true surrender, without the super ego or conceited urges playing decisive roles.

Eventually, this growing takes on a paradoxical course. Spiritually we do not become richer with the years, but poorer. According to Benedict, growing means to climb the ladder of humility by descending deeper and deeper. The person I have most revered as a man of

God, Fr. Charles van der Straten, said in the waning days of his life: "Yes, there are days when even to pray a Kyrie is difficult."[1] Few words have brought me as much consolation as those. He was completely immersed in God, even his back radiated light, not shadow. But his prayer was poor, dirt-poor, only with difficulty could he murmur a "Lord, have mercy!" At the same time, I heard him say this without any melancholy or sadness. I sensed underneath his words the consideration: "If this is what God now has in store for me, then that also is good. I do not need anything further, nothing more than what I have now." Even though poorer than poor, he was fully reconciled with that ultimate state. He was free and grateful, even in such extreme poverty. The limit had become limitless. In him, the paradox had become flesh, having left behind the traditional misconceptions of perfection: henceforth he has taken possession of that for which Christ Jesus has taken possession of him.

Can we have a check on whether we are growing or whether we are going backward? Measuring yourself was rejected by the Egyptian Desert Fathers of the fourth and fifth centuries as an idle occupation. Mindful of Paul, we should instead leave the trodden path behind and forget it, so that we can forge forward to lay hold of Him who laid hold of us. Nevertheless, there are small markers that can show us whether or not the path we are on is the right one. At least three perspectives can be useful here: Is our faith growing? To what extent do we make allowance for wonder? And how real is our gratitude?

If I cannot find gratitude in my heart, or if the source of wonder has run dry, or if my faith is badly in need of fresh air, then it is high time to question whether I am on the right path. "Now therefore thus says the LORD of hosts: Consider how you have fared" (Hag 1:5). Gratitude, wonder, and faith: three essential signs of a healthy spiritual life. Usually they go together. The person who can give thanks has faith and is able to remain ceaselessly in wonder.

See also: Beginning, Gratitude, Jesus and the Jesus Prayer, Paradox, Patience, Poverty, Wonder

1. B. Standaert, *Le père Charles, moine au coeur universel (1908–1979)* (Bruges: Zevenkerken, 1993), 100.

H

HALLOWING

Heiliging, the Dutch word for hallowing, is the name of a periodical that celebrated its fiftieth anniversary in the year 2000. In the early 1980s an attempt was made to give this spiritual magazine a new name, a moniker more in tune with the times. It sounded old-fashioned. But after much searching, the conclusion was reached that there was nothing better. Only a subtitle was added: *New and Old*. (See Matt 13:52, where the scribe who became a disciple is likened to the head of a family "who brings out of his treasure what is new and what is old.")

So, even though the word "hallowing" sounds hardly contemporary, it possesses an inalienable force. It refers to a process, an action. Hallowing *happens*. The real question remains: who is its subject? Biblical expressions focus on hallowing the Name or to let God be God in his hallowing radiance. As Ezekiel prophesies from his exile: "I [the Lord God] will sanctify my great name" (Ezek 36:23). His name had been profaned and now he acts to hallow it. And the whole process starts with the human person, in the heart. God will cleanse the mortal with water and pour a new spirit into him. From his body he will remove the heart of stone and he will grant him a heart of flesh. Complete renewal and sanctification begins in this way. The universe too shares in this rebirth: the wild animals, the trees and the plants will be abundant for the new person (see Ezek 36). That is the reach of the hallowing action of the Lord God when He sanctifies His name. When with Jesus we learn to pray "hallowed be thy Name," it is best understood as a courteous way to ask God himself to hallow His name. It is not we who hallow the Name of God; rather, we allow God to hallow his Name in us and in everything through us.

In Psalm 65 we also see this hallowing radiating out from God's house: "We shall be satisfied with the goodness of your house, your holy temple." And right away the psalmist describes the broadest movement imaginable that reaches out from the center to the ends of the habitable world:

> By awesome deeds you answer us
> with deliverance,

O God of our salvation;
you are the hope of all the ends of the earth
and of the farthest seas. . . .
Those who live at earth's farthest bounds
are awed by your signs;
you make the gateways of the morning
and the evening shout for joy. (Ps 65:5-8)

At the same time God blesses the earth that turns fertile and that in accordance with the seasons is clothed with delight:

. . . and blessing its growth,
you crown the year with your bounty;
your wagon tracks overflow with richness.
The pastures of the wilderness overflow,
the hills gird themselves with joy,
the meadows clothe themselves with flocks,
the valleys deck themselves with grain,
they shout and sing together for joy. (Ps 65:11-13)

Here we see hallowing as a transforming power that creates life, welling up at the temple and streaming to the ends of the earth and the universe.

For Paul this hallowing is our deepest calling: recorded in his very first letter, the oldest text of the whole New Testament, this thought surges powerfully to the surface. "For this is the will of God, your sanctification. . . . For God did not call us to impurity but in holiness" (1 Thess 4:3-7). And this process is closely linked with the workings of the indwelling Holy Spirit (1 Thess 4:8). Also in the First Letter of Peter, in the introduction, Christian identity is marked by the relationship between Father, Son, and Spirit, with sanctification attributed to the Spirit.

Paradoxically, Christians are, on the one hand, foreigners "dispersed" in the world and, on the other, at the same time God's "chosen" (1 Pet 1:1). And this election is "destined by God the Father" and "sanctified by the Spirit to be obedient to Jesus Christ and to be sprinkled with his blood" (1 Pet 1:2). At the heart of our identity lies this call to hallowing by transformation through the sanctifying operation of the Spirit.

In the letter to the Hebrews we read, in the midst of a number of exhortations, "Pursue peace with everyone, and the holiness without which no one will see the Lord" (Heb 12:14). The latter part expresses the ultimate purpose, the desire of Moses himself at the culmination of his search for God: "Show me your glory, I pray" (Exod 33:18). Well, this vision has everything to do with the transforming process that we call hallowing. Jesus said it in a similar way: "Blessed are the pure in heart, for they will see God" (Matt 5:8).

Hallowing is a momentous occurrence that can only be accomplished in us with timidity. The first Christians lived henceforth in the realization that they themselves were the holy dwelling and that the temple for God's abode no longer needed to be found in Jerusalem. The spirit that descended upon Jesus in his baptism was poured over the whole community at Pentecost. To give space to that spirit to do its work just as Jesus did with utmost devotion, *that* is to be fully Christian. In John, we hear Jesus say:

> Sanctify them in the truth;
> Your word is truth.
> As you have sent me into the world,
> So I have sent them into the world.
> And for their sakes I sanctify myself
> So that they also may be sanctified in truth. (John 17:17-19)

To be sanctified—another translation for "hallowing"—encompasses our mission in the world. Hallowing is the one process in which we can be sanctified in God with, and thanks to, Christ *and* take up our mission on earth. The whole process can start freely in us because of the free will with which Christ accomplished that hallowing on the cross. It's up to us, now, fully to accept.

With this thought in mind we can better understand how in Jewish tradition "to hallow the Name" became a well-established expression for those who die steadfast in the faith of their ancestors. We only hallow the Name definitively in the hour of our death.

When in the evening Rabbi Akiva, after having been tortured, lay dying, he started to pray the *Shema Israel* (see Deut 6:4). Never had he been able to pray it with this intensity, "with all his heart," and especially "with all his *nefesh*," his life's breath. His disciples who surrounded him tried to calm him: "It's really not necessary anymore." But he retorted promptly: "You don't understand a thing! My whole life I have tried to utter these words just as they are written, 'with all my heart and with all my *nefesh*,' and now that I finally have the chance, you are telling me that it's no longer necessary!" And he commenced again, powerfully: *Shema Israel Adonaï Elohenu Adonaï Ehad* (Hear, O Israel, the Lord is our God, the Lord is One). And drawing out the last vowel of *Ehad*, he gave up his spirit. He died and hallowed the Name, completely uniting with it, in the most literal sense, that most mystic name for the Unnamable: the ONE.

See also: Death, Fear of the Lord, Heart, One, Name, Spirit

HEART

If you have a heart, you can be saved.

—Abba Pambo

With or without heart: the difference is as great as the difference between heaven and hell, life and death, light and dark.

How horrible the sound of the word "heartless." How precious the insight of French philosopher Louis Lavelle (d. 1951) who once confided to this daughter Marie in passing: "Avoir du coeur, voilà ce qui importe dans la vie" (To have heart, that's what is important in life). Desert Father Abba Pambo put it just as tersely: "If you have a heart, you can be saved."[1] Our humanity is at stake here: do you have a heart or are you heartless?

Yet, these days nothing is less clear. More than once I have heard somebody say to himself: "I really don't know if I have something like a heart." People have apparently lost the entryway to their heart. They live from the head, driven by diverse tendencies and tempers, or, more than that even, they are taken over by crammed agendas and school programs. Even free time is nowadays programmed long in advance with different exercises, new obligations, tennis or skating lessons, music academy or judo. When is there time to spend "with your heart?"

This realization has been with us for centuries. Just listen to this archetypical story of the Baal Shem Tov, the Jewish master and founder of Chassidism in Central Europe in the early eighteenth century: "We possess a treasure chest, bolted with an enormous lock, but the key is lost. Now what?" God's treasure chest is wisdom, love, his eternal loyalty, promised in the Torah, God's self-revelation. The lock is the human heart. The key is lost. We lost the way to our heart. This is how the Baal Shem Tov outlined the spiritual state of his contemporaries. "Now what? Take a sledgehammer and smash the lock to pieces." Break your heart and you regain access to the treasure!

Blessed is the person who may rediscover access to the treasure of humanity via the way of the broken heart. Because "a broken and contrite heart, O God, you will not despise" (Ps 51:17). David, in

1. *Sayings of the Desert Fathers* (Pambo 10), 197.

Psalm 51, had already discovered this and commended it to the poor in spirit. The biblical person knows this with fitting certainty. God can do everything, except this: abhor the affliction of the afflicted, despise the contrite, spurn the prayer of the destitute (see Pss 22:24; 51:17; 69:33; 102:17).

But before the heart is truly broken, a great deal of patience may be required, more than we might at first expect. Abba Poemen (fifth century) knew how hard our hearts can be. Just like the prophets, he compared them to stone. Opposite that stands the Word of God, as soft as wax and as fluid as water. The only consolation, he said, lies in perseverance. If we let God's Word drip without ceasing onto the stone of our heart, the water will drill through the stone. Unremittingly applying ourselves to reverence and fear of the Lord will grant us a broken heart, and in this heart access to God lies totally open.

A heart in tune with God is the fruit of an intervening process. In a poetic text, Ezekiel spoke of a future in which God will remove his people's hearts and replace them with a new one, a heart of flesh! There is also mention of water at the inception of this heart operation: "I will sprinkle clean water upon you, and you shall be clean from all your uncleanness. . . . A new heart I will give you, and a new spirit I will put within you" (Ezek 36:25-26). Spirit and water surround the intervention of God through which the human person receives a new heart.

The early Christian theologian Irenaeus (ca. 200) says that God has two hands, the Word and the Spirit, and with both hands He kneads our clay and transforms it in the freedom and beauty of the Word made flesh, the Son. But our heart needs to be "moist," "soft," not hard, not dry. Because, when God puts his seal on a hardened wax tablet, the wax breaks into pieces and the imprint does not show. The moisture of the clay or the wax has to do with humility and inner vulnerability.

The new heart is soft, receptive, malleable. God wants to imprint his law and his will by his own hand, so Jeremiah tells us at the high point of his prophesy: "But this is the covenant that I will make with the house of Israel after those days, says the Lord: I will put my law within them, and I will write it upon their hearts. . . . No longer shall they teach one another, or say to each other: 'Know the Lord,' for they shall all know me, from the least of them to the greatest, says the LORD; for I will forgive their iniquity, and remember their sin no more" (Jer 31:33-34).

"Except for the heart, no law." This Chinese proverb, passed on by Buddhists in Japan, refers to the well-known tension between law and heart felt by all religious. In this respect, Jesus, in one of his most famous arguments with a group of adversaries, cites the prophet Isaiah: "This people honors me with their lips, but their hearts are far from me" (Matt 15:8-9). Is there anything worse than to have to hear this: service to God without heart? To honor the Holy One but with the heart "far from Him"?

Elsewhere we hear Jesus say: "For where your treasure is, there your heart will be also" (Matt 6:21). In a person, the heart is just as central as his dearest treasure. Thus it is with our heart that we discern what has the highest value in our life. "Follow your heart," urge several of the masters, meaning: your heart knows what is highest, what is most sublime, so follow it without hesitation.

"Blessed are the pure in heart, for they will see God" (Matt 5:8). Few sayings of Jesus have so touched his disciples as this one. The monastic tradition, under the sage guidance of master Evagrius, and followed by his disciple John Cassian, found in it, so to speak, the grammar of the whole spiritual quest.

The true goal of life is the Kingdom of God, which is the same thing as seeing God. The means of arriving at that transparent knowledge of God is the way of the purity of heart. That way consists of a systematic battle on three levels and eight fronts: body, soul, and spirit are refined and brought to the true purity of heart by doing battle with the eight well-known demons or passions: gluttony, covetousness, indecency, anger, sadness, listlessness, vanity, and pride.

Once this fight is over, the monk arrives at lack of passion or *apatheia*, which Cassian equates with purity of heart. It is also called *caritas apostolica*, the love described by Paul in his first letter to the Corinthians, the love that "bears all things," that "does not insist on its own way," but that "rejoices in the truth" (1 Cor 13:4-7). Possessed of this purity of heart, we are now able to see God and to start on the way of contemplation.

"My child, give me your heart" (Prov 23:26), says the wise man to his disciple. In the biblical perspective, the heart is the place of insight. That heart is complex, riddled with many propensities, good and bad. The true search for God has to work out these conflicting tendencies. Jewish tradition says "You shall love the Lord your God with all your heart," and this means the good as well as the bad proclivities in that one heart. Your whole person, your every inclination, is called to love God, to acknowledge his reign.

Thus we do not need to ignore any tendencies in our heart, we need to accept them all in one big sweep aimed toward God. "Give me an undivided heart" so prays the psalmist, "to revere your name" (Ps 86:11). Reverence or fear of the Lord is a power that can unify all the inclinations of our complex heart.

Returning to the heart is a great gesture (*reditus ad cor*). Sometimes we have to be able to pull away from everything else and truly, also literally, enter the desert in order to get back in touch with the promptings of our heart. Already the prophet Hosea tells of the initiative of the passionate godlike Lover, speaking of his unfaithful bride Israel: "I am going to . . . lead her into the desert and speak to her heart" (Hos 2:16).[2] The desert is an ideal place to encounter one's heart and there, through purification, to resume the conversation "from heart to heart" with the living God.

Let anyone who goes on retreat or who may, just for a day, retreat to the *poustinia*, make it a happening of the heart. Go there with empty hands, and keep vigil with that heart of yours until it weeps again in genuine brokenness. God cannot spurn such a heart. Isaac the Syrian bears witness as follows:

> Blessed is the man who knows his own weakness, because this knowledge becomes to him the foundation, the root, and the beginning of all goodness. . . . But no one can perceive his own infirmity if he is not allowed to be tempted a little, either by things that oppress his body, or his soul. For then, comparing his own weakness with God's help, he will straightway understand the greatness of the latter. . . . For the heart testifies inwardly, and reflects the lack of something by the fear which strikes and wrestles within it. And because of this, it is confounded, since it is not able to abide in a state of surety; for God's help, he says, is the help that saves. (Cf. Pss 59:13; 107:13) When a man knows

2. This translation is from the New Jerusalem Bible, Reader's Edition (New York: Doubleday, 1990) [translator's note].

that he is in need of Divine help, he makes many prayers. And by as much as he multiplies them, his heart is humbled, for there is no man who will not be humbled when he is making supplication and entreaty. "A heart that is broken and humbled, God will not despise." (Ps. 50:17) Therefore, as long as the heart is not humbled, it cannot cease from wandering; for humility collects the heart.

But when a man becomes humble, at once mercy encircles him, and then his heart is aware of Divine help, because it finds a certain power and assurance moving in itself. And when a man perceives [the coming of] Divine help, and that it is this which aids him, then at once his heart is filled with faith, and he understands from this that prayer is the refuge of help, a source of salvation, a treasury of assurance, a haven that rescues from the tempest, a light to those in darkness, a staff of the infirm. . . . From this time forward he revels in the prayer of faith, his heart glistens with clear assurance. . . . When he thus perceives these things, he will acquire prayer in his soul, like some treasure.[3]

See also: Fear of the Lord, Humility, *Poustinia*, Poverty, Psalmody

3. *The Ascetical Homilies of Saint Isaac the Syrian* (Homily 8), trans. Holy Transfiguration Monastery (Brookline, MA: Holy Transfiguration Monastery, 1984), 67–68.

HOSPITALITY

Hospitality is a practice. Hospitality is also meant to become a way of life.

All the great traditions have recorded tales of exemplary hospitality. Because, of course, the guest who arrives unexpectedly, unannounced, could be an emissary, an angel, a Hermes, yes, who knows, perhaps God himself coming to pay a visit. Homer's epic poems are replete with scenes in which a stranger is timidly received as an emissary of God. And the person who hosts in godly manner is rewarded in godly manner. In the first pages of the Bible, Abraham, the first patriarch, receives a visit from the Lord God at noon by the oak tree of Mamre. While Abraham's hospitality is proverbial, what God promises him exceeds all expectations: "I will surely return to you in due season, and your wife Sarah shall have a son" (Gen 18:10). Sarah, who had remained in the tent and prepared the whole dinner, laughs, laughs in disbelief. But a year later Isaac is born, the child of the laugh, the fruit of the old couple's generous hospitality.

"I was a stranger and you welcomed me" (Matt 25:35). This phrase from the beginnings of our Christian tradition appears in a tale dealing with what we will find out at the end of time, positively or not: You did indeed welcome Me; or, you welcomed me not! At some time we will be judged on our hospitality. This particular practice is *that* essential.

An African abbot tells the story of how in his home in the village on a certain evening a guest was received. As young children, he and his siblings ate in the rear kitchen with their mother. Suddenly mother interrupted the meal. They had to stop eating. All food was saved and formally served to the guest on a new platter. The children protested, but mother was implacable. The only explanation she gave was: "We don't even know who he is!" In the person of the guest a mystery is embodied, which refers to something greater. We have to receive him in the best possible way, even if it causes us to suffer.

Not all cultures have the same sense of hospitality. The mere fact that in some languages the same word can mean "guest" or "enemy" makes one wonder. The Indo-European languages have the same root for the words "guest" and *hôte* (host). The Latin words *hostis* (enemy) and *hospes* (guest), and the French word *hôte* (host, but also guest or visitor) are all derived from that same root. Language betrays a real ambiguity with respect to the experience of welcoming a stranger.

The German words *Gastfreund* and *Gastfreundshaft* refer to a remarkable victory: an enemy has been made into a friend thanks to the provision of hospitality. In French we see that the same word *hôte* can mean guest as well as host. This gives us a taste of another dimension of what is going on: the reciprocity of the experience, in which the distinction between who welcomes and who is welcomed may completely fall away. "Around the hearth's fire, host and guest can no longer be distinguished," says an ancient Zen proverb. We see this miracle occur also in the Gospel: in Emmaus the roles are suddenly reversed. The guest performs the role of the master of the house: "He took bread, blessed and broke it, and gave it to them" (Luke 24:30). Only then were their eyes opened: the Lord was in their midst, in the person of that guest, the person they had met on their walk.

Language reveals that enmity may be involved in the act of receiving a "guest"; who knows, by taking in the stranger are you not letting in a "Trojan horse"? Fear lurks around the corner of the house of hospitality. Monastic texts do not gloss over this: in the Rule of the Master, one of the most important sources of Benedict's Rule, the guests must be watched with great vigilance. Every guest is a suspect, a dangerous intruder, a possible profiteer, perhaps a false brother and a thief. So the guest better be checked out!

So it is all the more striking that we do not find any of this systematic suspicion in Benedict. The first thing to do is to pray with the guest in the oratory, and that is all that is necessary to be able to tell whom is being received. Only then is the guest invited to the table. Whoever actively welcomes the stranger has conquered a deep-seated fear that is known to the heart, individually and collectively, since time immemorial. The hospitable person is a new person: she has cast off a primal fear. In Benedict's Latin text, and thereafter, *humanitas* and *hospitalitas* are used as synonyms: people who provide hospitality show their humanity, or *humanitas*, and vice versa.

Hospitality is destined to become a hallmark of every civilization worthy of the name. More than dialogue, hospitality is a way of encounter with different civilizations, cultures, religions, and worldviews. The great challenge these days lies in having the courage to welcome each other in all sincerity. Clearly, this reaches deeper than the art of dialogue: in hospitality, the other is received with one's whole being, beyond our words. In dialogue there is always the notion of *logos* (word), and in the East a remarkable distrust prevails when it comes to "words." The concrete body language of sincere hospitality does not lie. You receive the other with actions that take time and that engage the heart.[1]

The future of humanity demands a qualitative leap. The race for more and more weapons and worldwide arms trafficking mirror the enormity of our fear, but also the indecency of our cynicism. Cardinal Jean Daniélou once wrote: "It is proper to say that civilization made a decisive step forward on the day that a foreigner became a guest instead of an enemy; on that day the community of man was established." It is high time to recall that step made once in the past and to adapt it to our day if we, collectively, wish to make that qualitative leap in the near future. Our small blue planet's viability and peace depend directly on the practical achievement of global friendship through hospitality.

One of the most original and creative thinkers about hospitality is Louis Massignon (1883–1962).[2] He was a pioneer in the dialogue with Islam. From an early age he applied himself to learning Arabic. During the high tide of colonialism he served in the French military carrying out scientific research in archeology and scientific history. He lived in Cairo and Baghdad.

In May 1908, during an expedition in Iraq, his life took a decisive turn, something he would continue to refer to for the rest of his life, even though he rarely discussed it openly or wrote at any length

1. See the many contributions on this topic by our confrère Pierre de Béthune in his collected essays, *Par la foi et l'hospitalité. Essais sur la rencontre entre les religions* (Ottignies: Clerlande, 1997), and his recent *L'hospitalité sacrée entre les religions* (Albin Michel, 2007). [Translator's note: English translations of Fr. de Béthune's work are *Interreligious Hospitality: The Fulfillment of Dialogue,* trans. Robert Henrey (Collegeville, MN : Liturgical Press, 2010), and *Welcoming Other Religions: A New Dimension of the Christian Faith,* trans. William Skudlarek, OSB (Collegeville, MN: Liturgical Press, 2016).]

2. See the anthology edited by Jacques Keryell, *L. Massignon: L'hospitalité sacrée* (Paris, 1997). See also C. Drevet, ed., *Massignon et Ghandi. La contagion de la verité* (Paris, 1967), 132–41.

about it in his many publications. Suspected of being a spy, he is arrested and taken prisoner, and he realizes right away that his life is in danger. To compound his misfortune, he suffers a serious bout of malaria. He briefly considers suicide. At great risk, a family takes it upon itself to harbor and hide him. That hospitality, based on the sacred law never to betray a guest or to break your word once given, was for Massignon, then 25 years old, a revelation of what is holiest under the sun. He saw in it a direct revelation of how God wants to be known. Thanks to Muslims he rediscovers his own Christian faith. In that moment of crisis, he appealed to God in the language of others, Arabic, and with expressions he had learned through his study with the Muslim mystic Mansour el Hallaj. His thoughts of terminating his own life changed in a breakthrough of divine fire: he understood his own total insignificance in the midst of an overwhelming blaze emanating from the Unnamable. In this context Massignon often cites a verse of the Persian poet Rumi:

> He whose beauty drove the angels to jealousy,
> Came by at dawn and gazed into my heart.
> He wept, and I wept until the break of day.
> Then He asked me: "Between the two of us, tell me, who is the lover?"

Said Massignon, "This probably renders best, in the least incomplete way, what I experienced early in my life."

That night when he was visited by the Stranger, to use Rumi's image, will become the force, for the next fifty-plus years, that motivates some of the positions he takes and organizations he becomes involved with. His life, no matter how busy with study and research, remains intertwined with mysticism and political action. So, the professor at the prestigious Collège de France also teaches weekly evening classes in French for North-African guest workers in Paris to help them integrate in society. He takes to the streets to protest torture and the irresponsible use of force, and, already an old man, he is arrested, transported to a location four kilometers outside of Paris, and forced to walk home in the middle of the night.

He establishes a circle of friends (called *Badaliya*) through which the members, who live in all corners of the world, pray and fast together and study current issues tearing at the fabric of the world. On every day of prayer he sends around an inspirational letter, through which we learn that in 1962, the year of his death, the friends had reached the ninety-third day of a common fast. Born and raised in colonial times, he becomes a fierce anti-colonialist, who loudly expresses his vexation when the powers-that-be do not keep their word to the Arabic countries.

"Hospitality," "non-violence" (the way Gandhi practiced it in the political realm), "compassion," "substitution" (a mystical offering up of oneself for others), and "intercession" are the key words of his religious philosophy.[3] He realized how the rediscovery of holy hospitality—in which the guest/stranger in our midst reveals the face of the Stranger—opens up whole new possibilities for relations among peoples and religions. Prayer, intercession, welcoming the other with open arms, identifying with and changing places with the other, will hasten the coming of God's banquet with all peoples at the end of time.

Let us honor this path-breaking pioneer with a few extracts from his writings. Massignon addresses Christians and Westerners, but you hear how he received a treasure from the Muslims thanks to his encounters with the Arabic peoples of North Africa and the Middle East. Hospitality, mercy, and "substitution" go hand-in-hand. We sense how in his life hospitality was no special niche, but part and parcel of a complete art of living in which several practices played constitutive parts—practices that are warmly recommended here as well: fasting, making pilgrimages,[4] intercession, the practice of nonviolence, etc.

3. "Massignon seems to have wanted to develop in the *Badaliyah* the meaning of substitution as it characterized the spirituality of Hallaj and to find there, like Charles de Foucauld, an approach to apostolate that is far more truthful than proselytizing." G. Zananiri, O.P., in *Catholicisme* VIII, col. 823 (1979). "In Massignon's thinking, the work, wholly and directly inspired by Pauline teaching and the Letter to the Hebrews, links up with that of de Foucauld" (ibid., col. 820).

4. Annually he went on pilgrimage to Jerusalem, and undertook pilgrimages to India because of Gandhi (whom he had met in Paris), to Uganda because of the martyrs Charles Lwanga and his companions, to Tamanrasset because of Charles de Foucauld (his friend, who had designated Massignon as his possible successor and to whom he had addressed a last letter the morning of the day of his murder), to Salette because of the appearances to Mélanie, to Baghdad and al-Bayda in Iraq because of the mystic he studied all his life—Mansur el Hallaj (born in al-Beyda, crucified in Baghdad), to Düllmen because of the seer Anna Catherine Emmerich, and to Damiette in Egypt because of Francis of Assisi (in 1931 he became a Third Order Franciscan and took the name Abraham).

✦

"It is the Arabs who taught me the religion of hospitality; forty years ago, I was arrested, accused as a spy for colonialism, and in mortal danger. But I was their guest and I was saved, set free after three days, out of respect for God, for the Guest."

✦

"The time has come for a reciprocal conversion in hospitality."

✦

"Hospitality is the highest realization of the works of mercy. . . . Even though it is said that there are eight works of mercy, at bottom there is only one: the holy hospitality that puts faith in the guest, that mysterious stranger, that unknown who is God himself, just as He, defenseless, wants to deliver himself to us in vulnerability."

✦

"The first form of contact between two civilizations, no matter how primitive and adversarial they may be, is the principle of hospitality. Hospitality presupposes that the stranger, the enemy, nevertheless possesses something of value to us."

✦

"One can only find truth by practicing hospitality."

✦

"We shall be saved only thanks to a certain spiritual technique of the right of asylum, the *salaam Allah*, the hospitality that we are offered."

✦

"The day comes when God will make us rediscover the eschatological meaning of holy Hospitality for the salvation of the world."

See also: Dialogue, Fasting, Intercessory Prayers, Name, Pilgrimage, Reciprocity, Serving, Yin and Yang

HUMILITY

Humility is not a way of life that transforms us. Neither is humility a virtue that one practices until it is achieved. "The person who strives too consciously for humility shall miss the mark, guaranteed," said the philosopher Max Scheler. Yet, humility is an essential part of our vocabulary if we are serious about the concept of spirituality.

Humility has to do with God. Lowliness is the garment God puts on when He wants to show himself in human form (Isaac the Syrian). Lowliness, meekness, or humbleness are three delicate terms to indicate a limit, a state where humanity and godliness are no longer distinguishable. They flow into each other imperceptibly, as in the heart of Hadewijch when she noted in one of her letters: "What God was in me, was human, and what human nature was in me, was God." Humility is one of these mysterious interfaces deep inside us where God and the human meet.

Only the humble person can answer the question, "Are you humble?" with "Yes, I am." Only in the presence of a meek person do you feel fully accepted and not judged in any respect whatever. How wondrous! Even animals pick up a certain scent when a person approaches who is humble through and through. According to Isaac the Syrian, the humble person has recovered the smell of paradise, a quality from before the fall, and animals—including wild animals, such as snakes—fall immediately under its spell.

A meek person cannot be trapped. Satan's wiles have no grip on her. Abba Anthony said, "I saw the snares that the enemy spreads out over the world and I said groaning, 'What can get through from such snares?' Then I heard a voice saying to me, 'Humility.'"[1]

Vanity, flattery, aggression, anger, gloominess, or sensual temptations: no longer do they appear to affect the meek. In the humble, something went through fire and water. They died to that firm center that we tend to from childhood on and that we call our ego. We invest in our own profile of this ego, consciously or subconsciously, in order to keep standing, in order to protect ourselves in all directions, outward as well as inward. Fear, shame, uncertainty, dependency:

1. *Sayings of the Desert Fathers* (Anthony the Great 7), 2.

the blows of life have taught us how to defend ourselves. But the meek choose a totally different way: they learn to dismantle all defense mechanisms. They stop investing in this vain set of delusions that we strive to keep intact and that always circle around that inner god, the ego.

The ego of Abba Macarius has completely disappeared, and the demons acknowledge their impotence when, in vain, they try to attack him:

> When Abba Macarius was returning from the marsh to his cell one day carrying some palm-leaves, he met the devil on the road with a scythe. The latter struck at him as much as he pleased, but in vain, and he said to him, "What is your power, Macarius, that makes me powerless against you? All that you do, I do, too; you fast, so do I; you keep vigil, and I do not sleep at all; in one thing only do you beat me." Abba Macarius asked what that was. He said, "Your humility. Because of that I can do nothing against you."[2]

To fast or to keep vigil at night are no signs of great spiritual liberation: you differ in nothing from the devil, says this ancient saying, if you don't have that distinguishing quality called humility. Macarius can no longer be threatened, hurt, or maimed. The scythe is powerless against him. How wondrously free he is! Even corporal temptations no longer tempt him, no matter what he eats or drinks. Something in him has been totally consumed as if by a spiritual fire that even marked his body: "Some Fathers questioned Abba Macarius the Egyptian, 'Why is it that whether you eat, or whether you fast, your body is always emaciated?' The old man said to them, 'The little bit of wood that is used to poke the vine branches when they are burning ends by being entirely burnt up by the fire; in the same way, man purifies his soul in the fear of God, and the fear of God burns up his body.' "[3] The result is a radical freedom from insult as well as from praise:

> Abba Macarius said, "If slander has become the same to you as praise, poverty as riches, deprivation as abundance, you will not

2. *Sayings of the Desert Fathers* (Macarius the Great 11), 129–30.
3. *Sayings of the Desert Fathers* (Macarius the Great 13), 130.

die. Indeed it is impossible for anyone who firmly believes, who labours with devotion, to fall into the impurity of the passions and be led astray by the demons."[4]

A brother came to see Abba Macarius the Egyptian, and said to him: "Abba, give me a word, that I may be saved." So the old man said, "Go to the cemetery and abuse the dead." The brother went there, abused them and threw stones at them; then he returned and told the old man about it. The latter said to him, "Didn't they say anything to you?" He replied, "No." The old man said, "Go back tomorrow and praise them." So the brother went away and praised them, calling them, "Apostles, saints and righteous men." He returned to the old man and said to him, "I have complimented them." And the old man said to him, "Did they answer you?" The brother said no. The old man said to him, "You know how you insulted them and they did not reply, and how you praised them and they did not speak; so you too if you wish to be saved must do the same and become a dead man. Like the dead, take no account of either the scorn of men or their praises, and you can be saved."[5]

True humility has to do with holy reverence for the Lord and sweet gentleness. Contrariwise, it is impossible to be humble with a heart full of pride. In the humble person, awe for God's holiness burns from the bottom of her heart. In her innermost self, she kneels before her God, in fear and trembling, and never without tears. To her comes the Comforter, according to Jesus' word: "Blessed are those who mourn, for they will be comforted" (Matt 5: 4). Gentleness is released in her. Within her or without, there is only grace.

In the humble person, there is not even humility anymore, there is only love. "Descend into what is lowliest and most humble in you, and underneath it you will discover God's glory" (Isaac the Syrian). The meek person experiences how he is supported from below by a godly power, by something that Isaac calls "glory." That glory is the limitlessness of love, a mercy without bounds, a compassion for all that exists, humans, animals, or plants, the little and oppressed first.

4. *Sayings of the Desert Fathers* (Macarius the Great 12), 130.
5. *Sayings of the Desert Fathers* (Macarius the Great 23), 132.

Humility is the inner gateway to these biblical "bowels of mercies" (Col 3:12), another place for the meeting of God and human being.

One of the Fathers said: "All work without humility is vain, because humility is the precursor of love. John was the precursor of Jesus and drew everybody to Him; likewise, humility draws to love, which means God himself, because God is love."[6]

"Learn from me; for I am gentle and humble in heart" (Matt 11:29). Many icons in which Christ is pictured with the open Gospel book feature this text from Matthew. Evagrius Ponticus, a Desert Father from the fourth century, wrote in a letter: "I want nothing but this: to become the disciple of the Gentle One, He who is Humble of Heart." This cry from the heart summed up his whole life. When Jeanne de Chantal testifies in the canonization process of her friend and spiritual father Francis de Sales, she said this at the end: "In nobody on this earth have I seen the embodiment of our Savior's words 'I am gentle and humble in heart' as in him." These words radiate in those who have followed Jesus till the end. Only in the Humble One is a meek person truly humble. Only in Christ are we completely who we are.

The great conversation among the world's religions is a question of humility. The poor and the humble readily find each other, regardless of all dogmatic and cultural differences among Buddhists and Muslims, Jews and Taoists. Those who are humble don't care to be in the right: against whom? for whom? They serve truth with disarming freedom. In them, the seeds of religious war are nipped in the bud.

It is only too true that through the ages religion has been the cause of terrible wars. Louis Lavelle even posited: "All wars are religious wars." But the meek Christian, the poor Sufi, the Buddhist mendicant-monk, and the Jew devoted to his psalms have learned not to conflate their ego with the absolute, in whatever subtle form. In that way they could destroy the seed that carries the urge to war in their own heart. A fire consumed in them even the roots of that pernicious weed. In all of time they are the true heralds of world peace, in the past as well as today.

Humility lies at the very beginning of the spiritual path and crowns the end result as with a seal. Christmas is the feast of godly humility. The Assumption of Mary is the feast that comes at the end,

6. Paschasius Diaconus, *Verba Seniorum* 36:3.

after the resurrection of her Son. The profound tone of both celebrations is heard in Mary's *Magnificat*, the song of humility: "My soul proclaims the greatness of the Lord, my spirit rejoices in God my Savior for he has looked with favor on his lowly servant." Here also, God and person have become indistinguishable. The fruit of her womb is God's own son, who in God's name praised the poor and the humble. Blessed is the longing that reaches for freedom in the school of humility.

See also: Dialogue, Fear of the Lord, Hospitality, Mary, Peace, Poverty, Psalmody, Tears

I

ICONS

Our spiritual life acquires depth when we surround ourselves with works of art. The beauty around us quietly and beneficently stirs our soul, resets our inner compass, and brings peace to our heart.

Icons are very particular works of art. In south Italy and Sicily, where a marked Byzantine influence can still be observed, ordinary homes have their own "corner of beauty." It features an icon, lit by a small oil lamp. Now and then the inhabitant tarries a moment when passing in front of it, with or without a word, a quick prayer, a glance, a sign of the cross. Something radiates out from that corner, bestowing grace on the whole house.

Icons can become guides on our life's journey. They surrender their secret only slowly, partly because they came to us from the East and hence from a different religious culture. When you have learned to give them a place in your daily life, you discover how they provide a resting place for the eye and can pacify the conflicting torrents of a seething heart.

Face to face with an icon, we become quieter and more subdued: inner doors are being opened. An icon is indeed a window, and it opens to God. You can consider the icon as a glass window that tempers the light, enabling us to gaze at the mystery and making it bearable. Even more: the icon furthers the incarnation. The Word has become flesh, image, icon. The artist is said in Greek to be an "iconographer," which means that he "writes" the image and thus continues the work of the incarnation of the Verb of God. That is the artist's belief—and we may adopt it as well.

Normally, the iconographer prays, applies himself to the psalms, does not shy away from a fast, reads the Gospel, and only then starts to "write," all in accordance with a venerable and tried-and-true tradition. He stands in this tradition and works as somebody who is initiated, who shares the secret. The initiated understand him. For others, the secret remains veiled, even mystifying, and perhaps utterly inaccessible for a long time. Some never really enter into it.

Behind the icon lives one or other word of Scripture. All of a sudden it is revealed to you, sometimes only after many years. A word gives meaning, reveals significance, and shines light on what you are looking at. From the text, a new light shines through the image and, even in your daily life, touches you.

Take, for example, the famous *Vladimirskaya*, the dark Virgin of Vladimir, who looks at us with her large almond eyes, the icon that inspired the sculptor Charlier when he made the image of Our Lady Star of the Sea—*Stella Maris*—in the dome of our abbey at Zevenkerken. You see the child reaching in haste to embrace his mother, both arms around her neck and head. And all of a sudden, in what you are gazing upon, you hear three, four verses of the Song of Solomon:

> Let him kiss me with the kisses of his mouth! (1:1)
> *Nigra sum sed formosa*—I am black and beautiful. (1:5)
> Look, he comes, leaping upon the mountains. (2:8)
> O that his left hand were under my head, and that his right hand embraced me! (2:6)

The icon illustrates the Song of Solomon, and the Song of Solomon gives meaning and significance to the image. Christ is the saving bridegroom of his mother and, in her, of us all.

Throughout the years, you notice an interaction among image, Bible text, and life. A dialogue springs up in the quiet contemplation of the image: you hear the Word and you murmur a response. "Here am I, the servant of the Lord; let it be with me according to your word" (Luke 1: 38). "And the Word became flesh . . . and we have seen his glory . . . full of grace and truth" (John 1:14). "Lord, have mercy." "When the goodness and loving kindness of God our Savior appeared" (Titus 3:4).

Silently in the night, momentarily keeping wake in front of an icon, you let your gaze rest on the image that looks at you. Then you can close your eyes: the image does not disappear like on TV, where an image is not allowed to remain on the screen for more than four seconds. Here the rules are exactly the opposite: the icon carries you and supports the attention of the prayerful heart. If you become distracted, you return to the steady resting point of the image, and you resume your prayer word, your mantra: "Lord Jesus Christ, Son of God, have mercy on me a sinner." "Hail Mary, full of grace, our Lord is with you."

Slowly the postures of the three angels around the table under the oak of Mamre (the Icon of the Trinity by Andrej Rublev) take form in my memory and body. Christ's hand in blessing or the imploring hands of the Blessed Mother in the Icon of Our Lady of the Sign already start influencing my prayerful positions. "Ask a sign of the LORD your God! . . . Look, the young woman is with child and shall bear a son, and shall name him Immanuel" (Isa 7:10 and Isa 7:14). This can be accompanied by a quiet, increasing joy. You may pay particular attention to what is happening in your shoulders: the interiorization of these practices has a healing and liberating power. Your whole person comes under its beneficent influence.

To honor icons is to go on a journey. We can only sketch the beginning of the path. "The longest journey is the one to the inside" (Dag Hammarskjold). Mindfully venerating icons is a way of inwardness and, hence, it is a long journey, a journey into infinity.

See also: Ejaculatory Prayers, Forms and Formlessness, *Lectio Divina*, Pilgrimage

INTERCESSORY PRAYERS

Intercessory prayers entreat God on behalf of people and situations, offering them up to his attention, to his care. They are part and parcel of the breath of every spiritual life and presuppose a certain mindset and practice.

I recall a conversation with a fellow monk from the Saint Andrew of Clerlande monastery in Ottignies, Belgium, in the late 1960s. In those years, the liturgy was one gigantic construction site. We had just left the sturdy house of the Roman liturgy in Latin and were trying out new forms in the vernacular. This happened *ad experimentum*, as we said at the time (still in the language of the previous generation!). In the Saint Andrew community, which then had only just been established, every prayer service included intercessory prayers, mornings and evenings, as well as during the noontime celebration of the Eucharist. Printed breviaries were not yet available, but nevertheless the brother in charge of the liturgies succeeded in having freshly formulated intercessions at every service, properly taking into account the readings and current events. He prepared them really well (he usually carried well-scribbled notepaper with him), and I asked him: "How much time must it take you to draft all these new intercessory prayers?" He laughed and said: "The time of a cigarette!"

So I discovered how he came to the intercessions spontaneously, as naturally as breathing, and yes, as routinely as having a smoke! It had become a normal form of paying attention to life and to the Word. He then knew how to bend this natural mindfulness into a prayer that, supplicating or praising, brought the matter at hand before God.

Ever since that day it has become a silent assignment for me to live my reality in such a manner that, whatever I experience or hear, I may offer it up to God in the stirrings of my heart.

Of course, this can take a wide variety of forms.

Close to the end of the day, we can recall all that happened and all those we met, bring them before God, and gratefully pray for God's blessing on them. We ask that everything may be completed in God because nothing in our world is truly finished. Everything yearns to be liberated and glorified in God, as Paul wrote.

As we get older, we can all compile a list of names of people who count on our prayers or whose life is dear to us. Friends, family members, even people we don't get along with too well, yes, possibly even enemies. A lifetime of quiet and seclusion has taught me to compile that list with utmost care and, whenever possible, to go over it daily.

Also the deceased have a place. Over the years I discovered how often I had to add a little cross next to the name of those who had occupied a firm place on the list.

Births are equally noteworthy. Every year, my prayers are pregnant with at least three or four expected children of friends or relatives. What initially was an open space in parentheses after the name of the mother, is filled in a few months later with a unique, irreplaceable proper name: Xavier, Olivier, Audrey, William, Amelie, just to mention the last five!

In the Orthodox monastery of Maldon, close to London, established by Starets Sophrony, the Jesus Prayer is practiced every day, morning and evening, for two hours on end. With the same formula, albeit in different languages, the name of Jesus is invoked: "Lord Jesus Christ, Son of God, have mercy on us." In these series of hundreds of invocations, a number of proper names are inserted: all of a sudden you hear a litany of first names, all friends and acquaintances of the monastery. The brothers apparently knew all these names, in order, by heart and could recite them in the semi-dark. These names by themselves already constitute a prayer.

This teaches us a lot about the importance of a name in intercessory prayer. The name, brought before God in its uniqueness, receives the prayerful attention of those present. It now belongs to the community. It lights up in the space where the Name of Jesus reigns. It is included in everybody's praise and supplication. It is like a star in the dark. God himself calls him by name, as he does with all the stars (see Bar 3:34). The living community of saints receives each of these names in its bosom.

Intercessory prayers extend to animals, plants, climatic conditions, and seasons. Cosmic misery such as the tsunami of December 26, 2004 and hurricanes Katrina and Rita in September 2005 are brought before God in humble prayer. Every disaster has a number of dimensions, including solidarity and unexpected forms of compassionate humanity. The prayer includes it all, not just as lament or complaint, but also as supplication and admiration for the creativity and generosity that come to the fore in such extreme emergencies.

A unique form of intercession can develop in our heart at the outbreak of war. The irrationality of war and our powerlessness in the face of it are best captured in a sustained intercessory prayer, in the humble prayer of psalmody, in an aching silence past all words. This is no time for seeking refuge in mute perplexity or in noisy commentary but, rather, it is a time for vigil and prayer, humble yet filled with hope.

That same prayer accompanies all who work diligently to eliminate torture and the death penalty (e.g., Amnesty International) and those who labor in peace movements for dialogue between adversaries and the conclusion of peace treaties (e.g., Pax Christi, Pax Romana, Justitia et Pax, Sant' Egidio, and others). The list of people and situations that can be prayed for is nearly endless. Just think of AIDS patients and their families, the millions of refugees, not only in Europe but throughout all of Africa, victims of traffic accidents and their families, drug addicts, children in prostitution rings, etc.

The important thing here is to keep the gate of intercession continually and actively open. It should be possible to pair a listening receptivity to all that happens on our planet with a beseeching and grateful disposition that implores God for his blessing over everything and that presumes God's presence in everything. Frequently then, the often superficial curiosity to be informed of all that is going on in the world on a daily basis slowly disappears, and we become more circumspect in dealing with newspapers and images on TV, reports, and rumors. "To want to be on top of everything is often to get stuck in the emptiness of everything" (L. Vander Kerken). The psalms are often the most appropriate vehicle for channeling the sometimes crushing quantity of information and bringing it before God.

Furthermore, the person who has learned intercessory prayer feels less and less the urge to judge. The world has no need for ever more magistrates to (pre)judge politics and society. The world is best served by prayerful souls who plead for God's intercession day and night, open and free of any partisan prejudice. The heart begins to resemble the sun of Jesus: "for [your Father in heaven] makes the sun rise on the evil and on the good, and sends rain on the righteous and on the unrighteous" (Matt 5:45), generously and without distinction.

Intercessory prayer also reaches into the future. Those praying for peace direct their gaze to what God intends for our world, for "what no eye has seen, nor ear heard, nor the human heart conceived, what God has prepared for those who love him" (1 Cor 2:9). Our future is a living reality in God. That is why we may allow our intercessory prayer to extend to that—for us—still unknown time. Thus our supplication expresses not only our love but also our hope. As our faith teaches, our world is geared to, and meant for, a fullness that we may call peace (*shalom*), righteousness, and the Kingdom of God. The prayer that implores all what is best for this world already anticipates that glorious future; it hastens the time and actualizes Jesus' own prayer: "Thy Kingdom come."

Isaac of Nineveh, a Syrian father from the seventh century, characterized intercessory prayer as follows:

> And what is a merciful heart? It is the heart's burning for the sake of the entire creation, for men, for birds, for animals, for demons, and for every created thing; and by the recollection and sight of them the eyes of a merciful man pour forth abundant tears. From the strong and vehement mercy which grips his heart and from his great compassion, his heart is humbled and he cannot bear to hear or to see any injury or slight sorrow in creation. For this reason he offers up tearful prayer continually even for irrational beasts, for the enemies of the truth, and for those who harm him, that they may be protected and receive mercy. And in like manner he even prays for the family of reptiles because of the great compassion that burns without measure in his heart in the likeness of God.[1]

See also: Breathing, Forgiveness, Heart, Jesus and the Jesus Prayer, Name, Peace, Psalmody

1. *The Ascetical Homilies of Saint Isaac the Syrian*, Homily Seventy-One, trans. Holy Transfiguration Monastery (Brookline, MA: Holy Transfiguration Monastery, 1984), 344.

J

JESUS AND THE JESUS PRAYER

The name of Jesus refers directly to a concrete person who appeared on the stage of history some two thousand years ago. His name means "salvation" or "the Lord who saves." In his name we find the salvation his disciples announced and passed on. In addition, the Greek church fathers made a connection between the name *Jèsous* and the verb *jâsthai*, "to heal." He is a healer. Whoever invokes his name receives a healing.

Christians call him their savior or redeemer. His proper name is enriched with the name "Christ," which means "anointed" in Greek and is a translation of the Hebrew "Messiah" (*Mashiah*, the anointed one of the Lord, expected as the one who heralds the end of time).

In the Christian faith tradition it is common practice to invoke that name, using a variety of formulations, under all kinds of circumstances. I am referring to what is called the Jesus Prayer. Starting about the twelfth century, one formulation became pretty well solidified among the Byzantine faithful in the East and, later, among the Russian masters: "Lord Jesus Christ, Son of God, have mercy on me, a sinner." The roots of this prayer practice can be traced back to the middle of the fourth century, specifically to the Desert Fathers in Egypt and their heirs in Palestine (including in the area close to Gaza).

Each element of the formulation can easily be traced back to the Gospels and the letters of the apostles. The prayer of the tax collector in the temple, according to the parable composed by Jesus himself, provides the original shape of the formulation. The professions added by Peter, John, and Paul complement each other and make up the first part. For the good thief on Golgotha, the invocation of only the proper name was sufficient: "Jesus," without any further title, "remember me when you come into your kingdom" (Luke 23:42).

Recitation of this prayer has a transforming power. Over the centuries, a whole library has been written about the art of continually reciting this prayer formula. At the end of the eighteenth century, two friends, Nicodemos, a monk from Mount Athos, and Makarios of Corinth, a Greek bishop, put together an extensive anthology: *The Philokalia of the Neptic Fathers*. It collects some forty treatises about this prayer and the spiritual life. These works date from the fourth to, and including, the fourteenth century. This Greek *Philokalia*, first printed in Venice in 1782, was later translated into Slavonic languages and by now has been translated into many modern languages (English, French, Dutch, Italian, etc.). Sometimes there were significant additions, such as, for example, in the Romanian version. One can justifiably say that wherever a new translation of the *Philokalia* was published, a new source of life emerged.

Also very famous is *The Way of a Pilgrim*, a nineteenth-century text. In it we read how a poor layperson and pilgrim is taught, with help from the *Philokalia*, to achieve a state of continual prayer by systematically being mindful of the words, "Lord Jesus Christ, Son of God, have mercy on me, a sinner."

Universally, we can see how a great love for the name of Jesus has taken on all kinds of forms throughout the centuries.

Luke the Evangelist and the church father Origen (ca. 200) were early examples of particular affection for the proper name "Jesus."

"Look at the sheep," said the Coptic desert father Macarius (fourth century), "see how they chew the tender grass and how you can tell from their cheeks how it profits them. So it is with those who unremittingly have the holy name of Jesus on their lips. Recall the old village women: they always had a chew of several herbs in their mouth. Masticating it was good for their stomach and bowels, it benefitted their whole digestive system! So it is with those who repeat the sweet name of their Lord Jesus: thought, imagination, feeling, everything in them experiences its beneficent power!"

In the West there were Bernard, Anselm, and Bernardino of Siena. They wrote long poems and treatises about that "sweet" name Jesus. In the *Lives* of St. Francis of Assisi, his brothers say of the *Poverello* that whenever he encountered the name of Jesus in prayer, his tongue moved over his lips. Also, he did not allow any written note to be left on the ground. He picked it up immediately. Who knows, maybe it contained the letters of the holy Name of Jesus and could be stepped on inadvertently?

Various old French poems provide witness to a passionate predilection for the name that encompasses all parts of us and our entire life, including death:

> Jésus soit en ma tête et en mon entendement.
> Jésus soit en mes yeux et en mon regardement.
> Jésus soit en ma bouche et en mon parlement.

Jésus soit en mon coeur et en mon pensement.
Jésus soit en ma vie et en mon trépassement.[1]

Another poem ends with "Jésus me soit Jésus le jour de mon trépas!" (Let Jesus be Jesus, and thus savior, on the day of my death!). Earlier, St. Anselm had expressed the same thing in Latin, *Jesus sit mihi Jesus in hora mortis. Amen* (Let Jesus be my savior in the hour of my death).

The Practice

It is a fine practice regularly to take the time to apply yourself to this prayer, consciously and tenaciously for, say, a half hour a day. If the prayer then occasionally returns in unguarded moments, it is no wonder. The invocations will flow as a gurgling brook at the bottom of the heart, even at night. When the prayer arises spontaneously, the formulation can take on considerably shorter forms: "Lord, have mercy," or even more to the point, "Jesus, Jesus, Jesus." Often the profession alone suffices and the supplication is eliminated. The profession contains everything: recognition of, and responsiveness to, God's attributes and an inner realization of their relationship.

A contemporary Portuguese anchoress near Bethlehem limited herself to: "Yes, Abba, Jesus, Love." Saying "Yes," the soul aligns itself with the Origin, the Father, who reveals himself in Jesus as the eternal Spirit of love. Little by little, the words may overtake each other: the first one can come last. The "Yes" of Mary of Nazareth finds its inner strength in the liberating "Yes" of the Son, which itself reveals and confirms the eternal Yes-amen of the Father and the Creator of all that is. The cross that encloses height and breadth, distance and depth, shines in the center of these four simple words. As other Names for God, they begin to glow and to blaze in the prayerful heart.[2]

1. Jesus be in my head and in my understanding.
Jesus be in my eyes and in my gaze.
Jesus be in my mouth and in my speech.
Jesus be in my heart and in my thought.
Jesus be in my life and in my death.

2. For "Jesus," see Matt 1:21 and Luke 1:31; for "Abba," see Mark 14:36; Gal 4:6; Rom 8:15; for "Love," see Exod 34:6; 1 John 4:8-16; Rom 5:5; for "Yes," "Amen," see Rev 3:14 and 2 Cor 1:20 (cf. Isa 65:16, in Hebrew: "Bless by the God of the Amen," with Amen rendered by translators by terms such as "faithfulness" or "truth").

Let's look for a somewhat secluded spot and a quiet moment of the day, and then we can start, without haste and in faithful mindfulness. In the beginning it is good to use your voice. As a rule, one prays the Jesus Prayer in multiple series of one hundred. Appropriate prayer strands exist for the purpose.

It is best to start slowly, paying attention to the words as well as to one's breathing. A half-hour for one hundred, so taught a Russian master of the nineteenth century, I. Briantchaninov—that is how slowly and mindfully the fathers prayed! We don't really need more than fifteen minutes for about one hundred prayers; so we can always stretch it out a bit. After ten or twenty times we find the right rhythm, which does not need to remain constant but should be driven by the silence that surrounds each word and that enriches it.

Similarly, the language in which we pray does not always have to be the same. With each language another culture and another church community enters the prayer. I once heard somebody pray the Jesus Prayer aloud in Serbian (*Gospodi Yèsoe Christye . . .*). How thankful I was that I knew it, so that I was able to repeat it during the interminable war in Kosovo.

You can keep your eyes focused on an icon. Every icon leads to the heart, and as soon as you are in your heart you may close your eyes. If you become a little distracted, one glance at the icon suffices to recover a wakeful heart. The icon supports the heart's prayer.

Always begin and end the prayer with the Holy Spirit. Never start without invoking Him first, instructed a monk from the East. Because without the Spirit there can be no prayer as the Father intended: "The true worshippers will worship the Father in spirit and truth, for the Father seeks such as these to worship him" (John 4:23). For that matter, the first word is "Lord Jesus," and Paul teaches that "no one can say 'Jesus is the Lord' except by the Holy Spirit" (1 Cor 12:3). So let us receive the Holy Spirit with the Jesus Prayer—this Easter present of God the Father in and through the risen Christ (see John 20:22). The mercy and forgiveness of sins that we seek come with the indwelling of the Holy Spirit. In this way, He is also the very conscious end of our prayer.

The attention we devote to the Jesus Prayer works a transformation. Not mechanically (and for some people this remains a temptation against which they must guard), but graciously, as a process deeply driven by the Spirit. This is about much more than a sustained effort. Here we let the Spirit do his work, which is our sanctification. Let the uninterrupted prayer then anchor us in this hallowing process, which started with our baptism and which can only find its fulfillment in our contemplation of God's face. In this joyous hope our thanksgiving becomes an unquenchable fire, fed by God himself, Father, Son, and Holy Spirit, now and forever.

See also: Aspirations, Ejaculatory Prayers, Hallowing, Heart, Name, Profession of Faith, Spirit, Yes-Amen

JUBILEE, JUBILATION

"Jubilee" and "jubilation," both words are intrinsic to life. The distant roots of the words lie in the Hebrew *yobel*, as it appears in Leviticus 25:10: "And you shall hallow the fiftieth year and proclaim liberty throughout the land for all its inhabitants. It shall be a jubilee for you: you shall return, every one of you, to your property and every one of you to your family."

The original meaning of *yobel* is "ram" or "ram's horn" (see Josh 6:5). At the announcement of the year of *yobel* a ram's horn is sounded as a trumpet; that is, presumably, the origin of the term "year of *yobel*."

The year of jubilee is a Sabbath year squared: 7 x 7 + 1! Then everything falls still in order to reflect, to thank, to forgive. Debts are forgiven, brothers turned into slaves are set free, properties that had been alienated are returned. This confronts us with an enormously powerful vision of the priestly tradition: every fifty years a general restoration is announced in the name of God.

The fact that we continue to read such texts means that we realize the necessity of redress and forgiveness, and that this takes priority over rights acquired at the expense of others. Nothing is settled forever. Because God is God, the Lord of all time, the Law dictates that from generation to generation we set right all that has become unbalanced in life. God alone ensures true continuity across the generations!

Since the fifteenth century, ever since Pope Paul II, it has been common practice in the Catholic Church to decree a year of jubilee every twenty-five years. And because in the traditional view Jesus was crucified in the year 33, customarily a special jubilee is announced for every year that ends in '33. In civil society, small jubilees are celebrated more and more frequently: after ten or twelve and one-half years of loyal service or as a family, and certainly after twenty, twenty-five, or forty years.

There is no jubilation without repentance, no year of jubilee without redress of all relationships within a community and among the various communities. According to Luke, at the start of Jesus' ministry he announced "the year of the Lord's favor" in the synagogue of Nazareth (Luke 4:19). In doing so, Jesus read the prophecy of Isaiah 61. This year of the Lord's favor was a jubilee year, and what that meant was unmistakable: "to bring good news to the oppressed, to bind up the brokenhearted, to proclaim liberty to the captives" (Isa 61:1)—amnesty in all its forms.

When the jubilee year of 2000 approached, Pope John Paul II endeavored to mend the relationship with the Orthodox and Protestant Christian communities. After all, the important schisms in the Church took place during the second millennium. On the political level, an attempt was made to have the debts of poor countries forgiven. The Bible's vision is more powerful than any restructuring measures we have in the toolkit of our modern society!

In common parlance, "jubilant" and "jubilation" designate elated joy and celebration. High spirits are definitely required.

The Latin church fathers and writers in the Middle Ages were quite taken with the terms *jubilare* and *jubilus*. They used them to express a certain kind of joy, an inner delight as well as one that is manifested publicly, in songs or shouts, and that actually obliterates the separation between inner and outer. In the world of music, the term *jubilus* came to mean a vocalization of the last syllable of the Hallelujah.[1]

Something we tend to forget these days is that *jubilatio* refers to a song of praise without restraint! Hilarius and Augustine were the first to elucidate this particular type of song. In *jubilatio* it is no longer a matter of articulated words: everything turns into pure sound! Thus, in Gregorian chant the text of the verse suddenly becomes pure a's and o's. The charismatic movement has rediscovered some of this when its followers pray in tongues. It's a way of learning how to give form to what is beyond words. There is a verse by Flemish writer Felix Timmermans (1886–1947) who, utterly unable to express what stirs his soul, finally admits: "The words rupture" (from *Adagio*).

Augustine discussed this more than once in his commentaries on the psalms.

> "Don't search for words," he says, "as if you can say how to please God. It is written, 'Sing to him a new song; play skillfully

1. In Greek, the words *alalazô* and *alalagmos* are used. In Hebrew the root is *roe'a* and *re'a*, with the noun *teroe'a*, which, among other things, was the war cry sounded to the Lord of hosts, or the joyful shout when the grape harvest was brought in. Over the centuries, this shout took on a more liturgical character, and it became used in the temple to call upon God as king of the celebrating community. The steady progression of this original shout can be clearly seen in the texts, becoming a pure expression of the shared belief.

on the strings, with loud shouts.' Only in this way do we properly sing to God: by starting a song of jubilation. What does it mean to start a song of jubilation? It means to understand that the song of the heart cannot be put into words. Because those who sing as they bring in the harvest of grains or grapes do not first express their joy in songs, they are filled with so much joy that it cannot be put into words, and so they drop the syllables and they sing shouts of jubilation.

"Shouts of jubilation are songs that express that the heart is bringing something forth that cannot be put into words. And for whom is this song of jubilation more suitable than for God, who is inexpressible? Indeed, inexpressible is He who cannot be uttered in words; and if you are unable to express him in words yet cannot be silent, what else remains but to burst forth in jubilation, to let the heart exult in wordless joy, and to allow the immeasurable joy not to be bound by boundaries of syllables? So sing for Him in shouts of jubilation!"[2]

For Augustine, jubilation starts in marveling at all creation and then focuses on the spiritual creature, which by grace is called to see God, despite the inequality. If the spiritual creature succeeds in transcending this inequality through love, it is capable of discerning God but remains unable to put the experience into words:

As long as you could not feel God, you thought you could express Him, but now that you feel Him, words fail you. Then shout with joy, jubilate to God and to Him alone, do not spread your jubilation over several things, because He alone is inexpressible. Jubilation is fitting only for Him, because he cannot be spoken, while everything else can be said one way or the other.[3]

This and other observations of the bishop of Hippo fed the entire Christian community throughout the centuries.

"Jesus, my jubilation"

—Bernard of Clairvaux

2. Translated from the Dutch translation of St. Augustine's Commentaries on the Psalms (Pss 33:3 and 100:3-6).

3. Augustine, Commentary on Ps 100:3-6.

Bernard of Clairvaux writes: "Jesus is honey in my mouth, a melody in my ear, and a jubilation in my heart" (*Jesus mel in ore, in aure melos, in corde jubilus*). Richard of Saint-Victor connects jubilation with a certain stage of the Christian life, namely the second-last one, the one just before perfection. He will be followed in this line of thinking by others.

In the first part of his treatise *Vanden XII Beghinen* (*The Twelve Beguines*), John of Ruusbroec describes the ascent of the soul in four ways. The first way is the one of *jubilus* or *jubilatio*, then comes *contemplatio*, followed by *speculatio*, and finally the highest form, the storms of love:

> When the human person is touched by this light and this contact, his joy and delight of soul and body are so great, in this heart lifted up to God, that the person does not know what happened, nor knows if he can endure it any longer. This is called *jubilus*, which nobody can express in words, and which can only be understood by the one who experiences it. It lives in the loving heart that is opened to God and closed to all creatures. And this is the source of *jubilatio*: love from the heart, a rising flame of devotion, this is thanksgiving and praise full of unending, holy awe for God. . . . This then is the first and lowest way in which God shows himself in a life of contemplation. (From the rendering in contemporary Dutch by L. Moereels)

John of the Cross counts jubilation among the highest steps of spiritual growth. In his *Spiritual Canticle*, he identifies jubilation with "the song of the sweet nightingale" (stanza 39). The Spanish mystic emphasizes how a transformation takes place in this phase: "in this union of the soul with God, the soul sings to Him together with Him" (Explanation, para. 12). "This is the Canticle which the soul sings in the transformation which takes place in this life, about which no exaggeration is possible. But as this song is not so perfect as the new song in the life of glory, the soul, having a foretaste of that by which it feels on earth, shadows forth by the grandeur of the magnificence of that in glory" (Explanation, para. 13).[4] In *The Living Flame of Love*

4. St. John of the Cross, *A Spiritual Canticle of the Soul and the Bridegroom Christ*, trans. David Lewis, with corrections and introduction by Benedict Zimmerman,

he describes that state of jubilation as a commentary on "dying you have exchanged death for life." Transformation and jubilation: they dovetail here.

There never is a great distance between Augustine and these later reflections.

Let us rediscover the path to jubilation in the heart that has learned to love. Marveling at God's creation and even more at what He is, in his inexpressible goodness, beauty, and unity, we surrender to a song that consumes all words in fire. Let us learn anew in the school of the psalms and with Augustine how a shout of joy can catch our heart and fill it with a plenitude of sounds and cries, unspeakably richer than what can be rendered in words or concepts. The ground of all this is that God is God, and that He, light from light, visits our heart in the hour of his grace.

See also: Blessing, God, Loving, Psalmody, Wonder

OCD, electronic edition with modernization of English by Harry Plantinga, 1995, available at www.ccel.org/ j/john_cross/canticle/canticle.html (accessed March 25, 2016).

JUDGE (DO NOT)

Do not judge. Do not speak ill of others. Imperatives such as these feature prominently in the Gospels and can frequently be found in the many aphorisms of our monastic rules. Yet we have to admit that we are too often tempted by our tendency to judge. We are constantly judging, especially in areas that we know all too well. We spot immediately what is missing, what is too much or too little, what doesn't belong, etc. Will we ever be freed from this, radically?

Archimandrite Sophrony, the publisher of the works of holy Staretz Silouan, was already more than ninety-years-old when I had the opportunity to talk with him for half an hour. I asked him: "Not to judge, as Jesus requires of us in the Gospel, how do we do it?" He laughed disarmingly and said: "That's easy!" And he explained: "Think of the Judge, and you will lose any need to judge others right then and there!"

Afterwards, I discovered to my amazement that every time "not judging" is mentioned in the New Testament, it is always accompanied by a reference to the Last Judgment. When the heart harbors great fear of the Judge, there is no more room for judging anybody, let alone condemning anybody.

Recently I put the same question to a venerable Indian, Sri Sri Ravi Shankar, when he was visiting Brussels. He smiled and said: "Look at a child, how she deals with her mother. The child does not ask if her mother has much learning, what diplomas she earned, at what university she studied, etc. A child does not judge her mother. You still have that child in you. You know how a child feels toward her mother. Become that child, and you will know how not to judge. Did someone not say: If you do not become like children, you will never enter into the kingdom of heaven?"

There you have two answers to the same question, both disarmingly introduced with a laugh or a smile.

Based on the above, we may be able to build a small ladder in the heart, with at least three steps.

First, let us become conscious of this inclination always and quickly to pronounce judgment, whether that judgment is totally crushing or not. Once we can do that, it is appropriate to question just how self-evident this need is, and then to let go of it. This may lead us to realize how useless, premature, unnuanced, and even how unjust this judging business is.

Through practice we can learn to let go of the impulse to judge as soon as we feel it coming up. Let go of the verdict. Lay down the gavel. Call on the angel of mercy. Or press the delete key of your inner computer. Erasing everything. Forgetting, purposefully.

The next step on the ladder could be to keep an inner eye on the wide horizon of the end of time. Eventually, God will be everything in everybody. The feast will arrive at some point. Everybody will then recline at the same banquet table. If we wish to participate in that later, we determine it *now.* So we say, " Don't get upset needlessly, don't build animosities, don't curse anybody or anything, avoid terminating relationships in such a way that they cannot be mended. Don't curse anybody in your heart, and don't tell anybody to go to hell. Because the stronger your reactions are now, the smaller the chances will be of participating in the heavenly banquet later!"

At the moment of his execution, Thomas More managed to say a prayer for the king who had ordered him to be beheaded. He hoped, so he prayed, to be able to meet the king again at the banquet in God's kingdom. He called to mind Stephen, who in the hour of his death prayed for Saul, and how these two now share in the same feast in the community of saints.

We can use the ladder in both directions: sometimes from down to up, other times from the highest step to the lowest. Those whose mind is fixed on the final end, the Last Judgment and the Feast of all feasts, can immediately change their feelings about current unpleasant life situations. And, the other way round: those who find themselves stuck, boiling with rage or seething with irritation, can, at the first impulse, hear a bell's tinkle with the message, "Delete!" or "Click here: erase!"

A third step on the ladder can be to turn inward to a silence without thought. Those who twice a day plunge into the great silence for half an hour remember those times fondly. Without too much trouble, they are able to cleanse their inner eye of any image and to be fully present, pure, naked, stripped, without preoccupation, without care. Those who do not regularly practice this exercise will find that kind of inner movement far more difficult.

There are two lessons here: first, it is extremely useful to have periods of prolonged, complete silence on a daily basis, and, second, it is particularly salutary to fall back on that silence for a moment or two during the day and to switch the inner radio off. Resetting everything to zero at least once every hour and deeply, mindfully breathing out, is an extremely healthy practice; it has powerful positive consequences for not-judging as well as for the inclination to speak ill of others. Doctors tell us that this kind of mindful breathing done once every hour is also very salutary for our health.

Those who judge are in part stuck in a "small" consciousness, sharp, to be sure, and perhaps even right on target, but certainly not wide and grand. So, if we want to get rid of our tendency to judge, we need to choose in our heart an awareness that is wide and open. We will teach our inner eye not to fixate too much on pointed targets. "The broadening of the heart is the product of its purity," we read in Desert Father Evagrius. There is a mutual effect: the purer the heart, the wider and freer it becomes. And vice versa: open the heart, as wide as you can, and many passions will give way.

Silent meditation, contemplation of icons, practice of *lectio divina*, the Jesus Prayer, psalmody, and night vigils are all practices that will induce a broadening of the heart. A habit of saying quick prayers will also help with that. Those who train their heart continually to murmur something that elevates the spirit will discover to their surprise that there is no more inner space left to judge whoever or whatever.

Hence, those who start their day with these practices for a couple of hours will certainly find it less difficult to be gentle and lenient, and will realize quicker how the impulse to judge influences the heart for ill. Those who every day can fall back on a word, an insight, a broadening light received in the early morning or during a night vigil, will be better equipped for the normal battles of every day. The power of God's grace surrounds them like a shield, as the psalmist assures us.

See also: Ejaculatory Prayers, Feasting, Fight, Jesus and the Jesus Prayer, Love for One's Enemies, Meditation, Peace, Psalmody

K

KEEPING SILENT

A brother asked Abba Poemen, "Is it better to speak or to be silent?" The old man said to him, "The man who speaks for God's sake does well; but he who is silent for God's sake also does well."[1]

Abba Macarius the Great said to the brothers at Scetis, when he dismissed the assembly, "Flee, my brothers." One of the old men asked him, "Where could we flee beyond this desert?" He put his finger on his lips and said, "Flee that," and he went into his cell, shut the door and sat down.[2]

"If only we could shut up," you hear somebody say once in a while. But keeping silent means more than keeping your mouth shut. Some people manage to keep their lips pressed together, but their whole body expresses rejection, condemnation, infinite displeasure. To keep silent on the outside and to keep silent on the inside: if only we could master that!

Silence is golden. Silence is masterful. The one who always wants to have the last word loses the argument, makes a poor impression, and is powerless against the person who has learned to keep silent at all appropriate times. William the Silent (aka William of Orange or William the Taciturn) received that nickname as a compliment. In turbulent, very troubled times he achieved more while keeping silent than all the agitators.

About the suffering servant in Isaiah, it is written, most paradoxically: "He will not cry or lift up his voice, or make it heard in the street . . . until he has established justice in the earth" (Isa 42:2-4). He appeared to be silent in the exercise of his authority, yes, even persuasive, although he never raised his voice.

"Abba Poemen said of Abba Nisterus [the Cenobite] that he was like the serpent of brass which Moses made for the healing of the people: he possessed all virtue and without speaking, he healed everyone."[3] Healing each other in silence—may this be the salutary end result of our steadfast application of practices that transform us and others, for the better, for more abundant life.

1. *Sayings of the Desert Fathers* (Poemen 147), 188.
2. *Sayings of the Desert Fathers* (Macarius the Great 16), 131.
3. *Sayings of the Desert Fathers* (Nisterus the Cenobite 1), 155.

See also: Adoration, Conversation, Dance, Form and Formlessness, Meditation, Music, Paradox, *Poustinia*, Spirit

L

LAMENT, LAMENTING

Contemporary man needs to learn again to lament, says Otto Fuchs in his commentary on Psalm 22. "To lament" in the biblical sense is quite different from the rather rampant current grumbling, sighing, protesting, venting, and other ways of complaining. Biblical lamenting can be seen, for example, in the Psalms. Analyses have shown that this lamenting, on the one hand, is aimed at offering praise—I lament *until* I can praise again, and, on the other, how it is embedded in a prayer of praise—I lament *because* once I was able to praise.

The biblical prayer of lament is rooted in an experience of covenant. I know that since birth I have been anchored in a vital bond with the living God. "On you I was cast from my birth, and since my mother bore me you have been my God" (Ps 22:10). From early childhood on, the biblical person has learned to praise God at pilgrim feasts or at home in the blessing of the daily bread or celebrating the Sabbath. Because I have learned to praise, now I lament, until I can praise again. A prayer of praise bookends the lament, at the beginning and at the end. Praise and lament are the two lungs of biblical prayer. The true rhythm of this prayer is praising—lamenting —praising.

We are deprived of the original experience of once having been allowed to praise God. This lack means that we lament without hope, without the prospect of any song of praise. Some people are so marked by this hopeless perspective that they are no longer able to muster a proper lament: faced with the emptiness, they are struck completely mute. No hope, no word, no lament, nothing.

A practice that can revive the lungs of the spiritual person is psalmody. All the sorrow suppressed in the intentional muteness may be expressed, even with the prospect of a festive life in which God, sooner or later, will be lauded in thanksgiving and praise.

In some modern spiritual movements, infants are learning to give praise and thanks to God and to express it in jubilation. How precious this is! And, in reverse, how sad if somebody has to wait till his or her twentieth year or longer to experience, in an uninhibited way and without the slightest social manipulation, a full evening, let alone a whole night, of beseeching and thanksgiving in a place like Paray-le-Monial or Taizé.

See also: Emptiness, Feasting, Jubilee, Praise, Psalmody

LECTIO DIVINA OR SCRIPTURE READING

Among all the arts and practices we can choose to focus on, Scripture reading or *lectio divina* is absolutely central and a true priority if we wish to live a spiritual life.

The expression *lectio divina* exists not only in Latin, but also in Greek (*hè theia anagnôrisis*) and reaches back to the golden era of the church fathers. In our current languages the term never received a literal translation: nobody speaks of *divine reading*! This is a remarkable thing, and could mean that the consistent practice of "divine reading" was already in decline when modern languages started to develop.

The expression means that in this practice we "read from (or 'of') God," as we have an adjective before the genitive of the object. The question then is: is this actually possible, to read from (or of) God? In Greek, just as in Dutch or in German, "to read" (*legein*) has to do with bundling, collecting, bringing into unity. Can we just bundle God by "reading from" Him, like a bunch of carrots strung together? Only by doing it do we discover, to our surprise, that it works exactly the other way round: we realize that in reading the word of God, we are "read" by God, yes, we are gathered in by Him and brought into unity.

The practice always occupied a central place in ancient monastic tradition. In the Rule of Benedict, the best hours of the day are devoted to it. Ordinarily, the day started with this form of paying attention to God's word, after the night prayer of Matins. One read and learned by heart. The rest of the day one continued to murmur God's word and to chew on it. What was committed to memory remained available in the monk's heart the whole day long.

Conscious and unconscious associations stemming from one verse in a psalm can illuminate the heart and sometimes even set it aflame. "His mother treasured all these things in her heart" (Luke 2:51), as the Gospel writer reminds us more than once. Mary constitutes the model for that particular activity of the monk: reading and praying, keeping vigil with the Word that is taken into the heart.

To shed further light on this art, let us elaborate on four particular aspects: two handicaps, three schedules, four stages, and one method.

Two Handicaps

Reading has become a threatened activity. At least two important handicaps are at work here. In the first place, there is competition from other media. Reading is outweighed by radio and TV. On average, we in Western Europe spend about twelve hours a week in front of the TV, according to reports of some fifteen years ago. So, how many hours are left for reading? Another item, this one gleaned at the Frankfurt Book Fair of 1985: one out of three Germans never reads a book in his life. Still other surveys have revealed that among those who entered upon monastic life, many had never read a book from cover to cover prior to their entry. They only managed to read certain books in their entirety by listening to works read aloud in the refectory or during the night office. Young university students in the United States live constantly with music in the background. Certain forms of reading that require quiet are slowly being pushed aside, until one day they will have disappeared entirely.

Another handicap is that our memory is poorly developed these days. A person completely without memory is no longer able to read. He reads a sentence, forgets it, and the next sentence has no connection to anything: the thread has been cut and he must start again from the beginning. The poorer one's memory, the more laborious one's reading. Conversely, meaningful, creative, nonliteral reading only gets going thanks to the interplay of allusions, memories, and ample associations—in other words, thanks to a trained and richly furnished memory.

According to cultural critic George Steiner, the contention of philosopher Theodor Adorno that there can be "no chamber music without a certain chamber" is also, in our culture, true for reading. It does not make a whole lot of sense to recommend reading the Bible if we do not address at the same time the obstacles to reading in our cultural environment. The time has come to create new book clubs for youngsters, and those not so young, so they can spend an evening together around a major text: one of Plato's dialogues, a couple of Seneca's letters, or an epistle of Paul.

Three Schedules

The Church has three timetables for reading the Bible, a threefold menu if you will:

1) The first timetable consists in a *weekly* reading of the Bible by looking up the three readings and the related psalm for the Sunday liturgy and reflecting on them. Throughout the world, this may be the most common way of reading the Bible today. The arrangement dates from after the Second Vatican Council. In three years you finish practically all the books of the Bible, especially those of the New Testament. With the three readings and the psalm, every week you receive a short synthesis of new and old, prophecy and fulfillment, historical recollection and relevant experience. The same texts are read and discussed the world over on the same weekend, not only among Catholics but also, for example, among Anglicans.

2) The second timetable involves *daily* contact with Scripture on the basis of the weekday missal. In this manner one goes through all four Gospels in a year. The first reading changes in odd or even years, but virtually all books of the Old and New Testaments are covered in two years, usually on the basis of a historical schedule. Thus, one reads books that belong to the same time period, even though they are not placed next to each other in the Bible (Isaiah and Micah, for example). The Scripture readings of the divine office correspond to this two-year schedule. Hence, the daily liturgy stimulates us to read the Bible without interruption and in a salvific, historical perspective.

3) An ancient timetable that was used by the monks of old involves reading the whole Bible in a *single* year. Already in the time of Jesus, the Torah—the five books of Moses—was read aloud in cyclical manner, in some synagogues in one year, in others in three. And each part of the Torah corresponded to an excerpt from the Book of Prophets. In the traditional divine offices of monasteries, every day you would hear the beginning of a Bible reading which you were expected to complete in your cell, your *lectio divina.*

In the figure that follows, all books of the New Testament can be found in the inner circle, in accordance with the four seasons and the liturgical calendar, and similarly for the books of the Old Testament in the outer circle. The Psalms are placed at the edge between New and Old. This table is based on accepted practices and ancient traditions adopted by Jews and Christians alike throughout the centuries. May this suggestion motivate the receptive reader to go through one Book in its entirety in accordance with the seasons in one year, and through the other Book in the next.

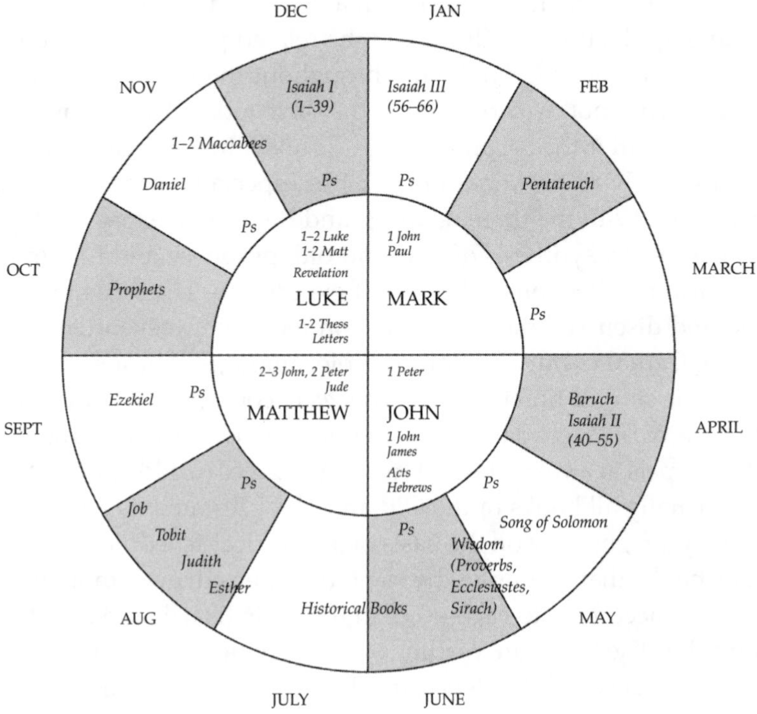

The Four Stages of Reading the Bible

We can distinguish four stages in reading the Bible and sooner or later everyone is confronted with each one:

1) *The fanciful Bible*. This is the child's Bible, with marvelous stories; it is the sacred history of former times: colorful, spirited, fantastic, and more than exemplary. Movies such as *Jesus Christ Superstar* and *The Ten Commandments* nourish this first level of familiarity with Scripture. Atlases and the whole history of iconography, namely that of cathedrals, serve this initial approach. Pilgrimages to the Holy Land deserve a place of honor: they imprint landscapes on our memory in which we can situate particular texts. In our modern era many young people lack this first Bible experience, and therefore have difficulty placing a particular story in a broader context.

2) *The Bible of the Curious*. The second stage corresponds to adolescence, the time of awakening curiosity. One wants to know, to verify, to check the text in every which way. How Egyptian in origin is this

Bible wisdom, and what was carried over from Mesopotamia? Does this story tally with archeological finds? Many folks tumble into the Bible through the gate of curiosity: they are young and want to know, even in retirement age! Modern exegesis deals with all these questions.

3) *A life-giving word.* In the third stage one reads only because of the life-giving power of the Book. One takes refuge under the Word that "is a lamp to my feet and a light to my path" (Ps 119:105). "In your light we see light" (Ps 36:9). We no longer need to read everything: we know how this page from Saint John, or from Paul to the Corinthians, or from the Wisdom of Solomon can infuse our heart with new life. We read and, especially, we re-read. We care less about knowing many things or comparing different texts; instead, we are intent on nourishing ourselves.

4) *The Book without books.* And then the stage arrives in which we live out of the Book, but without books. The spring no longer wells up outside the city walls; we draw from the well of our own heart, which has interiorized words a whole life long. Older monks are living proof of this kind of freedom. They may no longer be able to read, their eyes beyond fatigue, but delving in their memory they are able to run through whole pages of the Gospel or murmur psalms they know by heart. They remain resilient and exude vitality because they are nourished by the Word, without having to open even a single book.

One Method

Lectio divina is a practice. You start the day by opening the Bible. You read and you muse on what you just read. You read and re-read, you learn by heart. You read and become enlightened. The Word begins to live in you. You read and you pray, you give your response. "When you read, He talks to you. When you pray, you talk to Him" (St. Cyprian and St. Jerome). *Lectio* and *oratio*, reading and prayer, they go hand in hand, they are two sides of the same coin.

A rediscovery of this kind of prayerful reading appears to be under way. Some twenty-five years ago, the so-called Vigan method of reading in small groups was launched. It started in the catechetical center John Paul I in Vigan, a city in the Philippines. The center teaches Bible reading in small groups of six. This kind of reading involves three stages: text—word—response:

1) The first stage stays close to the written word. The text is read aloud, we listen in silence, and we make a note of words or expressions that strike us. These are then shared with the group, without commentary. The guiding question is: which expressions move us?

2) In the second stage, the text is read aloud a second time. Again, we become silent and we answer the question: "What does the Lord tell me through this text?" At that moment, the text becomes word. After a while we share with each other what the Lord tells me, personally, here and now, through this text. God is word. He speaks. We hear Him only rarely, or maybe even never, because our mind is elsewhere or, in any event, because we are really busy. But if we listen to his word together, then let us at least give Him a chance to speak to us.

3) In the third stage, the text is read aloud another time (by now we almost know it by heart, a big plus!). Again we become quiet as we formulate our response. The key question is now: "What is my response to what the Lord has told me?" This takes the form of a prayer. An intention or a promise may be part of this prayer: "What do I commit myself to, now that the Lord said this to me?"

Reading and praying: it's a kind of breathing. When I read, I hear His voice. When I pray, I respond. The Vigan method fits with the oldest practice of the early Christians. What is centrally important is not what I think of this text, nor all the things this text reminds me of, but rather what the Lord is telling me through the medium of this text.

The method is geared to small groups of on average six people, and if there are more of you, break up the group. But, of course, the method can also be practiced on one's own: I read in order to learn what God tells me and in my prayer I give Him my response. The method can also be a good source of inspiration when preparing a homily. The homily will then reflect the method's three stages: What struck us? What is the Lord saying through this story, through these sayings? And how do we react to what He is saying? Ultimately, all of life becomes a *lectio* and an *oratio*, a reading and a prayer. Everything that happens, also a conflict with my daughter, is a word or a text that makes me wonder: What is the Lord telling me through *this* text? And what is my response now? There will be plenty of reasons to give thanks and praise.

Read and pray, and walk in the great light of God's word, the Bible.

See also: Breathing, Culture, Meditation, Memory, Pilgrimage, Psalmody

LISTENING

What is the greatest commandment? What is the first? What is the most important? These three questions turn up in several places in the New Testament with, surprisingly enough, somewhat different answers each time.

In the letter to the Ephesians we read: "Honor your father and mother—this is the first commandment" (Eph 6:2). This comes as a surprise because in the Ten Commandments or great Words of the covenant, announced on Mount Sinai, it is certainly not "the first," at most the fourth or the fifth! Yet, it does mean something because we all start life as a child, and the first thing we have to learn is to obey our parents!

In the First Letter of Peter, where we hear a kind of Easter homily and instruction, the first commandment is: "You shall be holy, for I am holy" (1 Pet 1:15). This is a reference to Leviticus, the central book and the heart of the whole Torah (see Lev 19:2). Immediately following in Leviticus comes: "You shall each revere your mother and father" (Lev 19:3). So, according to Leviticus, honoring your mother and father is the first commandment to implement the imperative of holiness.

Strictly speaking, the first commandment in the Torah is, "Be fruitful and multiply, and fill the earth and subdue it"(Gen 1:28). Jews have often needled me on this: "What are you doing (with your celibacy) about this very first commandment?"

For philosophers like Levinas, the word from the Decalogue "You shall not murder" constitutes the foundational principle and the most important structural element of the Law. The whole Torah can be subsumed under this one word!

For Jesus, we may think that the whole Torah comes down to: "You shall love." But He gives different answers to the question as to what is the first commandment. When the young man kneels before him asking "Good Teacher, what must I do to inherit eternal life?" Jesus answers: "You know the commandments," and he cites a whole list. The first one he mentions is "You shall not murder," and the last one(!) "Honor your father and mother" (Mark 10:17-19), at least according to Mark, because Matthew adds, "Also, you shall love your neighbor as yourself" (Matt 19:19).

Even if we think that we know the answer by heart, we have to listen carefully and make subtle distinctions. Indeed, we read in Matthew: "He said [to the Pharisee], 'You shall love the Lord your God, with all your heart, and with all your soul, and with all your mind. This is the greatest and first commandment. And a second is like it: you shall love your neighbor as yourself. On these two commandments hang all the law and the prophets'" (Matt 22:37-40). There is much that can be said about this: why does Jesus give a double answer? Is the first one not sufficient? This has to be thought through carefully, because even though there are two answers, the second is of equal value with the first! And they both start with the same appeal: "You shall love." Could it be that we don't quite know how to love God other than in light of the second answer ("and you shall love your neighbor as yourself")? And vice versa: is it possible that we have to learn to love our neighbor as ourselves, not conditionally or incidentally, but just as exacting as God's love, namely, "with all our heart, with all our soul, and with all our mind"? A last reflection: In Matthew we read, "In everything, do to others as you would have them do to you; for this is the law and the prophets" (Matt 7:12). So we have at least two answers within the same Gospel that say how the "law and the prophets" are summed up.

Now let us consider the parallel passage in Mark, where a scribe puts the same question ("Which commandment is the first of all?") to Jesus in the temple square of Jerusalem. There the answer is just a bit different! "Jesus answers: 'The first is, Hear, O Israel: the Lord our God, the Lord is one; you shall love the Lord your God with all your heart and with all your soul, and with all your mind and all your strength.' The second is, 'You shall love your neighbor as yourself.' There is no other commandment greater than these" (Mark 12: 29-31). In Mark, there clearly are *two* commandments. They are superior to all other commandments but, if we look closer, they themselves are superseded by another commandment, prior to love, in the imperative: "Hear, O Israel." What a surprise, again! The deep wisdom in all of this is that we have to start by listening. The first important thing we have to learn is how we are loved and chosen by the one Lord and God who made us his people. You are loved. Love then, with all your heart. Love God, love your neighbor, love yourself. Love in all directions because He loved you first, gratuitously and without end!

What is the first, the most important, the highest commandment? If you ask a Benedictine, there is little chance that, mindful of the Rule of St. Benedict, he will answer anything other than the very first word of that Rule: "Listen." In light of what we discussed before, Benedict's choice to start his Rule this way appears all the more pregnant with meaning.

A monk is defined by his capacity to hear, to listen, to understand. He is a searcher for God because in his heart he has become a "hearer of the Word." His day starts with the appeal, "Today, if you hear his call, do not harden your hearts." He listens with the ear of his heart. "Whoever has ears for hearing should listen to what the Spirit says to the churches," admonishes Benedict in the same Prologue to his Rule (RB Prol.10). Our ears are always wide open naturally, and we did not even receive muscles to close those openings, while all other orifices of the body can be closed by the exercise of willpower. Yet, we can block the great listening by living insensitively to what God says, desires, indicates.

Blessed is the listener who keeps his inner ear constantly attuned to God's promptings. He hears them even in his sleep. He surmises them in nature, in world events, in illness or death, in the suffering of his body. God speaks. Whoever lives in silence, hears Him. "In an eternal silence God speaks without interruption his one Word, his Son. Whoever lives in enough silence, hears Him," says John of the Cross in one of his short, felicitous sayings.

Listening leads to a differently centered life: one's center of gravity shifts. The Other in me is dearer to me than I myself. With this great listening, existence always starts anew: life receives resilience. Benedict even sees his monks ultimately able "to race along the way of God's commandments" and their hearts enlarged "with the unspeakable sweetness of love" (*dilato corde inenarrabili dilectionis dulcedine curritur via mandatorum Dei*; RB Prol. 49). The loving voice that calls directs our march to God's tent so that we may dwell there, to his Kingdom in order to share in his glory, and nothing else.

See also: Beginning, Meditation, Peace, Sleeping

LOVE FOR ONE'S ENEMIES

Love for one's enemies is a central theme in Jesus' Gospel. Also in Paul and in the First Letter of Peter, as well as in the brief ancient church text called the *Didache,* the message is powerfully announced: Love your enemies, pray for those who persecute you, bless them who curse you, and also "fast for those who persecute you,"[1] in which "fast" denotes an even more intense form of prayer and intercession.

When we see where this instruction is propounded and how it is framed, we have to admit that it is never just an extra little chapter in the teaching of Jesus or the apostles. It has a central place in the Great Discourse in Luke (Luke 6:20-49), and in the Sermon on the Mount in Matthew it occupies as it were the top of the ladder, coming at the end of the five opposites and just before the call to perfection: "Be perfect, therefore, as your heavenly Father is perfect" (Matt 5:48). In the *Didache*, or *Teachings of the Twelve Apostles*, these imperatives are placed at the very beginning, as the basic principles for the Christian way of life. So nobody can simply put them aside and say: Yes, that's okay for the elites, for the "perfect ones," but that's not me and it's not something I have to worry too much about. We are faced here with something fundamental. Whoever passes over this point ignores the core of our Christian wisdom.

This is well understood in the monastic literature: love for one's enemies is one of its favorite themes. It is often called the true touchstone of our faith; as long as we are incapable of that kind of love, we don't have anything to show for our spiritual freedom or our true love of neighbor. Perhaps we are surprised: are monasteries not places of peace and friendship? Why is it exactly there that we find so much and such insistent talk about "love of one's enemies"? In Greece, even on holy Mount Athos the Russian Starets Saint Silouan (d. 1938) penned many pages about that love! So it looks like he must have had some experience of enmity there.

1. *The Didache Online* 1:3, trans. Tony Jones (Paraclete Press), available at www.paracletepress.com/didache.html, reproduced under Creative Commons license (accessed April 6, 2016).

One who finds himself in the crucifying state of hatred, enmity, contempt, or oppression cannot deal with that word from Jesus: the enemy has succeeded in exhausting the last reserves of benevolence and amiability. The first thing we must note is that love for one's enemies is a moral impossibility. But Jesus is not talking about morality here. He is asking something else: we must give what we do not have. We are plunged into the realm of mysticism.

Loving one's enemy poses a painful paradox. But Jesus already fathomed the other side of the paradox when he put the command to his disciples: "So that you may be children of your Father in heaven" (Matt 5:44). "For he makes his sun rise on the evil and on the good," without distinction (Matt 5:45). "And [he] sends rain on the righteous and on the unrighteous," regardless of the differences (Matt 5:45). "For he is kind to the ungrateful and the wicked" (Luke 6:35).

Jesus sees that God is indifferent to all the dissimilarities that we know or advance in order to set ourselves apart from others. His view, marked by God's abundant generosity, enables him to coin these new paradoxes: love the one who hates you, pray for the one who persecutes you, bless them who would curse you. Because God is God, and we want to be his worthy children!

Because the greatest enemy often resides in our own heart, it may be useful to build, in the way of the venerable tradition, a small ladder with five steps that bring us to the top rung: true love for the enemy. Matthew showed us how to do it in a series of opposing constructions. He starts low with the elementary, "You shall not murder," and ends with "Love your enemies" (Matt 5:21-44).

First Step: "An Eye for an Eye, a Tooth for a Tooth" (Exod 21:24)

In our Christian milieu we often deem this ancient biblical proverb primitive and inhuman. But in reality, we barely know what it is about. Otherwise, we would have to admit that we ourselves do not come close to practicing what is written here. This is so because the operation of the proverb presupposes three conditions:

a) In order to respect the rule, there has to be a third person, a judge. In other words, you never take the law into your own hands to knock out somebody's tooth when this person knocked out one of yours. That is not the way the proverb is supposed to work!

(b) The third person, the judge, determines on behalf of the community the extent of the damage and then imposes a penalty on the guilty party to repay the injured party.

(c) As soon as the penalty is paid, the account is settled: nobody harbors a grudge anymore; instead, those involved can now look each other in the eye.

Each step requires maturity and objectivity on the part of all three persons involved. Let us respect this operating procedure from childhood on: it will redound to everybody's benefit.

Second Step: "And You Shall Love Your Neighbor as Yourself: I am the LORD"

> *I am the LORD.*
> *You shall not hate in your heart anyone of your kin;*
> *you shall reprove your neighbor, or you will incur guilt yourself.*
> *You shall not take vengeance or bear a grudge against any of your people,*
> *and you shall love your neighbor as yourself:*
> *I am the LORD. (Lev 19:16-18)*[2]

This text is framed by a double "I am the LORD." Thus the paragraph constitutes a unit. The whole chapter starts with, "You shall be holy, for I the LORD your God am holy" (Lev 19:2). This is an application of the Holiness Code of Leviticus, the heart of the book, even the heart of the five books of the Torah of Moses. No wonder Jesus chose exactly this phrase to render the core of the Torah!

In the above-quoted text the sentences follow upon each other: the listener moves from one to the next. And the text ends with the fruit and the end result, "and you shall love." In your own reflection you can add the following subtlety: only then, after you have accomplished the foregoing things, will you be able to love your neighbor as yourself. Notice that "the neighbor" receives different names: "your kin" and "one of your people." The relationship grows and adjusts with every new step.

(a) Start with *hate*. We must be able to name it, not deny or suppress it. If hatred wells up in your heart, don't nurse it against your

2. At the author's request and in order to translate the Hebrew text more appropriately the conjunction "and" was used in lieu of "but" (as it appears in the NRSV) to begin the penultimate line [translator's note].

brother. Do not carry a hatred. In the Christian milieu, hatred is often too quickly suppressed. We have not learned how to recognize it in our own heart and to work with it.

(b) *Reprove your neighbor.* This presupposes that we are co-responsible within one family or one nation, *and* that we only do this after we have learned to drive hatred from our own heart. In addition, if we do not carry out that reprobation, we are accomplices and become burdened with the transgressions of the other.

(c) *Do not take vengeance or bear a grudge.* Something else is going on here than pure hatred: somebody has been insulted by another, has suffered an injustice at the hands of another. The sense of revenge is aroused in the body. Well then, says the lawgiver, do not exact vengeance and do not hold a grudge. Thus, in this mature, well-considered maxim your learn to distinguish in your heart hatred from vengeance. It gives you a chance to experience what this sense is arousing, as well as the whole gamut of feelings that go with it. And then learn to cast off every notion of revenge and, certainly, never to nourish vengeance by nursing it.

(d) *And love your neighbor as yourself: I am the* LORD. This love is the ripened fruit of a whole process, emphasized here by the conjunction "*and* love." The love that is referred to here is, in fact, a fully actualized form of the "love for one's enemies" of which Jesus speaks in the Gospel. Namely, you love the one for whom you felt spontaneous hatred or an impulse of vengeance because that person had hurt or insulted you. This is not a unique instance in the Old Testament. Elsewhere we find love for one's enemies commended, but perhaps we have never stood still to consider it. Thus, the law of Moses teaches: "When you come upon your enemy's ox or donkey going astray, you shall bring it back" (Exod 24:4-5; cf. Deut 22:1-4; Prov 25:21, "If your enemies are hungry, give them bread to eat").

Third Step: "Vengeance Is Mine"

Indeed, things happen that call for vengeance. We already encountered them in the previous step in chapter 19 of Leviticus. Paul writes in his Letter to the Romans: "Beloved, never avenge yourselves, but leave room for the wrath of God; for it is written, 'vengeance is mine, I will repay, says the Lord'" (Rom 12:19; see Deut 32:35).

Vengeance belongs to God, when He wants it, as He wants it. One who suffers innocently forsakes vengeance, does not reach for the sword, but leaves it to God. Our Bible-based faith tells us that He does not tolerate a poor man or woman being oppressed and exploited. The whole book of Psalms stimulates the human heart boldly to call upon the saving justice of God. If we cannot expect that from God, what then? What kind of world would we live in? "Can wicked rulers be allied with you, those who commit mischief by statute?" (Ps 94:20). No, that cannot be.

When in the Gospel Jesus tells the story of the poor widow who keeps pleading her rights before the unjust judge, he takes for granted that it makes sense to address God just as frankly, even to importune Him. In his faith he is convinced that God will not delay in granting justice (see Luke 18:1-6).

Paul also has to deal with incidents that call for vengeance. He mentions them in letters, alerts other to the threat of false brothers, but leaves judgment and reprisal to God. He even asks that it may not be counted against them. The following passage is a perfect example:

> Alexander the coppersmith did me great harm; the Lord will pay him back for his deeds (see Ps 62:12). You must also be aware of him, for he strongly opposed our message. At my first defense no one came to my support, but all deserted me. May it not be counted against them! But the Lord stood by me and gave me strength, so that through me the message might be fully proclaimed and all the Gentiles might hear it. So I was rescued from the lion's mouth (see Ps 12:13). The Lord will rescue me from every evil attack and save me for his heavenly kingdom. To him be the glory forever and ever. Amen (2 Tim 4:14-18).

In difficult, conflicting, and even vicious encounters, the apostle's heart prays vividly with lines from the Psalms; he entrusts everything to God's judgment and retribution. Ultimately, the only things that reign are the kingdom and God's glory.

Fourth Step: "Do Not Repay Evil for Evil . . . but . . . Repay with a Blessing" (1 Pet 3:9)

To pray, to bless, to fast, and to plead for another's well-being at one's own expense: this ennobles us in our core. As the Carolingian Rhabanus Maurus said, "Love for our enemies cleanses the heart and erases our daily sins."

At this step on the ladder much can be discovered in one's own heart, namely, how to deal positively with another person despite that person's negative attitude. "Develop in yourself the tastes of your enemy," writes the French Dominican Father Sertillanges, "love his good characteristics. . . . Let me discover all that he and I can do together, love what he—entirely appropriately—loves, or value that aspect of the truth that he is attached to."

Augustine, who explicitly deals with this theme more than once, says with respect to praying: "As far as you are concerned, pray that you may succeed in loving your enemies. As far as the other is concerned, do not pray because he loves God, but that he may love God."

The work on myself can be accomplished by looking deeply at the other whom I experience as my enemy or adversary. Eastern and Western spirituality show us several possible paradigms. Let us consider the following three:

(a) "Consider your enemy as your teacher." An ancient sutra, quoted by the Dalai Lama, states: "If I helped somebody to the best of my ability, and if that person insults me in the most scandalous manner, may I then consider that person as my greatest teacher." In his commentary, the Dalai Lama explains the text as follows: "If our friends like our company and are close to us, nothing can make us aware of our negative feelings or thoughts. Only if somebody opposes and criticizes us can we come upon true knowledge of ourselves and can we discern the extent of our love. In that, our enemies are our greatest teachers. They provide us the opportunity to test our power, our tolerance, our respect for others. When we, in lieu of nursing hatred for our enemies, love them more, then we are not far from Buddha-mind, the enlightened consciousness that is the goal of all religions."[3]

(b) "Consider your enemy as your physician and your benefactor," says Abba Zosimus in sixth-century Palestine. He teaches: "The enemy? He was sent to me by Jesus to heal my ill flesh, to free my sick soul from vainglory, and to burn them with blazing-hot iron. Thanks to the enemy it became impossible not to look our pride in the face, or not to find out our aggression, our impulse for revenge, and our

3. Jean-Yves Leloup, "Un maître spirituel, le Dalaï Lama," *Vie Spirituelle*, no. 134 (1980): 368.

hatred. Because of him we learn to name one by one all the passions that live in us and that consume us. . . . They—our enemies—are our true benefactors: they ensure for us the Kingdom of heaven." The whole life of Abba Zosimus circles almost constantly around the single theme of making good use of that invincible enemy: the one who does it successfully will be led to the true gentleness and humility of the heart of Jesus. "Accept that he is your physician and gratefully allow him to heal you."[4]

(c) "Consider your enemy your brother and see him as your future companion in heaven." Consider your enemy as your brother, says Augustine several times in his commentaries on Scripture (*Sermo* 56 and 1 John 8:10-11). The whole tradition remembers the example *par excellence* of the dying Stephen, for the conversion of Saul of Tarsus. "With the power of his love he conquered Saul, the violent persecutor, and obtained as companion in heaven the one he had to suffer as his persecutor on earth" (according to Pseudo-Fulgentius, homily for the Feast of Stephen, December 26 in the breviary).

Thomas More had thought deeply about Stephen's example by the time he learned of the sentence meted out to him by the King of England, Henry VIII. More was condemned to the scaffold. In one of his very last addresses to his judges, he is supposed to have said:

> More have I not to say, my Lords, but that like as the Blessed Apostle Paul, as we read in the Acts of the Apostles, was present and consented to the death of Saint Stephen, and kept their clothes that stoned him to death, and yet be they now both twain holy saints in heaven, and shall continue there friends together forever, so I verily trust, and shall therefore rightly pray, that though your Lordships have now here in earth been judges to my condemnation, we may yet hereafter in heaven merrily all meet together, to our everlasting salvation. And thus I desire Almighty God to preserve and defend the King's Majesty, and to send him good counsel.[5]

4. See Zosima, *Colloqui*, in *Parole del deserto. Detti inediti di Iperechio, Stefano di Tebe e Zosima* (Magnano: Ed. Qiqajon, 1992), 101–24.

5. Daniel Sargent, *Thomas More* (Freeport, NY: Books for Libraries Press, 1970; London: Sheed and Ward, 1933), 290.

A few centuries before Thomas More, Anselm of Canterbury wrote a long prayer about love for one's enemies. We would like to quote a few lines from this famous prayer. Seen from God's perspective, the enemy is equally a fellow servant, just as destined to glory as we are, and from this same high vantage point, we are no less fellow sinners than the one we now see as our opponent or enemy. Those who keep their sight fixed on God and only await his glory find words and thoughts that speak gently and sincerely also of others, even if those others are personal enemies:

> Your servant beseeches You on behalf of these fellow servants of Yours that they cease insulting the goodness of such a great and loving Lord because of me (*propter me*), but that, because of you (*propter te*), they may be reconciled with you and declare themselves in accord *with me* according to your will. This is the vindication (*vindicta*) that my innermost heart desires: that, as far as these enemies are concerned, who are servants and sinners with me (*conservi, conpeccatores*), we, of one mind, with love as our teacher, follow our common Lord for the communal good.[6]

Perhaps we can at least keep this thought of the fathers in our heart next time we find ourselves in a fierce quarrel: let's be mindful of the promised feast and never curse another, in thoughts or in words, as if we do not want to see that person at the future banquet table under any circumstances. Otherwise, we run the great risk of not being invited to sit at that table ourselves.

Fifth Step: "Pray for Your Enemies for the Love of Christ"

Our father Benedict writes in his Rule that we have to pray for our enemies *in Christi amore*, for the love of Christ, and not otherwise (RB 4:72). Starets Silouan constantly repeats: "We are unable to love our enemies except through the grace of the Holy Spirit." This is not human work. Here we are pushing through to the veritable mystical moment of that love. It is not us who are loving our enemies, but Christ in us, by the workings of the Holy Spirit who poured God's

6. Based on Fr. Standaert's Dutch translation of J. P. Migne, *Patrologiae Latinae cursus completus* 158:908–10 [translator's note].

love into our hearts (Rom 5:5; see also Gal 2:20: "It is no longer I who live, but it is Christ who lives in me").

In the writings of this holy Russian of Mount Athos we read other catecheses about the intentional loving of one's enemies. John Chrysostom notes somewhere that "loving your enemies makes us in the likeness of Christ." The whole tradition agrees. Let us allow Starets Silouan of Mount Athos to provide some additional explanation:

> Abba Païssios prayed for one of his students who had disavowed Christ and, while the abba was praying, the Lord appeared to him and said:
> "Païssios, for whom do you pray? Don't you know that this student has disavowed me?" But the saint continued to feel compassion for the student and then the Lord said to him: "Païssios, by your love you have become like Me!" Only in this manner shall we find peace; there is no other way. If somebody prays much and fasts often, but has no love for his enemies, he cannot possess peace of heart. And I myself would not have been able to speak of this if that love had not been revealed to me by the Holy Spirit.[7]

Isaac the Syrian (seventh century), a distant source that also nourished Starets Silouan, noted in a similar vein:

> [A merciful heart] is the heart's burning for the sake of the entire creation. . . . He offers up tearful prayer continually even for irrational beasts, for the enemies of the truth, and for those who harm him, that they may be protected and receive mercy. And in like manner he even prays for the family of reptiles because of the great compassion that burns without measure in his heart in the likeness of God.[8]

These are the precepts, set out in the form of a ladder. In our heart of hearts we sense that Jesus is telling us something that touches our innermost liberty and that has roots reaching back into the heart of God. No morality is proclaimed here, only a mystical lesson. As the

7. Archimandrite Sophrony, *Starets Silouane, Moine du Mont Athos. Vie, doctrine, écrits* (Sisteron, éd. Présence, 1989), 292.

8. *The Ascetical Homilies of Saint Isaac the Syrian*, 344.

saints teach us, without the Holy Spirit, without the interiorization of Christ, a person will not manage to love his enemies. The likeness of our love with that of God occurs in and through the fire of his grace. Similarly, Fr. Christian de Chergé, the murdered prior of the Trappist monastery in Tibhirine in the Atlas Mountains (Algeria, 1996), indicates in a testamentary letter (anticipating his assassination) where he hopes he may be led by the common God and Allah:

> I should like, when the time comes, to have a moment of spiritual clarity
> Which would allow me to beg forgiveness of God
> And of my fellow human beings,
> And at the same time forgive with all my heart the one who would strike me down.[9]

He ends by praying that, God willing, he and his assassin may "meet again as happy thieves in Paradise, if it please God, the Father of us both."[10]

See also: Blessing, Fasting, Forgiveness, Friendship, Intercessory Prayers, Mercy, Patience, Peace, Psalmody, Serving, Spirit

9. Christian Salenson, trans. Nada Conic, *Christian de Chergé: A Theology of Hope* (Collegeville, MN: Liturgical Press, 2012), 200.
10. Salenson, *Theology of Hope*, 201.

M

MARY, MARIAN SPIRITUALITY

We consider the Marian dimension of faith in a category of itself, although it is one of the most difficult to define. Yet, when the world appears harsh, pitiless, one-sided, and, in the end, scary, the absence of a Marian dimension is plain. The Marian aspect can be said to add an extra value dimension to any art of living.

The person of Mary, as it appears to us from the four Gospels, as well as, and perhaps even more so, from the Eastern tradition, has been enriched and has been developed into a true symbol of quiet strength, focused attention, inviolable freedom and resoluteness in action, compassion, motherly gentleness, and infinite patience. Her gaze, posture, clothing: they all reveal an attentive reverence and modest presence that are singularly Marian. "She is younger than sin" (George Bernanos). "She is more illumining than the most exalted choirs of angels" (Oriental liturgy). She faces all suffering under the sun; she does not shrink from anything. For only great purity can penetrate freely into the deepest recesses of shame and sorrow, not to condemn but to console and to heal.

Many incomparable works of art—the *Vladimirskaya* with the large almond eyes from Russia, the many Black Madonnas from the Middle Ages, Fra Angelico's *Annunciation*, and Michelangelo's *Pietà*—express something of that peculiar quality that we call Marian.

Certain psalms, her own *Magnificat*, and hymns such as the *Salve Regina*, are indissolubly linked with a unique Marian spirituality. The sermons of St. Bernard on the Gospel of Luke (e.g., *Missus est angelus*), Martin Luther's commentary on the *Magnificat*, and the *Akathistos* hymn of the Byzantine rite create new tonalities for the same Marian melody that resounds throughout the ages. Not everybody will connect with all of its aspects. The cultural factor here is real: some things that are thought acceptable in Southern and Eastern Europe, or deemed as not even coming close to the line, are systematically rejected in the Northern and Western countries as "exaggerated" and "insufferable." Yet, it should be possible to recognize the Marian aspect as a spiritual category in its own right and to make at least some room for it in our own lives.

Woe to the person who, consciously or unconsciously, is blind to the unique radiance of the Marian qualities. But blessed is the one who, intimate with the Marian dimension of faith, never allows him- or herself any thoughts or words, gestures or attitudes, that betray this unique spiritual dimension in his or her own life.

See also: Chastity, Poverty, Psalmody

MEASURE AND BEYOND MEASURE

Praise him according to
his surpassing greatness! (Ps 150:2)

The spiritual life, if it wants to grow at all, presupposes discipline. Any training demands discipline, as well as perseverance. How can you master an art without regular practice? How can you play the piano without knowing the scales?

"Everything in moderation." "Don't exaggerate." Sayings like that are rife in all self-help books and rules for life, past and present. "Too much of ought is good for nought" (*omne nimium nocet*, as the Romans already knew), or "there is no greater gift from heaven than the knowledge of how to do everything in moderation" (Confucius). We cannot dismiss these wisdom sayings lightly.

Yet, is it also not written, "The one who sows sparingly will also reap sparingly, and the one who sows bountifully will also reap bountifully" (2 Cor 9:6)? Or, "The measure of prayer is beyond measure." This last sentence comes from the Latin and can be found, for example, in Bernard of Clairvaux (eleventh century): *modus orationis est sine modo*. By using this proverb, Bernard puts himself in a much older tradition for the saying clearly has Greek roots. For *modus* and *sine modo* there are *oros* and *aoristos*, which mean "defined" and "undefined" or "infinite." Prayer cannot be defined. The end of prayer is without end. In the mystical tradition of the Rhineland, *modus* was translated by *wiese* (form, way of doing) and *sine modo* by *wieseloos*. So they said prayer has to become *wieseloos*, without form. No expression was dearer to Blessed John of Ruusbroec than this abyss-like "beyond measure" or "without form" in a God-centered life.

Deeply engaged in prayer and search for God, we sense how all of a sudden a mesmerizing depth opens up. The paradox is that we have to learn to toe the line in accordance with certain conventions right up to the moment when conventions and directions, limitations, and customs all have to give way. Our practice remains a practice that leads to freedom, even though it requires our obedient submission to a certain discipline. True archery is accomplished in an almost spontaneous act: the arrow that hits the target is always a gift, no longer the result of disciplined effort.

Sometimes it is beneficial to concentrate our meditation on all those verbs whose action can never be exaggerated. Anybody who is the least bit passionate will feel right at home with this. Can I exaggerate in blessing, in praising, in giving thanks? Can I overdo a mindful cultivation of silence? Did anybody ever hear the ultimate silence? Is every silence we achieve not inhabited by an even deeper silence? Does my patience go beyond what is required, or do I suddenly discover within my patient forbearance a limit that speaks exactly of the opposite, namely my forceful impatience?

There are delightful abysses in our life. Ruusbroec was eager to explore them, and he did so with a powerful calmness and an immense confidence. All that is beautiful, sublime, or gratuitous remains undefined, immeasurable, and unfathomable, and the person who ventures in its pursuit must learn to tune his or her desire to what is limitless and beyond measure. Sooner or later, they will discover how their yearning is permeated by a yearning of Another. Our seeking is suffused by His seeking—our most selfless love did not come first. Amazed, we continue on, in a thanksgiving without end.

See also: Blessing, Forms and Formlessness, Gratitude, Growing, Meditation, Paradox, Patience, Praise, You as "You"

MEDITATION

Meditation is one of the principal practices of every intentional art of living. Next to *lectio divina*, psalmody, and recitation of one or other form of the Jesus Prayer, nothing is as beneficent or as essential as the art of sitting in silence and meditating. These four practices can be said to constitute the backbone of our spiritual life. They support each other as the vertebrae support a straight back. They water the soil of our life and make everything bearable and vital. One who spends time in solitude can quietly engage in each of these four practices in turn and do some mindful walking in-between. Repose, harmony, insight, and strength are released. Effortlessly, we again become mindful of the rhythm of our breathing.

What Is Meditation?

The term has had quite a history in the West, and even today, influenced by the East, it continues to evolve. A quick look at that history is instructive: at least, we will see where we have come from and where we are today.

But first a bit of philology. Meditation (*meditatio*) comes from the Latin verb *meditari*, which itself is a variant of the verb *mederi*. *Mederi* means "to take care of," and among its derivations are words such as "medicine" and "remedy." The word *modus* is also derived from it and is translated as "measure" and "manner." We call somebody "modest" if he or she leads a life that is "measured." In ordinary usage, *meditatus* stands in opposition to *subitus*. The former means well prepared, practiced, worked out, thoughtful; the latter, suddenly, right away, immediately (*immediatus*).

Thus, the basic meaning of the verb and practice of meditation has to do with measuring, considering, practicing, assessing, taking care. One meaning that we need to exclude, however, is the oft-cited etymology of "going to the center" or "to be in the midst of things": *in medio stare*. The tendency to connect meditation with concentration can be detected here. While that is not *per se* objectionable, it is not a connection that can be based on the first meaning of the word itself.

The Greek for "meditation" comes from a completely different root, but its meaning is remarkably close to what *meditari* has given us. *Meletao* and *meletè* have as their root the three letters "mel" (see *melius* and *mala*), which in Indo-European languages means "strong." So *meletè* is care, treatment, but also practice, routine, study, preparation (as by an orator, for example). *Meletao* means to take care of, to occupy oneself with, to train, to prepare for (death, for example), to study, to reflect on, to nurse (in the vocabulary of the physician Hippocrates). So, one who makes a choice for meditation chooses to lead a thoughtful and careful life, preparing him- or herself with perseverance.

When we look up these words in the oldest Latin texts of the church fathers, we notice that *meditari* is very close to the activity of reading. To meditate is to read a text so intensely that it is known almost by heart. For example, in the Rule of Benedict *meditari* is synonymous with learning a text by heart. In the early morning monks commit the readings and the psalms to memory. Then they can reflect on them throughout the day, chewing them over. The Latin tradition, in this context, is fond of the verb *ruminari,* to ruminate. *Ruminatio* is the practice of going over a text again and again so that the finest nuances can be distilled from it. *Meditatio* and *ruminatio* complement each other. What somebody has thoroughly committed to memory during *meditatio* can effortlessly be ruminated on from all sides. It gives satisfaction, joy. It works in a refreshing, invigorating, illuminating way and always offers new, deeper meanings within the same text. Great texts are usually too strong to be understood immediately. We have to meditate, to ruminate, to digest them slowly.

Jewish exegetes and the first church fathers held the same interpretation concerning the priestly rule about eating meat: "Any animal that has divided hoofs and is cleft-footed and chews the cud —such you may eat" (Lev 11:3; Deut 14:6). Thus, pork and horsemeat are off limits because neither one chews the cud. We don't eat what doesn't ruminate. We don't want to resemble pigs or horses that devour just about anything! "To ruminate" must be understood here as reading critically, questioning, prayerfully opening up the primary meaning of a text. Feuerbach's assertion, "Der Mensch ist was er isst" (man is what he eats), has deep Jewish and biblical roots!

In the Coptic tradition of the *Sayings of the Fathers,* the following catechesis of Abba Macarius is told concerning perseverance in rumination:

> Another brother asked Abba Macarius: "What is the most appropriate spiritual labor during ascesis and abstinence?" He replied: "Blessed is the one who always carries within him the holy Name of our Lord Jesus Christ, without interruption and with a repentant heart. Because, truly, in a whole life of application to virtue, no work of the spirit is better than that holy nourishment. Keep ruminating on it without cease, just like a sheep that chews the cud and that savors ruminating until the cud that is chewed enters the innermost part of the heart and there breathes a sweet anointing that benefits its intestines and all its innards. Just look at the beauty of its cheeks, still full of the sweetness of what the sheep has chewed over in its mouth. May the Lord Jesus Christ make his grace evident to us by his sweet and unctuous Name."

Blessed are those who have mastered texts by heart and who are then capable of retrieving them at will from memory's treasure, enriching them constantly with fresh insights. Meditation lets them tap into an inexhaustible source.

Somewhat later in the Latin tradition, ladders were constructed with four or five steps, starting with *lectio* or the art of reading. On the basis of the passage that is read, through *meditatio* one ascends to affective prayer, or *oratio.* Affective prayer as the third step leads the spirit into the fourth step of *contemplatio* or contemplation. Some authors, such as Richard of St. Victor, add a fifth step, *actio.* Back to the action!

Thus, this well-known ladder, often called the Ladder of Guigo the Carthusian, puts *meditatio* as the second step; here the passage that is read is not only committed to memory but also charged with empathy, with imagination. One has to try to imagine the scene from the Gospel and become engrossed in it as if one were an eyewitness to the event. In the Dominican monastery of San Marco in Florence, painter Fra Angelico enriched the cells of his fellow monks with frescoes depicting scenes from the Gospels. Often, one sees a Dominican monk seated, meditating, in a corner of the tableau. He is witness to the action and reflects on it in his heart.

This technique was already practiced in similar fashion by the Desert Fathers. One example is:

> Abba Joseph related that Abba Isaac said, "I was sitting with Abba Poemen one day and I saw him in ecstasy and I was on terms of great freedom of speech with him, I prostrated myself before him and begged him, saying, 'Tell me where you were.' He was forced to answer and he said, 'My thought was with Saint Mary, the Mother of God, as she wept by the cross of the Saviour. I wish I could always weep like that.' "[1]

Abba Poemen listened to the Gospel account, and took it in. Furthermore, we may suppose that he found his place in the picture as the beloved disciple standing under the Cross. He was co-witness with "the disciple whom Jesus loved."

This manner of meditating, to make scenes of the Gospels come to life thanks to one's imagination, has been very successful throughout the ages. It is strongly recommended by Saint Ignatius of Loyola in his *Spiritual Exercises.* Maria Valtorta's writings bear witness to the same approach in the twentieth century. While Cardinal Carlo Maria Martini was archbishop of Milan, he actively promoted this way of reading the Gospel among priests and young people. Also, Enzo Bianchi, founder of the monastic community of Bose in Italy, included the text of Guigo the Carthusian as an addendum to his now classic handbook on *lectio divina.* To this day, we are the heirs of that golden period from the Middle Ages.

Yet near the end of the sixteenth century we hear a critical voice. It comes from the Carmel perspective. John of the Cross (d. 1591) believes that traditional textual meditation in which the imagination is actively engaged provides a useful moment to achieve spiritual reading and contemplation, but that sooner or later one has to let go of this method. To ponder an existing text and to make associations based on it can only be a small step; the soul itself will discover how after a while a saturation point is reached.

Then, instead of pressing on or delving into the text with even greater intensity, the wise Carmelite recommends that we be satisfied with "loving attention." We can stop thinking and worrying about new associations and deep reflections. Pure mindfulness in love is all that is needed; it will lead us into the mysterious reciprocity of loving

1. *Sayings of the Desert Fathers* (Poemen 144), 187.

and being loved. What matters is to discover the pull of the Other and completely to accede to it, in quiet presence and nothing else.

In the twentieth century, meditation receives whole new impulses albeit coming from outside. Western masters went to study with Hindus and Buddhists in the East, or the reverse: masters of the East came to us. Graf von Dürckheim, Jesuit Fr. Enomiya Lassalle, Benedictine Father Henri Le Saux (also called Swami Abhishitananda), Willi Massa, Dominican Fr. Vincent Shigeto Oshida, or Trappist Fr. Thomas Merton are just a few names of the many pioneers and bridge-builders between East and West in the field of meditation.

While there are many valuable resources available to us in this field, we would like to highlight one master in particular, namely, John Main (1926–1982), and to briefly introduce his method here. One reason for this selection is that his approach is straightforward, and anybody who seriously pursues it may be able to join an existing support group. Indeed, under the leadership of Fr. Laurence Freeman a worldwide movement has assured the dissemination of the method. John Main's books are easily available, and local groups may be available to provide both support and deepening of the practice. In this way, meditation becomes an art that we do not need to rediscover on our own because a supportive community can surround the meditating person and assist the individual in maintaining this unique practice.

John Main was an English Benedictine monk of Irish descent. Only toward the end of his all-too-short life—he died of cancer well before his sixtieth birthday—did he reveal himself as a meditation master with a sturdy and simple method. Almost everything he published dates from the last few years of his life, including his verbal addresses that were recorded and that were transcribed later. Reading him is a wonderful experience because his words bubble up from an inexhaustible well. He keeps saying the same thing in different words. There is nothing speculative in the way he expresses himself: his word sticks directly to the experience that he tries to impart in the most direct way. That is something than can be said of only a few of the masters.

The core of his method was born in the years before he became a Benedictine. While he was stationed in the Far East, he met a swami. The swami asked how he meditated. John replied that just about every day he tried to reflect on something from the Gospels. The swami then told John that meditation was really something else. Intrigued, John asked him what it was all about. They agreed to sit together at least three times a week, quietly and alert, while each repeated a prayer word by himself in silence.

It was only much later that John Main discovered that certain masters from our Christian tradition sat in silence with at most one verse or one short saying in the same, simple manner. He recognized in the writings of John Cassian (fifth century), the anonymous English author of *The Cloud of Unknowing* (fourteenth century), Augustine Baker (Benedictine, seventeenth century), and the Byzantine and Russian Hesychasts precisely the same ways of praying in silence and meditating. He sensed that in our day people might again be receptive to the technique, more than to many other methods of contemplation. His intuition proved correct. Under the leadership of his younger friend and successor Fr. Laurence Freeman, O.S.B., the initial movement has grown into a global community centered in London with branches all over the world. In Belgium more than fifty centers have sprung up in less than fifteen years, most of them led by lay people.[2] But let's stay with the practical side of things. Here is how John Main commends and summarizes the method:

> Sit down.
> Sit still and upright.
> Close your eyes lightly.
> Sit relaxed but alert.
> Silently, interiorly begin to say a single word.
> We recommend the prayer-phrase "maranatha."
> Recite it as four syllables of equal length.
> Listen to it as you say it, gently but continuously.
> Do not think or imagine anything—spiritual or otherwise.
> If thoughts or images come, these are distractions at the time of meditation, so keep returning to simply saying the word.
> Meditate each morning and evening for between twenty and thirty minutes.[3]

2. A list of meditation centers may be found at www.wccm.org, the website of the World Community for Christian Meditation [translator's note].

3. John Main, OSB, quoted at www.JohnMain.org (accessed April 27, 2016) [translator's note].

Ten rules and an eleventh one, as a big stick, to encourage you to keep to your commitment to yourself.

So let's do it, in all simplicity. There is no need to hope that tomorrow we'll do a better job of it: praying is now, here (*Ima koko,* as the Japanese masters repeatedly say), never yesterday or elsewhere. You don't become more proficient after x number of hours and there is no prize at the end. Be now. Naked. Poor. Devoid of any pretense, any urge to achieve. Motionless. The stillness becomes palpable when you track your breathing. Follow it quietly and unite your breath with your word.

Don't worry about results. Forget about appraising yourself. After meditating with the swami for a year-and-a-half, John Main asked him: "How should I think about the future? Shortly I will be returning to Britain." The swami answered: "Just go. In ten or fifteen years we can talk about it again!"

A Japanese master who had taught us quiet meditation gave us the following warning as we were leaving his monastery: "Do not reject what we are offering you. It is a gift. We received it from the Chinese via Korea. The Chinese received it from the Indians. This all took more than twenty-five centuries, and in the course of time the treasure passed through all these different cultures. We offer it to you. Do not reject this jewel."

Still, every day, I hear this warning resounding in my ears: Are we not way too predisposed to reject this meager, naked, quasi-thoughtless sitting as a waste of time, considering it senseless, sterile, dull, etc.? John Main's writings illustrate all too well how smart we can be in avoiding this disarming practice. He understands our cultural habits and deflates our clever notions one by one! With every page of his published works he cheers us on, he encourages, he pushes—gently, patiently, as if possessed by a quiet urgency. He knows how it is with us, spoiled children who flee from simplicity, carrying within us untold little devils that avoid every true moment of silence as the pest.

"Keep your mantra!" Coming from the mouth of somebody who has experienced it for more than thirty years, the exhortation keeps ringing in my ears. Evidently the Japanese Zen master knew us very well when smilingly he said, "Do not reject what we are offering you. It is a gift!"

We all need a bit of encouragement from time to time. Reading about meditation always has a stimulating effect. Meditating with others once in a while is a great blessing. Do not neglect either one of these support mechanisms, but the key thing is to actually do it. Each and every day.

See also: Breathing, *Dhikr*, Jesus and the Jesus Prayer, *Lectio Divina*, Memory, Name, Psalmody

MEMORY

Memory is a precious resource that is extremely useful in the spiritual life. Regrettably, the culture in which we live is not really adept in dealing with this resource because memorization is no longer developed systematically, and sometimes people regard it only with disdain.

As was taught in the time of Augustine, and passed on to Thomas Aquinas and the generation of John of the Cross in the sixteenth century (and even after that), human beings can be characterized by three faculties: intelligence, will, and memory. Here in the West, we still value intelligence, especially if it is fast, faster, or fastest. Will power typically is far less developed: if somebody has no great desire for something, how can that person nevertheless go about gaining it or achieving it? But who still talks about memory? It is as if we forgot that we possess this capability! Of course, nothing is as calamitous as somebody—or a whole culture—beginning to forget that there is something like memory! If memory itself should suffer memory loss, would that not be an insurmountable disaster?

To learn by heart, to commemorate, to remember, to take notes for one's records, to write things down in order not to forget, to recall, to bring the past to the forefront but also to wipe it clean, purposefully to try to forget or to forgive, to let a wounded memory recuperate, to heal memory's hurts with suitable balms—the field is unimaginably wide. Any facet discussed below is just a small step forward.[1] But for us to be thinking about memory is a good start to re-engage this precious faculty in our daily life.

1. There is no lack of historical studies about memory and its disciplined functioning. *The Art of Memory* by Frances A. Yates (London: Routledge and Keegan Paul, 1966) is a classic. Starting with the Greeks, then Quintilianus and Augustine, to Giordano Bruno and Leibniz, we see how a steady tradition became ever more finely honed. For a more recent scholar who primarily studies the functioning of memory (and imagination) in the Middle Ages, see Mary Carruthers, *The Craft of Thought: Meditation, Rhetoric, and the Making of Images: 400–1200* (Cambridge: Cambridge University Press, 1998) and *The Book of Memory*, 2nd ed. (Cambridge: Cambridge University Press, 2008).

Memory and Hope

The church father Augustine had a predilection for the number three. His fascination with the secret meaning of the Three-in-One led him to appreciate every kind of unity of three as a picture of the invisible trace left by God in creation. This led the Doctor of the Church to make a direct connection between the three faculties and the three virtues (faith, hope, and love). Love has to do with will, faith with intelligent insight, but what about hope? Hope fits with the faculty of memory.

Perhaps this comes as a surprise. Does memory not have to do with the past? And hope with the future? Indeed. But only those who can remember a past have a future, and not otherwise. The founder of Chassidism, the Baal Shem Tov (b. 1700 CE) said, "The one who has memory, has a future. The recollection of something enables it to be set free. The one who forgets has no way out. Forgetfulness gives birth to exile."

In the oldest Christian tradition, hope is oriented toward eternal glory. The hopeful person prepares for heavenly bliss because his whole being, body and soul, is destined to be received in glory, in pure light that is glow and open radiance. Even though every image falls short, we have a sense of this perspective. Paul talks about the expectation that pervades creation and is aimed at "the freedom and glory of the children of God." It is good to direct the power of memory so that our bearings remain set on that glorious transformation.

John of the Cross

The mystic John of the Cross (d. 1591) loved analyzing the human faculties as means to achieve unification with God. Each faculty—intelligence, willpower, and memory—must actually die to itself, and completely empty itself, if it is to live in complete unity with the living God. So, intelligence must surrender all thoughts and its natural brilliance; will is being asked to die to all attachments, no matter how sublime they may be. And memory? It has to be freed of all accumulated images and conceptions. Memory is like a warehouse that we are learning to empty out systematically. It must be "as if shorn bald." We ourselves should be "as if we no longer had a memory." Memory then turns into pure hope, completely aligned to God, not expecting anything other than Him. Let us listen for a moment to the Spanish mystic in this summarizing paragraph from *The Dark Night of the Soul*:

> For *faith* voids and darkens the understanding as to all its natural intelligence, and herein prepares it for union with Divine Wisdom.
>
> *Hope* voids and withdraws the memory from all creature possessions; for, as Saint Paul says, hope is for that which is not possessed (Rom 8:24); and thus it withdraws the memory from that which it is capable of possessing, and sets it on that for which it hopes. And for this cause hope in God alone prepares the memory purely for union with God.
>
> *Charity*, in the same way, voids and annihilates the affections and desires of the will for whatever is not God, and sets them upon Him alone; and thus this virtue prepares this faculty and unites it with God through love. And thus, since the function of these virtues is the withdrawal of the soul from all that is less than God, their function is consequently that of joining it with God.[2]

Elsewhere we read, simply and powerfully: "No supernatural forms or kinds of knowledge which can be apprehended by the memory are God, and, in order to reach God, the soul must void itself of all that is not God. The memory must also strip itself of all these forms and kinds of knowledge, that it may unite itself with God in hope."[3] In sentences that are balanced and almost poetical, the Carmelite explains further:

> The more the memory expresses itself,
> The greater is its hope;
> And the more it has of hope,
> The more it has of union with God;
> For, with respect to God, the more the soul hopes,
> The more it attains.
> And it hopes most
> When it is most completely dispossessed;
> And when it shall be completely dispossessed,
> It will remain with the perfect possession of God in Divine union.

2. St. John of the Cross, *Dark Night of the Soul*, trans. E. Allison Peers from the critical edition of P. Silverio de Santa Teresa (New York: Doubleday, 1990), 180.

3. St. John of the Cross, *Ascent of Mount Carmel*, 3rd rev. ed., trans. E. Allison Peers (Garden City, NY: Doubleday, 1958), 370.

> But there are many who will not deprive themselves of the sweetness and delight which memory finds in those forms and notions, wherefore they attain not to supreme possession and perfect sweetness. For he that renounces not all that he possesses cannot be the disciple of Christ.[4]

What we do not find as expressly in the body of work of the Spanish mystic is an idea that we find time and again in Paul, namely that hope points to eternal bliss, to heavenly glory. Only when the mystic talks about the soul's "transformation" by God can we surmise the theme of eternal glory and glorification. The latter is quite often present in the work of John of the Cross, but the biblical link between hope and glory is nowhere expressly considered or worked out.

We use our memory best when we learn to make it an instrument of hope. This particular intuition must be counted as one of the most important in the centuries-long reflection on the capability to remember and to know by heart. The best experience of hope is felt by training it on God's radiating glory. This godly action enters our created world to transform it into perfect beauty.

Further, we may assume that our memory not only has to do with our brain but, more broadly, also with our total corporality. As some psychologists tell us, the body accumulates everything and forgets nothing, such as, for example, any pain we once suffered. If we use the memory embedded in our body to align ourselves with hope, which itself has no other expectation than heavenly glory, then we open an interior pathway through which God and his transformative power can enter and conform our body to the heavenly body of Jesus. To say it with the words of Paul: "But our citizenship is in heaven, and it is from there that we are expecting a Savior, the Lord Jesus Christ. He will transform the body of our humiliation that it may be conformed to the body of his glory, by the power that also enables him to make all things subject to himself" (Phil 3:20-21).

To Celebrate Memory: Remember the Feast with Gratitude

Since ancient times, the liturgical celebration is "a grateful remembrance of the deeds of the Lord," as a church song expresses

4. St. John of the Cross, *Ascent of Mount Carmel*, 370.

it so well. The preeminent feast in Israel is the Sabbath, and on the Sabbath the Jew is commanded to "observe" that day by "remembering"—the two words that figure first in the third command of the Decalogue: "*Remember* the Sabbath day" (Exod 20:8), and "*Observe* the Sabbath day" (Deut 5:12). What must he remember? God's rescue in the exodus, when God with strong hand and outstretched arm delivered his people from slavery in Egypt. And also the act of creation of the origin, when God completed his work on the seventh day, hallowed and blessed it, rested, and was refreshed (Gen 2:1-4; Exod 31:17).

Here we see one of the most substantive dimensions of memory, which is to remember the past so as to stand meaningfully, significantly in the present. Memory does not bring back the past as the past, but brings it into the current moment. The touchstone of that significance is gratitude. Remembrance leads to thanksgiving.

If memory serves me right, there is a traditional Jewish tale that says that at the moment of birth an angel is dispatched to give us a good smack. Instantly everything that happened before is forgotten and we start life with a clean slate. Where a story like this comes from remains a mystery. But it creates an amusing juxtaposition: at birth we forget everything while, on the other hand, in a sudden near-death experience we remember the whole movie of our life. In fact, in every good liturgy we remember in one moment all moments, in one night all nights, and not just from birth to death, but even from before birth and before creation till after death and after the end of the world. So, in the one Easter Vigil all nights are remembered, starting with the first at the time of creation through the last at the end of time.

Thus, from a psychological standpoint, to remember liturgically provides an uncommonly powerful way of living, individually and collectively.

The Wounded Memory

Memory preserves just about everything, so psychologists and psychiatrists tell us. Past wounds pile up, consciously and, especially, unconsciously. Our usual way is to suppress everything, and painful memories accumulate from birth, starting even in the womb. For example, *The case of Dominique*, told by psychoanalyst Françoise Dolto, is instructive: Dominique was an eleven-year-old boy who remembered tunes sang by his father during the war, when the child was still in his mother's womb.[5]

Unmentionable memories often only come to the surface halfway through life, as the result of a crisis, a problem in a relationship, a great loss. Certain problems can be so shrouded in taboo that we have learned not to think about them, let alone believe that something like that actually happened to us. Any conversation with a third party about a father's tyranny or a mother's alcoholism is considered high treason by the inner policeman. Sometimes it is fear that wipes away every trace of memory. Although the reverse also happens: fear unleashes the imagination, and memory comes to believe that what it most fears really happened, much in the same way that dreams can give actual shape to certain fears.

Memory can also be wounded collectively. "A tumor in our memory," is how a Jew once expressed what Auschwitz continues to mean for him and his people. Any war cuts deep wounds in the collective memory, and often three or four generations need to pass before these kinds of wounds are healed. Europeans know that all too well. To suffer through two world wars in one generation should be enough reason not to cause such enormous hurt to others, whether in the Balkans, Iraq, or anywhere else in the world. Children, mothers, prisoners, and mutilated persons typically remain marked by the experience until death.

A wounded memory needs healing. Finding somebody with whom you can talk about it is a very good beginning. But how will that person react? Will he or she condemn me? Spur me on to take revenge? Or urge me to forget, or perhaps even to forgive that which I deeply feel is unforgiveable? How can you forgive an attitude? Or somebody who is no longer alive? Somebody who no longer has any intimation that I had been hurt so deeply?

In our day many authors are intensely engaged with these kinds of issues. Therapies and practices have been developed that allow people with wounded memories to experience healing. In this context, I mention with pleasure people like Nelly Astelli-Hidalgo and Fr. Alexis Smets, or Simone Pacot and Lytta Bassett. From their

5. See the revelatory work of Nelly Astelli-Hidalgo, *Le fruit de tes entrailles. La guérison des blessures reçues dans le sein maternel* (Paris-Fribourg: Saint Paul, 1993).

contributions we learn that recovery is possible. Furthermore, we learn that psychology and the life of the spirit work together in keeping us going not through magic formulas, but with a process that helps to come to terms with the deepest layers of consciousness and memory, thereby enabling the workings of the God of forgiveness and healing even there.

Paul Ricoeur ends his book *Memory, History, Forgetting* [6] with a paragraph devoted to "the difficult forgiveness," personally as well as politically. At the very end he deals with "the good forgetting" (*l'oubli heureux*), which he, just as Kierkegaard, likens to the carefree attitude that Jesus argues for in the Sermon on the Mount when he talks about the birds in the sky and the lilies in the field. Our humanity only comes through completely where there is room for that difficult forgiveness and this good forgetting.

Prayer from Memory

It is good and wholesome to learn certain poems by heart, to place entire psalms and beautiful refrains in the rooms and cabinets of our memory. If you learn and write down a short psalm in the morning, you can repeat it all day. A poem learned by heart is always available. It can go and live like fish in the waters of my deeper consciousness, yes, even in the layers of my unconscious. Sometimes I get up in the morning and hear myself pray with the verses that I repeated or sang as I was going to sleep. Sometimes verses from much longer ago pop up in our head, who knows why or how. They make a person happy, even before the day has started!

It is not sufficient to learn by heart. It is important also to learn to use this memorization. For example, when you are waiting emptymindedly for a train that is delayed, you can turn your attention inward and reach into your treasure room where all that is beautiful and meaningful to you is stored. You can engage your memory when meditating in silence in a half-dark room, immobile and without a book. You can think then of one of the great texts whose structure you have clearly in mind, for example a gospel with its sequence of chapters. Never mind skipping any number of passages—the key

6. Paul Ricoeur, *La mémoire, l'histoire, l'oubli* (Paris: Seuil, 2000); *Memory, History, Forgetting* (Chicago: University of Chicago Press, 2009).

thing is to recall a series of episodes, gestures, or words of Jesus from your memory's storeroom and to reflect on them in silence. In this manner you can meditate from memory, quietly, unwearied, easily for an hour. At the end you feel renewed, suffused again with the Spirit, the same Spirit that pushed Jesus beyond death on the cross and that remains a driving force today.

When God Remembers Us

Dulcis, Jesu, memoria—"How sweet it is to think of you, Jesus" is the opening line of a song from the Middle Ages; every one of the forty-two quatrains contains the name of Jesus. "With God in our thoughts" is an expression used in a somewhat original translation of a passage in the First Letter of Peter (see 1 Pet 2:19: "being aware of God"). To remember God who thinks of us, or to think of God who remembers us: the spiritual life is wholly bound up in this singular, reciprocal activity.

When, in his Rule, Benedict sets up a ladder with twelve steps of humility, he gives a long and extensive description of the first step which in essence boils down to this: Be continually mindful of God and never, nowhere forget him. This teaching goes back to the Desert Fathers but also, and even by name, to a theme that is taken up repeatedly by Saint Basil. To be mindful of God, to remember God, never to forget God, always to be focused on him: it is a central message in all the teachings of the Cappadocian. The verse from the book of Psalms most cited by Basil comes from Psalm 16: "I keep the Lord always before me; because he is at my right hand, I shall not be moved" (Ps 16:8). This says it all for Basil.

Monks have come up with all kinds of techniques to keep their attention continually focused on God and to ban distractions as much as possible. They concentrate on their breath or on their heart and try to match the name of God or of Jesus to their breathing. They keep repeating short prayer formulas all day and night; even in their sleep the prayer word carries on. Christian monks are not the only ones who do this. These practices can be found in all the great traditions.

We try to remember God. But does God do the same? For us to be in God's thoughts, does that make sense? The Bible does not hesitate in presenting God to us as One who thinks of us, remembers us, not just sometimes but ceaselessly, with a loyalty that knows no end. We are amazed at this, as expressed in the precious Psalm 8: "What are human beings that you are mindful of them, mortals that you care for them?" (Ps 8:4; see also Ps 144:3, Heb 2:6-9).

Not that everybody is thrilled with that: Job would prefer God to stop looking, to turn the other way, not to observe him so closely, like a drill sergeant or a warder: "Will you not look away from me for a while, let me alone while I swallow my spittle?" (Job 7:19).

Elsewhere in the Psalms we read: "The LORD has been mindful of us; he will bless us" (Ps 115:12). His thinking of us is a blessing for us. We are confronted with an enigma here, perhaps the most beautiful and intimate of all mysteries when we speak of memory and remembrance. God is constantly engaged with us in thought because He is pure Act continuously blessing, hallowing, liberating, healing, caring, reconciling, forgiving, saving. He is verb. He does what he says: his Name offers material assistance, all his Names are deeds.

Those who wish to apply themselves to not forgetting God and to keeping God continually before their eyes, as Basil and Benedict expect from their followers, will ultimately enter into these acts of God. To remember God means in the first place to make fully present God's remembrance, God's care, his loving attention for each one of us without distinction. In the end I shall share in what he does, in who he is, in the attributes that are his hallmarks. Silence descends on the house, but it is filled. God's light radiates in and through everything. Death itself, when I live in the *memoria Dei*, has scant impact. As I may now walk in God's light, so I hope beyond death also to share in that light, unencumbered, freer than ever before.

We arrive here at something very simple, which is that already today we dwell in the creative *memoria Dei*, in his memory, and this faithful insight fills us with joy and peace, regardless of what may happen tomorrow, even dementia or progressive loss of memory.

See also: *Dhikr*, Forgiveness, God, Gratitude, Jesus and the Jesus Prayer, Mindfulness, Name, Sabbath

MERCY

The word "mercy" (Latin, *misericordia*) has to do with "heart" (*cor*) and with "poverty" (*miseria*). In connection with the Psalm verse, *Abyssus abyssum invocat* (Deep calls to deep) (Ps 42:7), Augustine says that "the depth of our misery calls forth the depth of your mercy (*misericordia*)." Is the merciful person the one who has a heart for what is poor?

Many words invoke the idea of mercy: pity, compassion, graciousness, sympathy. Our biblical language is especially rich in describing the many shades of that goodness. The Jewish tradition distinguishes no less than thirteen attributes of God. Over the centuries, a short tract (*Tashlikh*) about these attributes was developed and is read on Yom Kippur, the Day of Atonement. On that day one reminds God, seated on his throne of justice, of all his attributes of mercy, as they were revealed to Moses in Exodus 34:6-7 and as we hear them again at the end of Micah (7:18-20): merciful, gracious, slow to anger, abounding in steadfast love, forgiving, full of compassion.

In the Semitic languages, such as Hebrew, Aramaic, and Arabic, "mercy" has to do with the innards or intestines (*rakhamim*) and with the uterus (*rekhem*): you only have to think of the *viscera misericordiae* (literally: the innards or bowels of mercy) that we hear every morning in the Canticle of Zachariah. The translations attempt to reflect this phrase from Luke, but it is usually rendered in English as "the tender mercy of our God" or "the tender compassion of our God"(Luke 1:78). In a reading of the Talmud, Jewish philosopher Levinas reflects on the name of God in Aramaic, *Rakhmana,* the Merciful One, and notes the following:

> First of all, what is the meaning of this word "merciful," *Rakhmana,* that keeps returning in the text? It means the Torah itself or the Eternal, the Eternal that is defined by Mercy. This translation, however, is totally unsatisfactory. *Rakhamim* (from the Aramaic term *Rakhmana*), or Mercy, comes from the word *Rekhem,* which means "uterus." *Rakhamim* is the uterus in so far as it is focused on the other, which is carried in her and born from her. *Rakhamim* is motherhood itself. "God is merciful" means that God is defined by motherhood. The depth of this mercy touches a feminine element. This feminine aspect in God's

> fatherhood is truly remarkable, just as in Jewish tradition there is the notable idea of a "masculinity" that needs to be curtailed, of which circumcision perhaps symbolizes the partial renunciation, the glorification of a certain weakness without implying cowardice. Motherhood is perhaps sensitivity itself, which was so denigrated by Nietzsche and his followers.[1]

Also in the Qu'ran all Surahs, or chapters, with only one exception, start with the acclamation "In the name of God, the Compassionate, the Merciful" (*b-ismi-llah al-rahmân al rahim*). In the biblical and post-biblical tradition, the term "mercy" evokes immediately a poignant, deeply human emotion. The merciful person is moved in his guts and feels what is going on with the other, especially the other's suffering.

From this first exploration we discover a dimension that does not directly classify mercy as a virtue. You acquire virtue by diligent application, such as temperance and courage, two of the four cardinal virtues of Aristotle. One of the most famous parables of Jesus is the one of the Good Samaritan. Of the Samaritan it is said that he "saw" the victim on the side of the road and "moved with pity" he approached him, poured oil on his wounds, put him on his donkey, and entrusted him to the innkeeper. This Samaritan is not in the first place "virtuous." He acts because he is moved in his guts. This is something stronger than himself. He is touched and acts because he cannot do otherwise. He recognizes himself in the other and acts accordingly, just as he himself would want to be treated.

The ultimate issue for the teller of the parable is not, Why he and not the two others? But rather, if you can feel in your guts like him, then act like him, be the neighbor of the person in need. Follow the impulses of your deepest gut, and you shall live!

A reference to the great Chinese masters, Confucius and Mencius, is not without interest here. What is the ultimate basis of morality? The inner movement that we feel instantly, for example, when we see a child fall. Follow this reflex, and base your whole conduct on this singular consideration.

For we can also shut off our gut response. John notes this in his first letter: "How does God's love abide in anyone who has the

1. Emmanuel Levinas, *Du sacré au Saint: Cinq nouvelles lectures talmudiques* (Paris, 1977), 158.

world's goods and sees a brother or sister in need and yet refuses help?" (1 John 3:17).[2]

In the language of the Bible, another paradox may be noted: this very human and feminine emotion is almost exclusively attributed to God. He—the very masculine God of the Bible—is, over and over again, the subject of this mercy! Yes, it is one of the most frequently recurring attributes of God. Is God's nature so human then? Or is what is so deeply human also characteristic of God? The church fathers reflect deeply on these matters: the virtue of human nature is, in its perfection, God himself, wrote Gregory of Nyssa (fourth century).

This emotion shows up three times in Jesus' parables. We already saw it when he talked about the Good Samaritan. Also the good father, perceiving in the distance his lost son who is returning, is "moved in his bowels" and runs to meet him, embracing and kissing him, in total acceptance, and planning a complete celebration with the killing of the fatted calf. Everything follows from the first verb, *splanchnistheis* in Greek, meaning "moved in his *splanchna,* his bowels." With this parable, Jesus does not simply want to explain to the Pharisees why he eats with tax collectors and sinners. Jesus tells them how God is filled with compassion ("moved in his bowels") and because of this, through his intermediation, deals with his son, meaning here the tax collectors.

In a third parable, which has to do with forgiveness, the king is similarly moved when one of his servants, who owes him an unimaginable debt, begs for his mercy. The king does not even entertain the servant's offer of delayed payment: he summarily forgives the debt. But later on in the story, the king reacts fiercely when he hears that the same servant was unable to show compassion when a fellow servant pleaded with him for mercy. Then the king turns furious. In this indirect manner, we gain insight into the intensity of the emotions in the heart of Jesus, the teller of the parables.

Among the many writers of the New Testament, Paul is the one who most often brings up "the bowels." For him, they are a tender

2. The Dutch Bible quoted by the author and the author's parenthetical note to it convey a response from the gut more clearly than 1 John 3:17 in the NRSV. A literal translation would read: "If somebody has sufficient money and sees his brother in need, but shuts him out of his innermost feeling (literally: his bowels), how does God remain in him?" [translator's note].

place of reciprocity and goodness that directly refers to existence "in Christ." Whoever acts or talks in Christ comports himself "from the depth of his bowels" and vice versa. In later Eastern traditions we see how Christ and the bowels simply become identical: so we read twice in the Acts of Thomas and those of John that Christ is "the perfect bowels of mercy" (*ta splanchna ta teleia*).

With the Tree of Ten Sephirot (Spheres), the Jewish mystical tradition reserves a key central place for *Rakhamim* or the Great Mercy in the Kabbalah. Instructive for us is that mercy, linked with beauty (*tiferet)*, stands in the center, as the sixth unit in the descending movement from God's highest pleasure (first unit) to the establishment of the kingdom on earth (tenth unit). Mercy flows from *hesed* or universal love, which passes through *din* or justice. This signifies that mercy always implies a singular vulnerability with respect to an injustice suffered or existential pain.

The Christian tradition sees in the whole Jesus phenomenon a breakthrough of God's mercy. In the Letter to Titus, the writer translates the old Hebrew attributes of God in new terms that sounded agreeable to Greek ears of that time: "the goodness and loving kindness of God our Savior" (Titus 3:4). For "goodness" the Greek has *chrèstotès* (which has the sound of the name, Christ, because in those days it was pronounced as *chrîstotîs*) while "loving kindness" is nothing less than God's *philanthropia*.

How horrible is a world in which none of this mercy can be found. How liberating, consoling, and blessed is a world of the merciful. Jesus pleaded for such a world, including in his beatitudes: "Blessed are the merciful, for they will receive mercy" (Matt 5:7). The merciful find themselves in the wonders of reciprocity, which is characteristic for those who keep their "bowels of compassion" open and receptive. They even stand in a reciprocity that connects God and man: what is more human than God's mercy, and what is more godlike than a humanity forged of compassion and patience? An abyss opens up in the heart of the world. Shall we be the keepers of such openness? As the monk Saint Isaac the Syrian said, the merciful man prays for irrational beasts, for the enemies of truth, and even for snakes.

Maybe we understand only half of this last point about love for snakes. Father Abbot Paisios (d. 1994) was a monk who lived on Mount Athos. According to a witness, he kept two snakes, Mohammad and

Arafat. He loved them very much and took care of them with great tenderness. Once, a young monk came to visit. He saw how a large snake entered from under the rocks and started to leave again. The young monk stepped forward to kill it but Father Paisios stopped him and said, "Do you want to murder my disciple?" The brother asked, "What disciple?" "Come and see," answered abbot Paisios.

Together they went to the tomb of Father Tikhôn, his predecessor in the hermitage, and Father Paisios pointed to a snake: "This is my first student, he comes during the noon hour. In my cell there are twelve rats and yet another snake that comes to play with them. But he played a nasty trick on me. I gave him milk, because snakes like that, and for three days long he did not come to drink. When he reappeared, I called him and said: 'Why don't you come?' I showed him the carton of milk but he remained in his corner. Then I said, 'You have sinned! Go to confession!' He opened his mouth and spit out a frog. I ordered him, 'Now you are going to fast for three days, and only after that will I give you more to drink!' 'But Father,' said the young monk, 'snakes give me the creeps. Why do you love them?' "

The abbot turned angry: "You are a monk and you are afraid of snakes. If we have cats or dogs, we play with them. There are only two kinds of animals that people do not want anything to do with: snakes and rats. If we, monks, are unable to love these animals, who then will do it? Are they unable to feel love? Are you not ashamed? Did your heart turn to stone?" He pulled three small leaves from a tree and said to the young monk: "Did you not hear the tree's cry of pain, and so don't you understand that all beings feel love? The world was created through God's love, because of love our parents were married, thanks to love we were born into this life and could grow up, it is out of love that other people get married and bring children into the world. And the last gesture of love is the funeral service. All of life is surrounded by love. . . . Our good God is total love, and he is moved by our pitiful offering. While we eat the bees' sweet honey and only give God the wax of a candle, yet God is happy and rejoices in our offering!"[3]

See also: Forgiveness, Intercessory Prayer, Love for One's Enemies, Patience, Peace, Profession of Faith, Serving

3. Fabian Da Costa, *Florilège du Mont Athos* (Paris, 2005), 245.

MINDFULNESS

Do little, but do it with an undivided heart. Do nothing, unless you can do it mindfully. Vietnamese Buddhist Thich Nhat Hanh tells the story of how his master said to him, after he had closed the door somewhat carelessly, "That door is not closed." Surprised, he wondered, "How come, it's not closed?" But the master continued, "Now really close that door. With mindfulness." This was the beginning of a complete turnaround in his life. The slim little handbook he had been given as a novice contained only this one line: how do you perform every act as conscientiously as possible? Rinsing a cup, folding a blanket, and so on. It was even drilled into him that on the toilet he had to eliminate conscientiously, while praying that the whole world may be cleansed and liberated.

Do everything mindfully. Start with your breathing, in and out, gratefully smiling because of life itself. It is better to wait before doing something than to do it in a nonchalant way, that is what the masters from the East teach us.

Praying with a distracted heart, can you really call that prayer? Mindfulness is the prerequisite to all prayer life. In Greek, the masters enjoyed the play on words between *proseuchè* (prayer) and *prosochè* (mindfulness). The former cannot succeed without the latter, and the latter is the entrance gate to the former. Simone Weil considers this link between mindfulness and prayer in the collection of her reflections entitled *La pesanteur et la grace* (*Gravity and Grace*): "L'attention, à son plus haut degré, est la même chose que la prière. Elle suppose la foi et l'amour" (Mindfulness, at its highest level, is the same thing as prayer. It presupposes faith and love).[1] In that same vein, she believes that any kind of focused study that demands complete concentration, whether it concerns mathematics or a translation from Latin, cannot be separated from the spiritual life and the deepest ground of prayer.

When at one time I passed on this teaching to Trappist monks, the abbot remarked to me afterward: "Is it also not true that we cannot pray except *with* distractions?" Praying without distractions is the goal, but only a few are fortunate enough to be able to do it, as Desert Father Evagrius (d. 399) wrote in his famous tract about

1. Simone Weil, *La pesanteur et la grâce* (Paris: Plon, 1947), 153–54, 158–59.

prayer. Pope John XXIII noted in his diary how that morning during quiet prayer he had been subjected to some distraction. The advice he gave himself was, "Return, then, to the point of departure, my soul, and do it gently."

In silent meditation, everybody knows what the Buddhist master refers to when he talks about those noisy monkeys that sway back and forth in our tree. "Swallow them," taught a Zen master, for to be mindful in total silence often requires a tough victory over all kinds of temptations. The interior repetition of a mantra or prayer word can return a scattered attention to powerful simplicity.

Mindfulness remains the abc of whatever practice we wish to apply ourselves to. To assume the proper posture without wasting energy or chasing after several hares at the same time remains the key challenge, every time.

The poet Ida Gerhard wrote, "Is composing a poem just paying attention?" and the thinker Charles du Bos noted, "Mindfulness is in the field of nature what the leading of the Holy Spirit is in the field of the supernatural, and the link between these two is this: outside an attitude of mindfulness we are completely inaccessible and closed to the workings of the Holy Spirit, even if the Spirit wanted to assert itself."

"The kingdom of God is not coming with things that can be observed; nor will they say, 'Look, here it is!' or 'There it is!' For, in fact, the kingdom of God is among you" (Luke 17:20-21). We can pay attention to observable phenomena, but it appears that full attention must be able to observe itself and, thus, must be able to look inward. There is a light that shines in the glow of mindfulness itself. Only converted hearts see the kingdom of God within themselves. They surrender to what always comes first, not to what comes only after attentive observation. They feel the source welling up, experience the inner push, discern even in their breath the gift of life: that what comes from God is received very directly. They accord with it, unconditionally. They believe.

See also: Breath, Ejaculatory Prayers, God, Smile, Source

MOURNING

Mourning occupies an essential place in all cultures—it is a signal characteristic of our true humanity. Yet now we see, at least in the West, that our generation is turning away from mourning, sometimes to such an extent that people have to defend the right to express their grief. Many people in mourning have a hard time of it: they are shunned, systematically left on their own by just about everybody, or have to endure hurtful comments like: "Isn't it enough now? Haven't you gotten over it yet? How many months has it been now since he passed away? You really have got to learn how to deal with this." We not only hear this from others, we often also hear it in ourselves, as the voice of what passes for "normal" these days.

Mourning is something we owe to ourselves but it is too often neglected. It is our right to mourn for a considerable period of time upon the loss of, for example, a child or a spouse. To mourn alongside those in mourning is a high virtue. It is necessary that we draw attention to just how important this mourning is, because in our day it risks completely being lost.

Mourning is difficult: grieving well enables you to go on with life, humanizes your heart, increases your capacity to understand another's sorrow, and makes you reach previously unknown depths of your human existence. Some people get stuck in a grieving process that does not do them any good but, rather, is destructive. Proper mourning, measured yet without suppressing anything, is a difficult art.

Faced with our grief, we may feel completely powerless: the other's death took us totally by surprise. It befell us, unprepared, and here we are now, lost, not knowing what to do. In other cases, death can be anticipated and is experienced as liberating rather than destroying. There is the feeling of loss, but the thought that the other no longer needs to suffer and now abides where he or she ought to be, offers much consolation.

The loss is felt as a wound, a mutilation cutting deeply into the very flesh of our heart. That wound demands to be treated with salve, not with knives or salt or vinegar. Mourning well means handling the wound carefully, protecting it whenever necessary, regularly, and carefully covering it with fresh ointment, and not allowing it to fester or to get worse by irritating it. Certain conversations are harmful to the inner wound. Silence and the company of gentle fellow sufferers are some of the best lotions. Time is an important factor, but cannot be determined by anybody else. The grieving process does not run a straight course: We rightfully expect the pain to lessen over time, but sometimes we suffer a terrible setback that, after the first few weeks, we no longer had thought possible.

Many cultures use rituals to channel the grieving process and to lessen it gradually, such as wearing black for so many days or weeks if the deceased is a spouse, a child, a father, a mother. Occasionally people dress in black for a whole year: a sure sign of mourning carried on too long. That does not help anybody, not the person in question nor those around him or her. Others no longer dare to laugh, to be happy, or even to forget momentarily that they are carrying such deep sorrow in their heart. They are immediately made to feel guilty vis-à-vis the deceased if he or she for an instant is no longer uppermost in mind. The struggle against these kinds of guilt feelings requires courage: we must muster a healthy will to live, making a choice for life and, with Jesus, "letting the dead bury their own dead."

The sorrow that assaults us has to do not only with the feeling of loss: our grief appears to have so many layers, stacked as it were on top of one another. The emotion that goes with it can at times be so keen that it leaves us unable to concentrate or to remember anything. To our surprise we find how all-powerful sadness can be. It can return unannounced, after days or weeks of rest and self-control. Even after three or four years it can burst forth as sharply as in the early months, God knows why. The only thing that can be said about it is: be accepting of yourself and, with patience and without giving yourself over to despair, carry on.

Our memory is one of the most important powers at our disposal when we are in mourning. To mourn well, I have to be selective: I remember the words that invigorate my life, not those that hurt me deeply. Or better, in light of the positive words I learn to give a place to the less fortunate ones and to accept them in a somewhat different fashion.

A deceased person is a spiritual space. That space is filled with light and freedom. At death a person undergoes a purification. Everything that was petty, grasping, pusillanimous, and selfish disappears in death, while everything that was pure and authentically spiritual triumphs in full freedom. We must force our memory to concentrate on the imperishable that was released in the deceased's life and of which we were fortunate to receive a spark. Everything else will fall away regardless. Only deeds of light and intense good works continue to radiate in death, in the hereafter and in our life on earth.

Whoever has been able to interiorize the person who is now deceased has acquired a wellspring in his or her own spiritual space. By thinking about the people who went before me, I receive a portion of their life force, their deepest gospel. It gives me strength and inspiration. In everything I do, I want to be worthy of them. Jesus' Gospel words directed to his disciples also pertain to our dearly departed: "Abide in me as I abide in you." This reciprocal remaining in each other is the fruit of an interiorization of the spiritual space of the other in mine. This is a process: it occurs slowly, after the deep wound is somewhat healed.

To facilitate the healing of our memory, which can be thoroughly disturbed by emotion, it is good to repeat for ourselves short sentences that the deceased spoke tenderly or sayings that were typical of her and that made her walk tall. We can repeat these phrases as quick prayers: they banish all brooding thoughts and prevent certain depressive feelings from washing over our interior world.

Mourning also has to do with certain other processes that have nothing to do with the passing of a loved one. We mourn the end of a task we loved or the move from the house we built with our own hands to a much smaller apartment. When we turn over a completed page of the book of our life, we have to go through a process that has much in common with mourning. To map out a new, meaningful future against the backdrop of a rich past is an art—an art that we have to tackle with as much resolve as patience.

The lesser mourning can be helped by the greater mourning: remembering the greater grief we strip the lesser of excessive drama. But also the reverse is true: if I have learned to react well to lesser forms of grief, I will also find the necessary strength to overcome the greater ordeal.

See also: Ejaculatory Prayers, Friendship, Memory, Mindfulness, Reciprocity, Rituals

MUSIC

De la musique avant toute chose.[1]

—Paul Verlaine

Music unites North and South, East and West, black and white, young and old. No matter how many the reasons for discord between cultures, traditions, or generations, one pure voice or one melody from the flute may be all it takes to touch everyone's heart. No politician can rouse young people as effectively as a jazz band.

Music elevates. In the celebration of Mass words attempt to do so too, but if during the Offertory the organ pulls out all the stops or a Gregorian choir interprets an antiphon in a particularly penetrating way, all thoughts come to a standstill and for a moment all present hold their breath. The ensuing silence remains alive. "The silence after Mozart is still Mozart," noted Julien Green in his diary. Or as bishop Arthur Luysterman proposes, "Great music refers to something beyond ourselves. Because, especially in instrumental music, nothing is expressed with complete precision, music probably allows one to express more feeling than many other art forms." He cites the philosopher Ernst Bloch by way of example: "Music expresses what remains mute in man. Even if its theme is the experience of death, as in a requiem, it leaves room for transcendental experience: the realization that the limits of existence can be exceeded."

Music consoles. It opens the world to more, to otherness. "Music is the art of otherness. The otherness of Bach is God," as Julien Green put it. For music stirs the voice of the muse. Regrettably, not everybody is receptive to that otherness. People do not always wish to step outside themselves. They prefer to stay imprisoned in their own cocoon and refuse to let anything "other" enter.

Jesus described his mission and that of his predecessor John the Baptist as music. Both appeared as if they were playing, like children in the marketplace. But their music was not gratefully accepted: "We played the flute for you, and you did not dance; we wailed, and you did not weep" (Luke 7:32). But he is not discouraged. Jesus goes on

1. Music before all else [translator's note].

and draws his own conclusion: "Nevertheless, wisdom is vindicated by all her children" (Luke 7:35).

Music cannot do everything—it may charm yet not get people to move. People come to Ezekiel, the prophet in exile, even with a certain eagerness, but he hears the Lord saying to him: "They come to you as people come, and they sit before you as my people, and they hear your words, but they will not obey them. For flattery is on their lips, but their heart is set on their gain. To them you are like the singer of love songs, one who has a beautiful voice and plays well on an instrument; they hear what you say, but they will not do it. When this comes[2]—and come it will!—then they shall know that a prophet has been among them" (Ezek 33:32-33).

Music calls for song and dance, rhythm and poetry. It calls on them in a superlative way for what we call "a feast": life at its very best, its Easter best! "We have to celebrate and rejoice," says Jesus in the parable of the two sons (Luke 15:32). The eldest returned from the field but would not enter: he had heard the music and dancing as he approached, and all that because his younger brother had returned home after so many years of licentious living! For him, the music and the celebration were too much of a good thing. He did not want to share in it.

Sometimes silence is experienced as the purest music. And this paradox is itself the source of new melodies: is there anybody who does not know "The Sound of Silence?"

Elijah encountered God on Mount Horeb, not in the thunder and lightning, not in the earthquake, in nothing else but "in a sound of sheer silence" (1 Kgs 19:12).

For the poet and mystic John of the Cross there is no higher experience of happiness when approaching God's deepest mystery than precisely that paradox: the music of silence (see his *Spiritual Canticle of the Soul*, stanza 15: "The tranquil night/at the approaches of the

2. Ezekiel is referring here to a prophecy immediately preceding: "They shall know that I am the LORD, when I have made the land a desolation and a waste" (Ezek 33:29). This is clear in the Dutch text, but less so in the NSRV translation [translator's note].

dawn,/the silent music,/the murmuring solitude,/the supper which revives and enkindles love"[3]).

Spirituality and music go hand in hand again. At least, that is the thesis of Jan Christiaens in the art periodical *Vlaanderen* (Flanders), April 2006. In an issue entirely devoted to art and spirituality, he writes: "Music and spirituality are children of the same father. Authentic spirituality is marked by its potential for a transcendent dimension that has an inviting rather than a compulsory character. The same is true for authentic music: it is irresistible yet not compulsory, it is radically different, yet still its own."

In a true art of living, there will be room for music as well as for pure silence in the attentive heart. The spiritual person is animated, guided inwardly by a spirit capable of transporting him outside himself. What music lives in my bones, what silent dance pervades my heartbeat and my breathing, what is my life other than a song welling up from a Source that raises me up and nourishes me?

See also: Dancing, Feasting, Keeping Silent, Mindfulness, Paradox, Source, Spirit

3. St. John of the Cross, *A Spiritual Canticle of the Soul and the Bridegroom Christ*, trans. David Lewis (Veritatis Splendor Publications, 2013), 625.

N

NAME, TO NAME

He took earth
and fashioned my hand
five fingers for writing
a palm with lines
a language in code
that was the last thing
he made for me
then I asked for my calling
and he said:
name me.

—Maria de Groot

What is more exalted in a language than the Name?

A proper name causes words to open up and the cohesiveness of a language system to collapse. The name is the high point of our speech. "Name me!" is the way the poetess perceives her innermost and highest calling.

We name, and we are named: the one who names also reveals himself. The one who says "You are my son" also reveals "I am your Father." The more frequently and the more exalted you are able to name, the loftier your own name is carried along, recalibrated on each occasion. There is even mention of receiving "a new name that no one knows except the one who receives it" (Rev 2:17). And we find in the third part of the book of Isaiah, "You shall be called by a new name that the mouth of the LORD will give you" (Isa 62:2).

Words are joined and become systems, but a theology of the Name pierces through the tight enclosure of any language system. A proper name is irrevocably and irreducibly Other. Searching for the highest Name that we can name, we enter into the unique dynamic of the sublime. And are we not rediscovering the Sublime in our time? Here we are facing one of the most compelling practices of the spiritual art of living.

At the beginning of the Christian mystical traditions of the East and the West stands an author named Pseudo-Dionysus who wrote a tract called *About the Names of God*. When we are called by our own name we know that we are known and we grow quiet until we, made new, hear His unnamable Name resound in our proper name.

God has many names. In India one learns from one of the oldest Upanishads that the wise men gave "it" many names. "It" here means: the origin, the first, the godhead. With respect to the multitude of names given to gods by the people on earth, it is notable that some flourished for enormous periods of time, while others have completely disappeared. Who still calls on Marduk, Nimrod, Isis and Osiris, Bel, Rha, Zeus? Apparently, names of gods are as mortal and as perishable as human civilizations. Religions also create new names: a Christian can invoke his God with at least three or four new names: *Abba,* Jesus, Lord (in quite a different sense than used by Jews), and Christ.

In India one of the more than two hundred Upanishads teaches that it is liberating to call on God's name: "Name Him by name, and you are saved." "Repeat the formula and the sixteen forms of the name, and the sixteen bands that make your earthly existence unfree will be loosened." The fact of naming is all that matters: the one who keeps repeating the Name shall "gain entrance to heaven, cohabit with the Lord, become one with Him forever." "Repeat the mantra up to thirty-five million times and the worst possible sins a person can commit disappear into nothingness." "Even if you have forsaken all the rules of the Teaching, repeat the Name, and you receive the Purity and complete Liberation. So says the Upanishad."[1]

From China comes the teaching that "a principle, a way, a Tao or a 'god' that can be named is not the true God, not the true Way, not the true principle." The ur-principle, Tao, or God is and remains unnamable. This also is food for thought.

The Jewish tradition has an original approach to naming God. In any rite, the revealed name, written with four letters, YHWH, is never spoken the way it is written. Punctuation marks indicate how the letters of the text must be pronounced when read aloud in the liturgy: sometimes as *Adonaï* (Lord), at other times as *Elohim* (God). Outside of the liturgy, if one cites a text in which the tetragram appears, one simply reads *ha-Shem* (the Name) without more. Thanks to this rite a person learns to show respect in dealing with God: the reader admits that he never can grasp the secret he is naming. We can learn a great deal from such a humble practice.

1. Jean Varenne, *L' Upanishad Kali-Samtaran,* in *Sept Upanishads* (Paris: Seuil, 1981), 127–50.

A Chassidic Jewish master of the nineteenth century taught this: "When you pray, the words only become a prayer if they include the Name. So we say: *Baruch attah Adonaï* (Blessed, You, Lord). So, by the inclusion of the name *Adonaï* the row of words becomes a prayer. Moreover, the true master of prayer will teach you how every word comprises a Name for God: "*Baruch* (Blessed) is his Name, *Attah* (You) is his Name, *Adonaï* is his Name."

It pays to run through the Psalms and to check how God's name rings out in a variety of ways. Rabbis teach how each name connects with a different attribute and a specific action. It is well to sense these differences in one's reading:

> And God said to Moses: "You wish to know my name; I am called according to my deeds. Sometimes I am called 'El Shadday,' 'Tzveo'ot,' 'Elohim,' 'YHVH.' When I judge the creations I am called 'Elohim' [Judge]. When I am waging war against the wicked I am called 'Tzveo'ot' [Lord of Hosts]. When I suspend punishment for a man's sins I am called 'El Shadday' [Almighty God]. When I am merciful towards my world, I am called 'YHVH,' for 'YHVH' only refers to the attribute of mercy, as it is said: 'The Lord, the Lord (YHVH, YHVH), God, merciful and gracious.' Hence, 'ehyeh asher ehyeh' [I am that I am, or I will be that I will be]—I am called according to my deeds." (*Shemot Rabbah* 3:6)[2]

So, whenever in the Psalms we encounter one of these attributes (merciful, compassionate, gracious, filled with pity), in fact we hear also the name of God evoked in the way it was revealed to Moses. Often the Psalms give us whole lists of verbs, as in Psalm 146: "The LORD sets the prisoners free; the LORD opens the eyes of the blind. The LORD lifts up those who are bowed down; the LORD loves the righteous" (Ps 146: 8-9). Each verb says his Name and confirms: "I am called according to my deeds."[3] The search has a clear beginning, but the end is not in sight.

2. *Shemot* (Exodus) *Rabbah*, available at www.sefaria.org (accessed August 2, 2016). In the quote, El Shadday can be translated as "The God who knows when to stop" (information provided by Fr. Standaert) [translator's note].

3. For a more systematic study of God's names in the Psalms, see B. Standaert, *In de school van de Psalmen* (*In the School of the Psalms*) (Gent: Carmelitana, 1997), 93–104.

In Muslim practice there are beautiful litanies composed of names of God. These series are largely taken from the various Surahs in the Qur'an. God is the merciful one, the all-knowing, the bountiful, the patient, the long-suffering, the omnipotent, the savior, etc. The lists go up to ninety-nine. The hundredth name cannot be spoken. That led the mystics on a passionate search for that Most Sublime Name, the one that cannot be spoken! In a tract dating back to fourteenth-century India we hear a master tell this story: "Ibrahim Adham—may God have mercy upon him—was once asked: 'Do you know the Greatest Name? Tell us which it is.' 'Yes, I do know it, and I will tell you about it,' he replied. 'First you should cleanse your stomach of unlawful food, then you should empty your heart of love of this world, and after that by whatever name you call upon God *that* is the Greatest Name!' "[4]

Dying while hallowing the Name
Bless the LORD, O my soul,
and all that is within me,
bless his holy name. (Ps 103:1)

In the three Abrahamic religions, whole tracts have been composed about the names of God. In these quests the whole of creation, visible and invisible, is explored to reach, each time again, the ultimate limit: how far can we go in naming Him, He, the Unnamable? "O You, beyond all things —how else to call you, the Unnamable One, You?" (Gregory Nazianzen, in the famous prayer that he borrowed from Proclus, a Neoplatonic philosopher).

Nowhere is this limit as palpable as when death approaches. For what is at stake in death is one's identity and name—not just your proper name but the name of your God and the relationship you have with Him. That is why in Judaism dying is called "hallowing the Name." Jews, Christians, and Muslims all have preserved tales of martyrs who went to their death united with God by the invocation of his Name.

4. Nizam Ad-Din Awliya, *Morals for the Heart: Conversations of Shaykh Nizam Ad-Din Awliya recorded by Amir Hasan Sijzi*, trans. Bruce B. Lawrence (New York: Paulist Press, 1992), 193.

Rabbi Akiva died a martyr under the Roman occupation in the year 135 CE. In the evening he was tortured with metal combs. Yet he still insisted on praying the ritual evening prayer: *Shema Israel* (Deut 6:4-5). His disciples came to join him and said: "Master, it's really not necessary anymore. . . . You are suffering so much already!" But he replied: "You don't understand a thing! My whole life I have endeavored to say this prayer just as it is written: 'You will love the Lord your God with all your heart, all your soul, and all your strength. . . .' Thus also with all my life's breath (*nefesh*)! And now that indeed for the first time I can pray with all my *nefesh*, you tell me, Rabbi it's no longer necessary! You don't understand a thing!" And he repeated the prayer: *Shema Israel, Adonaï Elohenu Adonaï Ehad* (Hear, O Israel, the Lord is our God, the Lord is One). And while pronouncing the word *Ehad* he drew out the last syllable until he breathed his last: *Ehaaad.*

His death was accomplished while pronouncing the mystical Name: the One. In this way, he hallowed the Name until the very end. He died by joining his life breath as completely and as literally possible with the word that says: the One. What was intended as the greatest possible separation, he experienced as the greatest union.

A Russian monk of the nineteenth century, who became bishop for a short while and then returned to the ranks of the monks, Holy Ignatius Briantchaninov, tells the following story in an instruction on the Jesus Prayer: At the martyrdom of his holy patron saint Ignatius of Antioch (barely twenty-five years before Rabbi Akiva's martyrdom), the executioners were totally bewildered: where did Ignatius get the strength to face the wild beasts so courageously and so fearlessly? They examined his mortal remains and reached into the ribcage for the heart that was left intact. They cut it in two. Then they understood: in both halves they read the six letters of the name, *Jèsous.*

Ignatius, who liked to use the name *theofoor* (carrier of God) in his correspondence, knew he was being carried by God just like he carried Him, in his life and death. He loved the Name so much to the point, as the legend tells us, that the Name had branded itself in his heart.

In Baghdad, the Muslim mystic Mansur Al-Hallaj (tenth century) also died a martyr's death in a final confession of the One. "In me the One, whose essence is unique." He was systematically mutilated by his executioners and ultimately decapitated. From all his limbs one heard the cry: "I am the truth!" while the blood that spilled on the ground spelled the name Allah. His ashes were thrown into the waters of the Tigris River, but also there one read the holy letters of the name of God.

The martyr carries the Name so intimately in soul and body that everything in and from him, consciously and unconsciously, living or already killed, exclaims the Name of the One, the Beloved, the Unnamable. The meaning of our existence and our death corresponds directly with the profundity that we accord to the Name of God in our being. The holy Name is our freedom and our jubilation, our passion and our consolation, in this world and the next.

See also: Death, *Dhikr,* Ejaculatory Prayers, Fasting, Jesus and the Jesus Prayer, Jubilee, One, Profession of Faith, Psalmody

NIGHT VIGIL

In the morning, while it was still very dark,
he got up and went out to a deserted place,
and there he prayed. (Mark 1:35)

Never get tired of staying awake to pray. (Eph 6:18)[1]

In the first few centuries of the Common Era, Christians regularly passed the night praying and singing, often more than once a week. This practice has become extremely rare. Even the great Easter Vigil, the mother of all vigils (as Augustine said), gets pushed back to the early evening of Holy Saturday. To stay awake, to keep vigil, just to celebrate God: how can we bring people, young and old, around to that practice in our day and age?

The reformed breviary, or book of hours, provides for prayer at any time of the day, but says nothing about the night. It barely mentions vigils. The office of readings that in the past was called Matins, namely, the office that was prayed very early in the morning before daylight may now, it says expressly, be prayed at any moment of the day. The night is no longer given any thought.

In the breviary the psalms have pride of place. Well now, starting with the very first psalm, there is praise for meditating on the law of the Lord "day and night" (Ps 1:2). Psalm 134 also addresses those who stay in the house of the Lord and pray into the night: "Come, bless the LORD, all you servants of the LORD who stand by night in the house of the LORD!" (Ps 134:1). Other psalms mention those who pass the night in the temple (see, e.g., Pss 3, 4, 91) in hopes of being enlightened by a word from God, just like little Samuel.

We no longer know how to keep vigil. It is an art that is no longer taught anywhere. So, let's go and give it a try and see where it leads.

Whoever experiments with night vigils from time to time discovers that it is a very special way of praying. Such a vigil is not an office like morning prayer or evening service. When keeping vigil the important thing is to expend as little energy as possible and to tap into a new and

1. This translation is from the New Jerusalem Bible, Reader's Edition (New York: Doubleday, 1990) [translator's note].

different source of energy. Dispense with the thought of finishing up a task or an incomplete project. Nothing needs to be done. Everything is possible. The Word resounds. The response wells up by itself, at times in nothing more than an inhabited silence or a subdued humming, at other times in a spontaneous song or refrain. Short litanies make their way into our heart, repetitions of precious invocations: "Lord, have mercy, Christ, have mercy, Lord have mercy." "Holy, holy, holy, Lord God of Hosts, heaven and earth are full of your glory."

So let us begin anew and resolve to do at least this: Once a week, to get up in the middle of the night and quietly take a seat or use a prayer stool. Let us be present to the night and pick up a text, for example from Scripture. Let us read and become still, keeping vigil with the Word. God speaks in the night. He speaks always, but we are usually somewhere else, busily occupied, our attention divided among two or three different things at the same time.

Nighttime favors concentration: distractions are minimal. Read and keep vigil. Learn and receive. "Give your blood and receive the Spirit," as the Desert Fathers used to say. This is easy in the dark of night. There is nothing to be accomplished, except to let God be God. Totally. For this, let us prepare a space, perhaps even in our bedroom, with a minimum amount of stuff: a *prie dieu*, an icon, a candle, one or two books, a warm scarf or a coat.

Whoever does this regularly discovers that the second part of the night becomes brighter, and sleep more serene. After a night vigil, the day also feels different. The light of the night stays with you all day—a joyful power, always present, never failing.

To keep a night vigil with two or three people because of a special occasion such as a feast can be organized similarly. You can choose a private reading, with a communal song or refrain (for example, one of the songs of Taizé) as a complement. A sober ritual of light starts the vigil off. The alternation of reading, silence, and response in the form of song and intercession or expression of gratitude happens spontaneously. An appropriate breakfast ritual can cap it all off.

A longer night vigil offers the opportunity to read, for example, a complete Gospel such as Mark in six turns. Each turn lasts just a bit over an hour: twenty minutes of reading, a quarter hour of silence, and a quarter hour of sharing around the Word in song and intercession. Then comes a short pause to stretch the legs, to experience the night, to have a cup of coffee or tea. The morning is shared around the Eucharistic table, followed by a festive breakfast.

Such a night serves as a full-fledged initiation because none of the participants will ever say afterward that he or she forgot Mark. Even years later, the memory of that night with Mark stays with us, as if burned into us forever. We form community because we receive the same initiation and share the same secret. A person who is initiated is somebody who has a secret that is shared with other initiated persons. To betray the secret is impossible because it is buried too deep within us. Even without talking about it, we all know there is a secret. Whoever did not share in the night could not possibly guess it.

Here are some of the texts that we have tried out in the course of longer or shorter night vigils: Mark, John, the Revelation of John, the Letter to the Romans, the Letter to the Hebrews, the First Letter of Peter, the Letter to the Galatians, the Letter to the Ephesians, the First Letter to the Corinthians, the Gospel of Mary (bundled from the four Gospels, Acts, and Rev 12), the Song of Solomon, Ecclesiastes.

A long night vigil of eight or nine hours does not necessarily exhaust the participants. The next day most of them will lead their normal lives till evening. The second day one may feel a weakness early in the afternoon, a slump, nothing more, and it does not even last that long. The light of the night vigil keeps burning much longer, often a full week! The fatigue accompanies you for about twenty-four hours, but the light inhabits you for seven days.

One who has learned again how to keep vigil in the night can also keep a vigilant attitude during the usual busyness of the day: working mindfully, without raising one's voice, remaining very open and using little energy. In the presence of ill people, in situations of great excitement, or in the spiritual direction of others, such a calm posture, without raising any fuss, can be very appropriate and beneficial. It is as if one is able to listen to deeper layers of what is happening, and to lift the veil on them at the right moment.

The key to understanding lies frequently on an altogether different level than the one that everyone is preoccupied with. Being vigilantly present, one often perceives that there are different levels to the story. With complete mindfulness, one can see a solution that presents itself from an unexpected angle. The vigilant person does nothing special, but has learned to operate out of a different zone. Keeping vigil becomes second nature. Control of one's inner energy becomes considerably more circumspect. Power is always readily available.

So the paradox is that the one who keeps night vigils enjoys more energy than the person who has a full night's sleep. Dom Helder Camara ascribed his considerable energy to his habit, which he had taken up in the seminary, of getting up at 2:00 a.m. each night ("I made a contract with my alarm clock"!). Between 2:00 a.m. and 4:00 a.m. he prayed, read, and kept vigil. Then he went back to bed. His resilience was demonstrated to us during a late evening conference—there was no stopping him, by young or old.

The person who fasts *and* keeps night vigil doubles his or her power because the former strengthens the latter, and both have to do with proper use of energy. Worth a try, no? And especially, let us not wait until it is too late to try something new! The younger you start, the better—witness Dom Helder Camara!

Keeping Vigil in the Night, How Do You Do It?

Here are a few concrete tips:

1) Find a place to pray. This can be a corner in your own room, which is the simplest, or a chapel, or some other place.

2) Determine a certain moment: once a week, at the start of the night, in the middle of the night, upon suddenly awaking, or early in the morning, an hour earlier than usual. Everyone picks their own preference, taking into account age, overall health, and life and work habits. Experience has shown that large numbers of people prefer the traditional moments: early, middle, or the end of the night. So, everybody should make the choice that suits them best.

3) Sit still, squat, or kneel, perhaps facing an icon.

4) Choose a text: the Psalms, a chapter from one of the Gospels, or another basic text (e.g., the Rule of St. Benedict, a page from Starets Siloan, a passage from the tales of the Russian pilgrim, etc.), or simply use the prayers you know by heart.

5) Read for a while, a little, but in an open manner, not brooding over any point or entertaining an inner argument, with an

attitude of surrender. After that, silently keep vigil with the One, loving, thanking, musing on his Presence.

6) Let God be God, receive his radiance, his workings, his Goodness and Mercy, not just for yourself but for everybody and everything, in a sweeping intercession. People, names, or situations may then rise to the surface, or innermost layers of self that have been hurt. Then let them go, poor and full of confidence. For, as we know, He heals, He reconciles, He forgives. He brings peace, He renews. He completes. He integrates. He renders everything bearable, meaningful, illuminated, different from anything else. End with a conscious moment, a true conclusion that you can hold onto. It may be a thanksgiving, an Our Father, the final Psalm (Ps 150), a Gloria ("Glory to God in the highest, and peace to God's people on earth").

See also: Dreaming, Fasting, Gratitude, Icons, Intercessory Prayers, *Lectio Divina*, Psalmody, Sleeping

O

ONE, THE ONE

Nothing is one as the One. Everything is disjointed, everything is one thing or another, only the One is One. One as no other.

Anything that to some extent is one and inherently unified carries the seal of the One.

In the Bible story of Martha and her sister Mary (Luke 10:38-42), Jesus tells Martha that she worries about many things, but *only one* is needed. Not "one thing," as many translations have it, but one that refers to Somebody: the only One who can fulfill the human heart, the One—the true magnet for all that exists. Jesus was fascinated by this One.

"Good Teacher, what must I do to inherit eternal life?" Jesus was asked by a certain ruler. Jesus surprised him with his reply: "Why do you call me good? No one is good but God alone" (Luke 18:18-19). Jesus is filled with the One and wants no distraction from that One by anyone or anything else, not even by his own role as a recognized good teacher.

"The one who made them at the beginning made them male and female . . . and the two shall become one flesh. . . . Therefore, what God has joined together, let no one separate" (Matt 19:4-6). Upon hearing of "one flesh" (*basar ehad*), Jesus understands that this flesh has to do with the One, and thus with God: "Therefore, what *God* has joined together." In this one flesh God is present, God is engaged with it—it would be unthinkable to have God separated from it.

Rabbi Akiva, a master who lived about two generations after Jesus, taught the same thing. He noted that when man (*iysh*) and woman (*ishah*) are joined, they have to make sure that the Name of the Lord, and hence the letters of the Tetragram, are respected. In *iysh* we find the *yod* and in *ishah* we have the *hè,* which together form the first two letters of the Tetragram (YHWH): *yod hè* (YH). Take those away and what you have left is *esh* and *esh*: "fire" and "fire." The story degenerates into an all-consuming fire.

The same Rabbi Akiva died a martyr after having been tortured. In the evening, he prayed the ritual *Shema Israel*. He prayed with the greatest intensity and poured his whole life-breath into it, as it is written: "You shall love the Lord your God with all your heart, *with all your soul*—all your *nefesh* or life-breath—and with all your strength."

He prayed, *Shema Israel, Adonaï Elohenu, Adonaï Ehad* (Hear O Israel, the Lord is our God, the Lord is One). He stretched out the very last syllable, *Ehaaad.* He died while pronouncing this final profession; in death he joined his breath with the most mystical Name of God in all of tradition: the One.

A monk searches the One in solitude (*monos*) and fashions a lifestyle that enables him to track that One in everything he does. Aside from the Greek word *monachos*, in which we recognize the root *monos* (alone, one) from which our word "monk" is derived, the Syrians had a name for the faithful who sought God in seclusion: *yehidya*, derived from the root *ehad*, one and unique.

There is a tiny monk living in every one of us. There is a voice in everybody's heart that chooses oneness with the Name. As the psalmist sings, "Give me an undivided heart to revere your Name" (Ps 86:11).

> Deep in the silence known alone—
> like the fish,
> like the fish
> only knows its own element—
> knowing the One who was and is. (Ida Gerhardt)

See also: *Abba*, Aspirations, *Dhikr*, Ejaculatory Prayers, Name, Psalmody, Simplicity

P

PARADOX

Blessed are the poor in spirit. Blessed are they who mourn.
Those who want to save their life will lose it.
Unless a grain of wheat falls into the earth and dies,
it remains just a single grain;
but if it dies, it bears much fruit.
The one who serves is great; the one who kneels will be exalted.
Love your enemies, bless those who curse you, pray for your persecutors.
When I am weak, then I am strong.
What is foolish is chosen by God to shame the wise.
An Other in me, more myself than me.

This is just a sampling of sayings from our Western and Christian tradition. If we dipped into Jewish tales from the Chassidic masters or cracked open a wisdom book from the *Tao*-Chinese tradition, we would have no trouble finding just as many contradictory reflections in which weak and strong, empty and full, poor and rich, foolish and wise, death and life are juxtaposed in paradox. Paradoxes call into question, in a very direct manner, the logic of common sense. The paradox is essential: no proposition deserves to be fully accepted if it is not suffused by the paradox's own particular radiance, which is found in the heart of the Gospel and marked by the seal of the Spirit.

In our Western tradition, paradoxes are inventoried and classified as technical expressions from the manuals of rhetorical tradition. A paradox, we learn, points to an intensification of a statement by which the speaker wants to surprise the listener and force her to approach the subject other than by common understanding. The mind is put to the test. That which is *para-doxical* goes against (*para*) or "alongside" the *doxa* or the "opinion."

Standard logic and the habits of common sense within a given culture are destabilized when paradoxes are used. Handbooks of style and rhetoric urge caution in the use of these devices lest the speaker loses the audience's attention. Paradoxes can be off-putting to some people. And that does not serve anybody, say the old masters, because traditional rhetoric is meant to be practical. What matters is that you make your case!

A separate literary form of paradox usage is the oxymoron. The word itself joins two totally contrary meanings: *oxus* means "sharp," while *môrus* signifies "dull." Some oxymora have become nearly proverbial, such as "sweet sorrow" and "deafening silence." Here are a few more: O night, clearer than the days; a sober intoxication; a luminous cloud; a living stone; a motionless dance; the voice of silence; learned ignorance (*docta ignorantia*).[1] In the First Letter of Peter we find a veritable collection of oxymora, all relating to the paschal faith: Christ as a "living stone"—rejected yet chosen—the ultimate paradox, the very model of Christian life. By his wounds we have been healed, we who live as the chosen people but also as exiles, nowhere and everywhere at home. We are blessed if we suffer for doing what is right; if we are reviled unjustly the Spirit of Glory rests upon us!

Certain gentle forms of paradoxical discourse force the mind to avoid coarseness or bluntness. Short moments of quietude, distancing, slowing down, or mindfulness for the here and now can change one's perception in a flash. In Asia we see how in very subtle ways paradoxes can become part of our sensory perception. I remember a piece of calligraphy by the Japanese master Sengai with only two signs: one was translated for me as "Far" and the other as "Clear." Brought together, the piece expressed something forceful. Because something that stands at a distance usually looks hazy or blurred, not at all clear. Now I was challenged to see far *and* clear, together. Let the meditation begin!

In the Japanese tea ceremony (*cha no yu*), we learn to treat each object with utmost attention, to accept it, to let it go. In this manner what is light and what is heavy are entered into paradox. The little bamboo teaspoon filled with a measure of ground tea weighs virtually nothing, but is the most precious thing in the whole ceremony. So move this little spoon slowly and accord it its full weight! The porcelain water pitcher is quite heavy so handle it as though it were light as a feather. And so we learn that what is far, experience it as if it were close by, and what lies right next to you, approach it with the necessary distance. Reverse the common perception for a moment

1. See Pierre Fontanier, *Les figures du discours* (Paris: Flammarion, 1968); Henri Morier, *Dictionnaire de Poétique et Rhétorique* (Paris: PUF, 1961); and Chaïm Perelman and Lucie Olbrechts-Tyteca, *Traité de l'argumentation. La nouvelle rhétorique*, 5th ed. (Brussels: Ed. de l'Université de Bruxelles, 1988).

and experience how light a yoke becomes, how easy a burden. Constantly acting in this fashion creates a space of unique freedom and loving attention for the objects themselves. The guest whose privilege it is to witness this will be touched and refreshed.

In the Byzantine rite we find a similar preoccupation with concrete gestures that are explained by a paradoxical interpretation. When the priest prepares the bread and slices it into four pieces with a knife that is shaped like a lance, each piece marked with two initials (IC, XC, NI, and KA, "Jesus Christ triumphant"), he says, "The Lamb of God, the Son of the Father, is broken and shared; He is broken but not divided, He is eaten everywhere and not consumed, but He hallows those who partake." Each verb is at the same time powerfully pronounced and immediately negated, while the gesture renders visible one side of the greater reality.

So, also, in the Eastern rite we read during the ritual gesture of the Offertory, in which we offer up the concrete gifts of bread and wine: "You are the one who offers sacrifice and who is being sacrificed, You who receives and You who are shared, O Christ our God. We glorify You." The words reveal the gesture's mystical paradox: it is not we who give, but He who offers himself up in our gifts. He receives and He shares himself, and all this happens in that single gesture.

A paradox is not just a means to an end. If you accept paradox as a basic way of seeing things, you discover that path and purpose are inseparable, that, strangely enough, they seem to coincide. Thanks to paradox we learn that we can lift up common opposites and find a new perception of reality. Paradox then becomes a key, a finger that points past itself to what is other. The foolish person, however, stares at the finger and does not see the moon at which the finger is pointed. The foolish person is the one who remains stuck in the paradox, determined to resolve the contradictory logic. An extreme example of meaningful nonsense can be found in the following Taoist dialogue between Wushi ("Without Beginning") and Taiqing ("Highest Clarity"):

> Wushi then terminated the meeting and said: "He who does not know is deep, he who knows is superficial; he who does not know lives inwardly, he who knows lives on the surface; he who does not know penetrates, he who knows is coarse." Taiqing raised his eyes to heaven and sighed: "So, not to know is to

> know, and knowing is not-knowing? Who, then, is able to understand that knowledge is not-knowing, and that not-knowing is knowledge?" Wushi replied: "The Tao cannot be understood, and what is understood is not the Tao. The Tao cannot be observed; what can be observed is not the Tao. The Tao cannot be spoken; what can be spoken is not the Tao. Who has ever understood that what gives shape to forms is itself without shape?"[2]

Where we encounter the biggest paradoxes—heaven and earth, life and death, all and nothing, Creator and creature—we also find the greatest challenges. Thus the Greek church fathers consider the incarnation as "the paradox of all paradoxes," when the Word, that was with God and that was God, agrees to take on human form, and He who is without beginning risks being born from a woman, willingly taking on human mortality. All the great spiritual traditions display a predilection for paradoxes whenever they need to express the inexpressible.

Reciprocity

Some of the aforementioned paradoxes may show a surprising opposite, in perfect reciprocity.

A paradox includes an opposite that approaches pure contradiction, but as soon as the paradox is fully accepted an unexpected free space opens up, and that space is graced with reciprocity. "All things have been handed over to me by my Father; and no one knows the Son except the Father, and no one knows the Father except the Son and anyone to whom the Son chooses to reveal him" (Matt 11:27).

At the heart of this pronouncement by Jesus, in which he reveals himself, we must as it were pass through the wall of the first three statements before we gain access to knowing the Father, which is reciprocal knowledge of Son *and* Father. Indeed, to know one is coincident with knowing the relationship between the two.

From beginning to end, the pronouncement is held in an inner tension of paradox, because the Son appears in full power—he receives everything, he is the only Son, to him the whole inheritance is due. "All things have been handed over to me." Nobody knows him except the Father, and this in a transparent and reciprocal manner that is initially not accessible to anyone. "No one knows. . . .

2. *Philosophes taoïstes*, Part II (*Huainan zi*) (Paris: Gallimard, 2003), 103.

No one knows." In contrast to these definite declarations, Jesus concludes with a purely inviting openness: "and anyone to whom the Son chooses to reveal him." Here, in utter benevolence, he allows the other to enter so as to share in the knowledge of Father and Son, to discover how "poor," gentle, and humble of heart he is, and that in his school the yoke is easy and the burden light. This imagery perfectly testifies to the experience of paradox.

Transformation

A paradox that is fully accepted works a transformation. What we are looking for turns out to be what we are gradually becoming. We enter into the object of our searching, and suddenly, then, that other appears to be more us than we are. We are caught up. "We will be like him, for we shall see him as he is," as we read in the First Letter of John (1 John 3:2). To see Him we have to become Him.

Thus, to be is what matters, that is to say, we must share in the "Act" that He is. To experience the gratuitous we have to assume an attitude of gratuitousness ourselves: outside the realm of the gratuitous, nobody can enter it. The divine Act always comes first and supports from the inside all my searching, loving, and knowing. To know Him as an object appears to be impossible because He is Subject, more subject than my own subjectivity. So stop considering Him as an object outside yourself. Become God and He shall know you, and that knowledge will fill you. The paradox lies in the play between object and subject.

French philosopher Louis Lavelle repeats on nearly every page of his posthumously discovered notes about God that we cannot turn God into an object. The turnabout consists in recognizing Him always as the first Subject in ourselves and trying to honor Him. "Aimer Dieu, c'est éprouver l'amour que Dieu a pour moi" (To love God is to experience the love God has for me). "Dieu n'est pas une idée de l'homme, c'est le contraire qui est vrai" (God is not an idea of man, it is the contrary that is true).

The object is Subject, and by understanding that I allow myself to be loved, to infinity. "Be God. And if you don't succeed, at least stop being yourself!" said a Sufi master. The marvelous reciprocity offers itself up only to the one who is prepared to die to his own small ego. Then "we will be like him, for we shall see him as he is." Making that our aim, that is what matters. Not just to see but to become, in an absolute unification after a total renunciation and a complete silence.

What Can We Expect from a Culture without Paradoxes?

Paradoxes are essential: they challenge the self that is focused only on itself and that seeks to bend the other toward itself so as to reduce the other to itself. They deal hard and wholesome knocks to a culture of small egos and petty narcissism. Woe to a culture that does not know how to handle paradoxes: as it only knows the systematic denial of what is different from itself, blind violence is the result. The only thing still alive in such a culture is a horrible totalitarian dream.

But where can we find paradoxical thought these days? Where does the vital transmission of paradoxical thinking occur? In high school, where youths are being taught to be competent and competitive? In college or university, where each new research program is judged on the basis of cost/benefit analysis? Through newspapers? TV? Politically correct debates?

The wisdom of Chinese swordsmen teaches that the one who always wins, loses. But our sports culture with its fierce competitiveness challenges athletes, teams, and trainers to an exhausting and ultimately boring battle to win always and everywhere.

Paradoxes are essential. They add irrationality even to the wisest life philosophies. Where can we discover nowadays that strength is to be found in weakness? Is the Church such a place? Do abbeys and convents provide environments where life is consciously lived in this way? We urgently need a culture of paradox to awake from our sleep. The wise Desert Father Abba Poemen once said, "'All the virtues come to this house except one, and without that virtue it is hard for a man to stand.' Then they asked him what virtue was, and he said, 'For a man to blame himself.'"[3] A paradox questions the self and its blind urge to reduce everything to itself.

Our Western culture systematically smothers all breathing space for wonder at anything that is not itself. The global culture we need today and tomorrow will of necessity have to be able to sustain encounter and coexistence with different cultures. It needs to rest on a different basis than one of self-sufficiency. The wisdom model of

3. *Sayings of the Desert Fathers* (Poemen 134), 186.

the Tao, with its fertile polarity of yin and yang, offers a far greater chance for survival.

African thinking, too, can be full of surprising turns that manage to integrate opposing differences rather than brushing them aside or reducing them to sameness. So, for example, here is a thought by Amadou Hampate Ba, a Muslim, that I read recently: " If you think the same thing I think, you are my brother. If you think differently from what I think, you are twice my brother! Because then you will enrich me with your difference, and I will share mine with you, and we will be brothers not once but twice." The same thinker said: "If somebody else does not understand me, that does not mean that person is dumb. If I get to know him better I shall realize how to make myself understood, and then he will understand me."[4]

Wonder of Wonders

The *l'arche* communities of Jean Vanier or humble places of prayer such as the grotto of Massabielle in Lourdes are, in our times, remarkable signs of promise for the future. There the weak are not further marginalized by the alliance of the strong but, rather, they occupy center stage—just like the child in the community of Matthew, according to Jesus' teachings (Matt 18:1-3). In Lourdes, thousands stand in line to make their way to the grotto yet nobody pushes. Spontaneously, everybody allows the frail to go first. In all languages, without one word needing to be said, everybody understands how to behave in that one, proper way.

In Mary's company all of humanity finds again its paradoxical "correct" way of behavior. Wonder of wonders! Key sayings from her *Magnificat* turn into reality before everybody's eyes: "He has cast down the mighty from their thrones, and has lifted up the lowly. He has filled the hungry with good things, and the rich he has sent away empty." So, against all hope, there is reason to hope!

See also: Culture, Emptiness, God, Mary, Poverty, Reciprocity, Wonder, *Wu Wei*, Yin and Yang

4. Both quotes are from Jacques Levrat, *Une expérience de dialogue: Les Centres d'Étude chrétiens en Monde Musulman* (Altenberge: Christlich-Islamisches Schriftum, 1987), 19.

PATIENCE

Patience is to impatience as day is to night, as light is to dark. When impatience appears, patience is gone. True patience knows no limits. "The inside of patience is still patience," a confrère once said in a homily. Many people experience patience as a suppressed impatience. Whoever has developed the great patience in him- or herself discovers that the inside of patience does not harbor disguised impatience, but only patience!

Impatience is part and parcel of our digital culture. Everything has to happen as fast as possible, immediately, preferably without a single breather! "Everything right now, twenty-four seven," demands the youngster raised on technology. Patience is a waste of time, and time is money. A culture of patience stands at loggerheads with what is valued in our day and age. Yet, every sensible person knows that impatience can be ridiculous at times. Does grass grow faster by pulling on it? Does a son turn into an adult sooner by slapping him or giving him hell?

Sometimes our patience can be severely tried, and physically experienced, in the most ordinary circumstances, such as waiting for a train, or a guest, or the result of a medical test. During a silent meditation, time can suddenly grip us with fear. If waiting involves pain, our patience can be severely tested. Then patience and impatience stand like twins in the same emotional state. Both desire an immediate change. Patience wins out when it can say to itself: "Hang on, here and now. Don't worry about what's next and what comes after that. If the pain is tolerable now for a moment, why doubt that it will be tolerable the following moment?" And all of a sudden, the pain appears to be less bothersome. A half-hour later it may be almost forgotten. In Zen meditation one learns to live *ima koko*, now and here.

In our mind, patience and impatience may exist together in paradox, with the result that impatience gets its way but is never allowed to dominate the scene. In fact, Lady Patience learns to play tricks on her twin, Impatience. Every patient person knows how impatient he or she can be: it is our inalienable shadow side. To want to get rid of it forever is an illusion, but that is no reason for patience's light to be overshadowed by the shortsightedness of impatience.

Truly patient individuals are like initiated members of a traditional society. They have access to a silent and inalienable secret. Even in the midst of torture such people cannot be robbed of their patience, not out of pure stubbornness or obstinate denial of another's authority, but because they are animated by a different power, a power unknown to the torturer. In times of persecution, just as in times of totalitarian delusions in the media or in politics, a culture of patience is an indispensable tonic.

Patience has many synonyms, for example, forbearance, tolerance, endurance, steadfastness, resilience, trust, and love.

When Paul talks about love (*agapè*), the first characteristic he ascribes to it is patience. The greater your patience, the greater is your love in practice. This passive capability to wait, to have patience, to bear and to forbear is so essential for Paul because behind every form of magnanimity or generous commitment there can always lurk a hidden attempt at self-realization. But with great patience you allow Another to triumph within you. When all is said and done, your power no longer derives from yourself. True love, so teaches Paul, is the "Christ in me" whose love abides. To really allow Christ to enter into me, all I have to do is to faithfully open myself up with forbearance and patience. In his famous hymn on love, Paul shows that one's faith can move mountains or make one give up his body, but that without this mysterious *agapè* all is vainglorious and without consequence (see 1 Cor 13:1-3).

However, when the great queen, the Agapè, enters into the soul, she allows herself to be recognized by these remarkable traits of resignation, selflessness, and infinite patience: "Love is patient; love is kind; love is not envious or boastful or arrogant or rude. It does not insist on its own way; it is not irritable or resentful; it does not rejoice in wrongdoing, but rejoices in the truth. It bears all things, believes all things, hopes all things, endures all things. Love never ends" (1 Cor 13:4-8).

Love is in the first place patience, and patience is love, extreme love that knows no end. The patient person no longer suffers time because he or she is in touch with that which is without beginning and without end, with the eternal and the divine. Yes, patience has to do with God. No one is more patient than He is and nothing makes us more like Him than infinite patience.

An early Latin church father, Saint Cyprian of Carthage, wrote a short treatise on patience (*De patientia*) for his contemporaries. Stoics had already done the same thing about two centuries earlier, but Cyprian lived in an exceptionally difficult period for the Christian movement, one marked by systematic persecutions here and there. Cyprian himself was unable to escape them and died a martyr's death. The principal reference of the North African bishop in *De patientia* is Christ himself, ridiculed and tortured. We can profit from reading a page of the treatise here. It is used in the Liturgy of the Hours during Holy Week, when we enter with Jesus into the night of suffering and death.

> And moreover, in His very passion and cross, before they had reached the cruelty of death and the effusion of blood, what infamies of reproach were patiently heard, what mockings of contumely were suffered, so that *He* received the spittings of insulters, who with His spittle had a little before made eyes for a blind man; and He in whose name the devil and his angels are now scourged by His servants, Himself suffered scourgings! He was crowned with thorns, who crowns martyrs with eternal flowers. He was smitten on the face with palms, who gives the true palms to those who overcome. He was despoiled of His earthly garment, who clothes others in the vesture of immortality. He was fed with gall, who gave heavenly food. He was given to drink of vinegar, who appointed the cup of salvation.
>
> That guiltless, that just One—nay, He who is innocence itself and justice itself—is counted among transgressors, and truth is oppressed with false witnesses. He who shall judge is judged; and the word of God is led silently to the slaughter. And when at the cross, of the Lord the stars are confounded, the elements are disturbed, the earth quakes, night shuts out the day, the sun, that he may not be compelled to look on the crime of the Jews, withdraws both his rays and his eyes. He speaks not, nor is moved, nor declares His majesty even in His very passion itself. Even to the end, all things are born perseveringly and constantly, in order that in Christ a full and perfect patience may be consummated.[5]

5. Cyprian of Carthage, *Treatise 9*, para. 7, available at www.newadvent.org/fathers/050709.htm (accessed October 6, 2016).

The rhetoric of this page, with its intensive contradistinctions, is impeccably thought out; what's more, it allows us to peek into the secret of patience: the patient person is able to bear the strangest paradoxes of life and in so doing testifies to an unknown freedom.

Every single person is called to this freedom. The school of patience leads to the right results. For it orients us to Jesus *and* to the One he unceasingly and lovingly gave witness to, his Father. Moses on Mount Sinai had already learned the lesson that the Lord is "long-suffering" and "abounding in steadfast love," even unto "the thousandth generation" (Exod 34: 6-7).

See also: Forgiveness, Love for One's Enemies, Mercy, Night Vigil, Paradox, Peace, Serving

PEACE

"Grace and peace." These two concepts are often paired together in the oldest letters of the New Testament as well as in the liturgical greeting, then and now. Together, they signify God's complete salvation. If "grace" refers to the origin, the source of salvation, "peace" denotes the end goal. "Grace" and "peace" together express the beginning and the end of the Christian salvation experience. It is a wish, but also a confession of faith.

Peace—*shalom*—is an all-encompassing concept in the Jewish tradition. The word *shalom* embodies health, prosperity, fruitfulness of the land, posterity, peaceful relations with neighboring countries, cosmic harmony, covenanted faithfulness with God, and blessing upon blessing. This peace is what we expect and what is coming to us: it is first and foremost a notion of the future.

Rabbinical thought about peace is very systematic: the three axes of existence (study, prayer, and action) must be geared toward peace. The Talmud, as the greatest synthesis of rabbinical thought, leads to peace. The last paragraph of the first treatise (*Berakhot*) is wholly devoted to the subject, just as the final paragraph of the last treatise of the whole *Mishnah*[1] provides a summary account of everything that peace accomplishes.

By studying the Talmud, the God-fearing person seeks and pursues peace (see Ps 34:14).

Prayer also needs to be aimed toward peace. As stated in the *Derekh Eretz Zuta*,[2] in the chapter that deals with peace, those who pray but do not seek peace shall not be heard. Conversely, those who seek peace may be confident that their prayers will not return to them unheard. The liturgical order itself bears proof of this orientation toward peace because in the closing lines of all prayers, peace is always the object.

In the *Midrash* on Leviticus we read: "Peace is great, because all blessings and words of consolation brought to Israel by the Holy

1. The first major written rendering of ancient oral Jewish tradition [translator's note].

2. A noncanonical tract of the Babylonian Talmud [translator's note].

One, blessed be his Name, end with the prayer for peace"; after the recitation of the *Listen, Israel:* "You who erects the tent of peace"; in the Benedictions (*Amidah*): "You who brings peace"; and in the priestly blessing of the sons of Aaron: "May He give you peace" (Num 6:26) (*Vayyikra Rabbah* 9:9). According to Elie Munk, a contemporary rabbi, "all this means that in Jewish understanding peace never is the point of departure but is the final purpose of all our desires and aspirations."

This also implies that even in the experience of conflict, let alone in wars, we must always keep in mind the ultimate peaceful outcome because at some moment in time, understanding and real peace will again have to reign between the opposing camps. Thus, let's not get carried away and make sure we are mindful of the worst possible outcomes of every action we take, lest we sow never-ending feelings of revenge.

Peace is a name of God, one of his most precious attributes. God's names are actions. Whoever seeks peace wants to allow room for God's workings as peacemaker. "He who creates peace on high, let Him also establish peace among us and all of Israel," is one of the best-known peace songs in Israel. Obviously, human action is required for peace, but if in faith we are able to discern a Name of God in it, we realize that peace is also a gift from God's hand. He "creates" peace, He "establishes" reconciliation. What we accomplish is only patchwork if it is just the work of our hands. At best, our work is constructive cooperation with his will. Do the prophets not assure us that God has plans for our *shalom*, for a future with hope (see Jer 29:11)?

The city of Jerusalem stands as the symbol of this divine end goal because its name is often translated as *visio pacis*, vision of peace (*Yeroe-sjalaïm*). All peoples are called to ascend the mountain "shoulder to shoulder," humble, poor pilgrims who profess the One from one mouth, one heart.

This vision arises toward the end of the great compilation that we call the Old or the First Testament. The end of Isaiah (Isa 66), the final sentences of 2 Chronicles 26, Zephaniah 3:9, and many psalms point in the same direction: a grand pilgrimage from all peoples to this mysterious center that coincides with *Yeroesjalaïm*. Unquestionably, the current movement by representatives of the world's faiths to build, together, a culture of peace and understanding, embodies that prophetic dream, a dream once recorded in the First Testament.

Adonaï shalom! Right in the middle of the Book of Judges (Judges 6:24), where the most horrible pages of the people's history are recorded, we hear Gideon's surprising cry: *Adonaï shalom!* (The LORD is peace). The peace is Somebody. For Gideon this profession signified that he could completely shake loose from the idolatry of the Baals and that a way out was in sight, despite the raids of the Midianites and other tribes from the east. In the name *Adonaï* we hear the early faith, the faith of the fathers; in *shalom* resounds a hopeful look toward salvation, notwithstanding the precariousness of the besieged situation. Because of the Name, professed with force, hope returns: "I will deliver you," also in the new situation in which nomadic tribes were trying to invade the land (see Judges 7:7).

Even in the difficult times of the seventh century BCE, the prophet Micah sees a sign of hope because in Ephrathah, in the small town of Bethlehem in Judah, a Messiah shall be born. "And he shall be the one of peace," the visionary declares forcefully (Mic 5:5). Peace in the form of a person! But also a very threatened peace, because immediately following his declaration Micah raises the specter of the Assyrians and their new civilization based on iron. Thus, peace shall come, but under threat of the sword. It will not be a comfortable peace, but the promise is, for that matter, not any less epoch-making and hopeful.

Also in the New Testament we find that peace is a Person. "He is our peace," professes the writer of the letter to the Ephesians (Eph 2:14). He had read in Isaiah of "peace, peace to the far and the near" (Isa 57:19). This double peace the writer now sees fulfilled in Christ. He brought both Jews ("the near") and heathens ("the far") into unity, broke down the wall of separation, established the new person, and "through him both of us have access in one Spirit to the Father" (Eph 2:18). Father, Son, and Spirit appear together in that one sentence, and define the familiar movement in a cultural space in which the old temple structures are broken wide open.

"He has made both groups into one" (Eph 2:14), yes, every duality, every dissension, partition, or separation He brought into unity. This foundational act converges with his death on the cross and the spilling of his blood. That which cost him his life is precisely what brought the new into being.

We hear a powerful paradox here, in line with what we read in John or in the book of Revelation. "I have said this to you, so that in me you may have peace. In the world you face persecution. But take courage; I have conquered the world," says Jesus to his disciples just prior to his passion (John 16:33). He secures this victory by dying on a pillory. When he reappears to his disciples, after his death was accomplished, they see a person pierced who greets them with a strong, and repeated, "Peace be with you!" and who shows the scars in his hands and side (John 20:19-21).

In the middle of the book of Revelation, a lamb appears, "standing" yet "as if it had been slaughtered" (Rev 5:6)! The Lamb is greeted as the conqueror, the lion of Judah, the one privileged to open the seals of the book that records the will of God, the peace of the world.

Peace is a Person: accepting Him occurs with a faithful assent in which we allow ourselves to be sprinkled by his innocent blood and to be pulled along in his extreme surrender to the Father.

People of peace are always ahead of what still has to come. They are occupied by a vision. As humble pilgrims, they journey to a sanctuary that far surpasses them and all the particularities of their own traditions. You see more of their backs than their faces, because in their passion they are always a few yards ahead of those who try to understand or to follow them. They are a lighthouse in the night of the world. Jesus even calls them "sons of God," our Father in heaven who, peaceably and without distinction, "makes his sun to rise on the evil and on the good, and sends rain on the righteous and the unrighteous," all in perfect impartiality and with royal generosity (Matt 5:45). Blessed are such peacemakers!

See also: Forgiveness, Intercessory Prayers, Love for One's Enemies, Mercy, Patience, Profession of Faith, X

PILGRIMAGE

Happy are those whose strength is in you,
In whose hearts are the highways to Zion.
They go from strength to strength;
The God of gods will be seen in Zion. (Ps 84:5, 7)

A good number of religious edifices have been swept away by the wave of secularization, but, to the surprise of all analysts, places of pilgrimage have remained upright in the surf. Marian venues such as Lourdes, Banneux, and Beauraing continue to receive visitors, and some, like Compostela and Medzugorje, are far more popular these days than twenty or thirty years ago. Apparently that journey to a grotto, mountain, holy site, or apostle's tomb packs meaning and hidden power stronger than modern cultural patterns can change or erode. That should give us food for thought.

Going on pilgrimage is a medium that is being widely rediscovered. It stirs discussion surprisingly easily. Whenever somebody says "I am going to walk to Compostela" (or go on a bicycle, let alone on horseback), they will be amazed at the unexpected sympathy: colleagues at work, neighbors, family members, everybody wants somehow to stay in touch and convey best wishes. To go on pilgrimage jars something loose in everybody, including unbelievers, the unchurched, even the modern, nonreligious citizen.

The Universality of Pilgrimages

Only the human person goes on pilgrimage. Only the human person experiences life as a journey, pointing to an "elsewhere" that he cannot reach except by taking leave of himself. Stars and stones, mountains and oceans, horses, buffaloes, snakes, and sparrows: no being under heaven has the urge for pilgrimage in its heart the way humans do.

People of all time periods have gone on pilgrimage. Ancient Egypt, distant Japan, India, Madagascar, Brazil, and Mexico: the oldest roads are often pilgrim routes to holy places, temples, graves of one or other ancestor, king, marabout, or holy monk.

On the Japanese island of Shikoku, eighty-eight holy places are connected by a single trail. The route is 1,240 km long.[1] It used to be

1. 770 miles [translator's note].

that young women walked the pilgrim trail in preparation for marriage. Whoever could manage the journey was certainly ready for the tribulations that married life might bring.

India has pilgrim routes from north to south, from east to west. In Buddhism pilgrimages are an act of faith: to go the way of the pilgrim lends the faithful access to true happiness, to nirvana. According to tradition, just before his death the Buddha imposed on his disciples four places of pilgrimage, the four principal places of his own journey: his native village, the place of his enlightenment, the place where he started his teaching, and, finally, the village of his death. Three centuries later, a pious king distributed his mortal remains over 84,000 stupas: each one of these small votive monuments became a place of pilgrimage.

In addition to the Buddhists, the Hindus also have their own pilgrim shrines in India, as do Jains, Sikhs, Muslims, and yes, even Christians. The tombs of the Apostle Thomas (near Madras/Chennai) and Francis Xavier (Goa), and the holy sites of Our Lady of Fatima (Velangani) and Our Lady of Lourdes (Villenour) are much frequented: Catholicism and Indian culture are interwoven.

One of the most beloved poets and mystics in all of India is the poor Hindu pilgrim Tukaram (1598–1650). Singing, he traveled from holy place to holy place. Due to his status as an outcast he was not allowed to cross the temples' thresholds, yet what he received in piety he gave back in short passionate songs, a collection of which the French priest-author Guy Deleury (1922–2015) translated and called *Psalms of the Pilgrim*.[2] Transmitted by word of mouth, Tukaram's poetry lives on in the crowds of pilgrims around India's holy places, even today, four centuries later.

Also fascinating is the story of Swami Ramdas (1884–1963), who in the twentieth century discovered his calling to the service of Ram and walked as a pilgrim across all of India. The teachings of Krishna, Buddha, and Jesus accompanied him on his wanderings as so many

2. G. A. Deleury, *Psaumes du Pélérin: Toukaram* (Paris: Gallimard, 1956). There are a number of English translations of Tukaram's poetry including Daniel Ladinsky, *Love Poems from God* (Penguin, 2002); J. Nelson Fraser and K. B. Marathe, *The Poems of Tukaram, Motilal Banarsidass*; Dilip Chitre, *Says Tuka: Selected Poetry of Tukaram* (Penguin, 1991) [translator's note].

torches of light. Step-by-step, the way he trod through the Indian subcontinent was an entering into the Reign of universal love and goodness.

From time immemorial, the Abrahamic religions—Jews, Christians, and Muslims—have remained equally familiar with pilgrim feasts and customs.

Every Muslim is required to make a pilgrimage to Mecca during his or her lifetime, one of the five principal pillars of Islam. According to Al Ghazali, the pilgrimage can be considered the fulfillment of the religion. For the Qur'an says in connection with that pilgrimage: "This day I have perfected your religion for you" (5:3).

The Kaaba in Mecca is the house of the Lord on earth, the center of the world, the place visited by angels and mortals. Muslims use the word *hajj* for the pilgrimage. The Arabic word means literally "to direct oneself toward," but also "to dominate, to obtain or achieve." Indeed, according to Muhammad Hamidullah (1908–2002), by approaching His house one directs oneself to God and one tries to control oneself to the point where the self is forgotten and one is lost in God. If somebody did not manage to make the pilgrimage in his or her lifetime, the heirs have to undertake it in their stead. That is how essential the *al-hajj* is for Muslims.

In Israel it was a holy duty to "go up to appear before the LORD your God three times in the year" (Exod 35:23-24). From the time of the patriarchs, going on pilgrimage from holy place to holy place was a nomadic tradition. Bethel, Shechem, Hebron, Mamre, and Beersheba are some of the holy places that were visited regularly in ancient times. "In every place where I cause my name to be remembered I will come to you and bless you" (Exod 20:24).

Starting with the reforms of King Josiah (622 BCE), worship and pilgrimages became concentrated on the shrine in Jerusalem. On three great pilgrimage festivals the whole people come together in the holy city: Passover, Pentecost, and the harvest feast in the fall Sukkoth, also called the Festival of Booths (see Deut 16:1-13). There was not only feasting and offering, in the city also stood "the thrones for judgment" (Ps 122:5). Jerusalem was considered the city for ultimate judgment, a place of study, a university *avant la lettre.*

In later Judaism the tombs of patriarchs, prophets, and famous rabbis, within as well as outside the Holy Land, remain sites of visitation and annual pilgrimages.

Christians are also familiar with the pilgrim's journey. From the very beginning they called themselves "Followers of the Way," and their master said unequivocally: "I am the Way," He who was born while on a journey and who started life as a fugitive. His public life was the journey of a wandering prophet who said of himself: "The Son of Man has nowhere to lay his head" (Matt 8:20). As recorded in the Gospels, he will die outside the city, crucified as a public scoundrel, as a slave without rights, in-between two other "criminals." So, right from their beginnings, Christians have plenty of reasons to take the pilgrimage movement seriously. Nothing brings them closer to the center of their faith identity than a completed journey on foot. The path teaches Christians who they have been for centuries: people on a journey.

The basic model of every Christian pilgrimage consists in tracing Jesus' footsteps and following Him in the Holy Land by going from Bethlehem to Nazareth, from Galilee to Jerusalem, from Gethsemane to Golgotha, and from the Cenacle to the Mount of Olives. The pilgrim completes with a conscious literalness Jesus' own pilgrimage to the Father. For, of course, the life of Jesus as shown in the four Gospels is a peregrination from village to village, ending in Jerusalem on the pilgrim feast of *Pesach* or Easter.

The first Christians honored the place where martyrs bore witness to their faith with their blood. As a result, pilgrimages sprang up to the burial sites of martyrs and apostles—especially to those of Peter and Paul (*ad limina*) in Rome, and to the grave of Saint James in Compostela, in the northwesterly corner of Spain (*finis terrae*).

Marian shrines constitute a third type of Christian pilgrimage destination where humble and needy humanity gathers around the Savior's Mother.

Speaking Figuratively

Christian tradition's very identity is conceptualized in metaphors of pilgrimage, crossing, initiation. The *Summa Theologica,* Thomas Aquinas' great thirteenth-century synthesis, is internally shored up by this singular movement: coming from God in order to return to God. Spiritual treatises that describe such a movement can be found in just about every generation. Both the Prologue and the Epilogue of Benedict's Rule sketch out for the monk, who after all spends his whole life within the seclusion of his monastery, a veritable pilgrim's path where there is talk of rising, setting out, progressing, persevering, following guideposts, and, ultimately, in the very last chapter, of arriving "at the pinnacle of perfection."

Saint Bonaventure wrote an *Itinerarium* for the spirit's movement to God, Ignatius of Loyola recorded his life's journey as that of a pilgrim, Teresa of Avila described a "path of perfection," and John of the Cross analyzed the stages of the spiritual life as a systematic ascent of Mount Carmel. And who is not familiar with the marvelous nineteenth-century Russian work *The Way of a Pilgrim*? In our own generation, cardinal Basil Hume, a former abbot, published his reflections under the title *To Be a Pilgrim.* A short formula, recently distributed as an aid to silent meditation, expresses precisely what is envisaged by the pilgrim's way: *Weg von mir, Hin zu Dir, Ganz in Dir, Neu aus Dir* (Away from me, Toward You, Immersed in You, New through You) (quoted by Graf von Dürckheim). The way is completed in a radical renewal.

Homo Viator

In Western civilization perhaps nobody embodied the pilgrim's way as much as the vagabond Benoît Labre (1748–83), who lived in the century of the Enlightenment. From his twenty-first year until his death, he was constantly on pilgrimage throughout Europe, ending his days as a mendicant and a hermit in Rome, the eternal city. At the news of his death, the street urchins called out: "The saint is dead! The saint is dead!" At his funeral, the church was too small to hold all who wanted to attend. The authentic vagrant of and for Christ, home nowhere and everywhere, had captured everyone's heart, no matter how rootless his life had been.

The practice of peregrination shows just how the message is part and parcel of the medium or, to use Marshall McLuhan's felicitous phrase, how *the medium is the message*. The path will teach you everything, you only have to walk it. Wisdom comes from your feet, prayer arises from the rhythm of your pace, from the cadence of your step. Heart, respiration, walking pace: slowly they fuse into one reality. The whole art consists in carrying on, without ever making the purpose anything other than walking the path.

A French specialist in pilgrimage shrines once defined the dynamic of going on pilgrimage as *Partir ailleurs pour revenir autre* (To leave for other parts in order to return a different person). You go elsewhere to return home changed. Just as you only really realize where you live after you have stayed elsewhere for a while.

You start the trip as an unbeliever, as an admirer of culture looking for the most beautiful monuments, or as a sporty cyclist intent on having a great ride, but the road imprints its strange mark upon you. Gradually, we might say step-by-step, it changes your motivation, your goals, your self-image, your deepest identity. "He is no longer the same person," said a woman whose husband trekked to Compostela with horse and carriage and who had to give up half-way because of the horse. Even a half-traveled road sufficed to work a radical transformation.

Pray for us at Compostela is the unapologetic title that two nonbelieving authors gave to their book about the centuries-old pilgrim's route to Santiago de Compostela in Spain.[3] The way makes you poor. The pilgrim arrives and begs for intercession: "Pray for me." But the pilgrim's poverty is disarming; people would entrust their life to him. When the guest-pilgrim leaves the house, a "pray for us" accompanies him as an echo on his way out the door. He carries and is carried, he travels on as if inhabited. He discovers that true life is nothing other than being underway, letting go of many things, treating others with blessing and being blessed in return. Even though the pilgrim is alone, he or she lives henceforth connected with everybody. The old psalm of David becomes engrafted in his or her whole being:

> For the sake of my relatives and friends
> I will say, "Peace be within you."
> For the sake of the house of the LORD our God,
> I will seek your good. (Ps 122:8-9)

See also: Blessing, Hospitality, Intercessory Prayers, Peace, Psalmody, Quest, Walking

3. Pierre Barret and Noël Gurgand, *Priez pour nous à Compostelle* (Paris: Hachette, 1999).

POUSTINIA

Poustinia is the title of a book written in English by a Russian woman, Catherine de Hueck Doherty (1896–1985).[1] The word means "desert" but also refers to a practice of devout Russians that was familiar to Catherine when she still lived in Russia right before the revolution of 1917. In that sense, *poustinia* basically means a wooden cabin furnished with nothing but a table, a chair, a couch, a bible, an icon, a jar of water, and a piece of bread. The cabin is built at a certain distance from the village, in the midst of the forest. Lay people—*poustiniks*—go there on retreat for twenty-four hours or for a couple of days. The true menu offered by this cabin in the "desert": silence, solitude, Bible reading, and worldwide intercession.

Catherine fled Russia in the aftermath of the revolution and after much wandering settled down in Canada and the United States to give new form to this spiritual practice. The book describes the practice and deals with the fruitfulness this God-centered solitude in a tiny, isolated place brought about in her and her co-workers. The whole work demonstrates her conviction that people nowadays need the "desert" (*poustinia*) more than anything else if they are to stay spiritually healthy. Did Blaise Pascal not write that all misery is due to the fact that we are no longer able to stay in our room in quiet isolation? In our day we witness a renewed demand for quiet cabins. But it still takes courage to turn one's back on "the village" and "the world" and to stick it out in relative solitude for twelve or twenty-four hours, by one's lonesome self, alone with the One.

We can pose the question to anybody who is looking for deeper meaning: do you have such a *poustinia* nearby, for three or six hours, for half a day, for a twenty-four hour period? Don't say too quickly, "I'll never find that! That is pure luxury!" Well, luxury it is, but of the humble kind, and whoever searches, finds! Talk it over with the superior of a quiet convent or monastery in the neighborhood where, perhaps on the second or third floor or in a deserted cabin at the rear of the garden, you may find exactly what you are looking for: a table,

1. Catherine Doherty, *Poustinia: Encountering God in Silence, Solitude, and Prayer* (Combermere, Ontario: Madonna House Publications, 1993).

a chair, a bed, an icon, a Bible. Anybody who really wants this can find it if asked for, but without adding anything to, or subtracting from, the formula.

Every convent in our region should be able to prepare one or two *poustinias* for lay people. There are still plenty of convents, and they have many empty rooms. A person who respects the formula of *poustinia* in its simple, uncomplicated way will surely find it, wherever he or she may live.

The oldest model of *poustinia* can be found in the Bible. A devout woman suggested to her husband to add an upstairs room to the house for when the man of God passes. "Look, I am sure that this man who regularly passes our way is a holy man of God. Let us make a small roof chamber with walls, and put there for him a bed, a table, a chair, and a lamp, so that he can stay there whenever he comes to us." And so, as told in 2 Kings 4, when Elisha passed through one day he was able to go to the upper room and take a rest. We see here how a devout woman organizes a room for a man of God, an early precursor for what would later become the life dedicated to the Holy. So maybe now the time may be ripe for service in the other direction by having religious orders prepare rooms for lay people who in their spiritual hunger long to catch their breath in the quiet of an upper room.

It takes a couple of seasons before the fruits of the *poustinia* are ready to be plucked. Any practice demands time and regularity. As the Japanese saying goes, "Any practice done with perseverance becomes a source of strength."

Losing in Order to Gain

Poustinia is a kind of Sabbath in a space rather than time. I know a father who once a week goes away to spend a day alone in silence. Social policy could encourage us to work part-time, when feasible, so as to share part of the total time devoted to work with those who are unemployed. If in any given company five people work one day less, a sixth person can be gainfully employed. Apparently, these social mechanisms actually exist. It is true that people earn a little less, but actually not that much less because governments subsidize these kinds of initiatives. And who says that we always must make as much as possible? Between less and enough lies an interesting margin. People embrace it because they realize the social benefit of enabling another to leave the unemployment line. At the same time they can immerse themselves in the great silence on a weekly basis. That something like this can constitute gain is a paradox understood by anybody who tries it.

Out of this kind of experience of silence arises another way of dealing with common work-related stress. Deep reflection, liberation from rut and routine, capacity for wonder and reverence, learning to keep a healthy distance, humor and freedom from addiction and from being caught in the daily grind: all these and much more will flourish when you learn to honor silence in your life. Whoever goes into the *poustinia* discovers step by step how to become engaged with universal values.

For Nothing

We must try to seek the deepest solitude, such as keeping an authentic fast, for no compensation or benefit at all. Initially, many practical concerns may motivate a practice. Yet it is proper to implement a spiritual practice like *poustinia* gratuitously from the start. I sit in silence for nothing, for nobody, only for Him. I fast not because of my weight, or my balance, or out of respect for a ritual. I fast for nothing, for nobody, I fast only for God. In this manner we get close to Jesus' sublime words of the Sermon on the Mount: Whenever you pray, whenever you fast, whenever you give alms, don't do it "before others in order to be seen by them." Do it "in secret" and "your Father who sees in secret will reward you." If you really want to pray, "go into your room and shut the door and pray to your Father who is in secret" (Matt 6:1-18). So Jesus apparently also knew about this practice with an inner room and a closed door! In the *poustinia* you learn to pull further and further away into your innermost sanctuary, there where consciousness of room or door has disappeared. There is only He, our Father who is and sees in secret.

What is *poustinia?* A silent desert in the heart, open to His actions, a Sabbath in the space in which the Lord of the house refreshes the soul and stirs it to new life with unspeakable words.

See also: Emptiness, Fasting, Gratuitous, Paradox, Sabbath, Sunday, Silence, Unapparent Virtue, *Wu Wei*

PRAISE, TO PRAISE

Alleluia! This well-known exclamation (*Hellelu-Yah*) is nothing but a passionate appeal to praise the Lord, put in the imperative form of the verb *hallel*, which means to praise, followed by the abbreviated Name *Yah* (instead of YHWH, the Lord). So the word Alleluia means: "Praise the LORD!" Many psalms begin or end with that call. In the book of Psalms, in addition to the great *hallel* of Psalm 136, we find two series of *hallel* psalms. The first one goes from Psalm 113 to 118; it is also called the Easter-*hallel*: these psalms are prayed serially at great feasts, especially at *Pesach* or Easter. At the end of the book of Psalms there is another such series of psalms, from 146 to 150, introduced by 145, the great psalm celebrating the kingdom of the Lord (its title is *tehillah*, or "song of praise"). So, as we can see from the literary structure of the book, psalmody leads to praise.

It is imperative to praise. To praise is part and parcel of the art of living for a person grounded in the Bible. We can never exaggerate in giving praise. We will always fall short; there is no reason for shame in this but, rather, a spur to praising all the more abundantly. The wise Jesus Sirach repeats more than once: give praise but know that your praise will always fall short. In Psalm 150 (in which "praise" appears thirteen times!) we read: to "praise him according to his surpassing greatness!"

That is the paradox: we try to give thanks and praise in a manner worthy of his "surpassing greatness." We will never succeed, but that is no reason for distress, for in the very act of trying we already feel nourished with happiness. While giving praise the heart feels larger, beats faster. A wholesome haste permeates our life. Benedict, at the end of his Rule's Prologue, sees the monks "race along the way of God's commandments," and their hearts "will swell with the unspeakable sweetness of love."

Throughout the Rule we get a taste for this strange hurry that typifies existence. The monk leads a life that is alert, detached, and free to follow another's commands, time and again. No hesitation, no dawdling, not in rising at night or in answering the guest knocking at the front door. Promptly, the guest hears from behind the door the sound of a *Deo gratias* (Thanks be to God!). Giving praise and thanks precludes every dejection or melancholy, every inclination to depressive thoughts. It appears that praising has a therapeutic effect. If we only knew it—we would certainly do it more often, and with conviction!

Giving praise comes out of the roots of our existence. The short Psalm 100 invites "all the earth" to give praise to God. Why? "Know that the LORD is God. It is he that made us, and we are his; we are his people, and the sheep of his pasture" (Ps 100:2-3). We did not create ourselves, we received life from his hand. The ground of our praying and praising is the sense that our existence is a present handed to us by the Other. In the last stanza of the same poem we read: "For the LORD is good; his steadfast love endures forever, and his faithfulness to all generations."

The root of our praise is that we have learned to know the Lord not only as our creator but also as our Shepherd, faithful and loving, who wants to share history with us. Our historic existence is rooted in his goodness, which lasts forever. To give praise is an existential act. The more tranquil we become and the deeper we push through to the wonder of our existence, the freer the song of praise will rise from our innermost being.

Augustine, who studied the psalms with uncommon passion and perseverance, and who animatedly explained them to his Christians, comes to the conclusion that in the psalms God readies praise for himself. The call to praise is not just a brotherly exhortation by the choir leader to the whole community, or an appeal by the angels in heaven for people also to sing the heavenly Alleluia on earth—we find this in the writings of the church fathers as well as in those of the Jewish exegetes.

Indeed, in the book of Revelation we see liturgies of praise flow from earth to heaven and vice versa. No, God prepares for himself a song of praise in the psalms. Here we recognize a deeper enigma that runs throughout our spiritual life which is that at the high point of almost every practice a mysterious reciprocity opens up, suddenly, unexpectedly, and undeservedly. Giving praise is a human act, embedded in an act of God. And even if our songs of praise are only fragmentary, by sharing in God's act, sooner or later God will bring our meager prayer to immortal conclusion. Who, then, would not give praise?

"Those who do not give praise here on earth shall be mute for eternity," wrote John of Ruusbroec. Our praise continues into the other world. Our songs of praise here are just preparatory to the jubilation without end in heavenly glory. The source of our praise is the discernment of God's unspeakable and immeasurable goodness. This realization can set our hearts aflame: words fail, and we jubilate for God, in God, and together with God. Only in the glorious hereafter shall we be able to bear and grasp the full extent of God's immensity. Then there will be laughter and joy. We sing this already in one or other psalm, as a foretaste: "When the LORD brought back the exiles" (Ps 126:1).

See also: Feasting, Gratitude, Heart, Jubilee, Lament, Psalmody, Reciprocity

PROFESSION OF FAITH

"You are the Messiah." "Truly this man was God's son." "Yes, Lord, I believe that you are the Messiah, the Son of God, the one coming into the world." These are classic professions of faith from the Gospels. Many psalm verses also contain short and powerful professions: "My help comes from the LORD, who made heaven and earth." "The LORD is my shepherd," is the opening phrase of Psalm 23. All that follows illustrates and confirms precisely that "You are with me . . . your rod and staff, they comfort me. . . . You prepare a table before me . . . my cup overflows." Every verb in this poem confirms my profession: He is indeed my shepherd, there is nothing I shall want!

Many antiphons in the liturgy constitute pure professions of faith, often borrowed from a psalm. "You have forgiven the guilt of my sin." "You have lifted up my soul from the grave." "You have known me." "You are my Father." Antiphons like these play in our head, live deep in our memory, and function like mantras: words that we repeat or almost unwillingly hear echoing at the bottom of our heart, even in the most unguarded moments of our daily routines. The reverse is also true: many of the mantras commonly recommended are in fact professions or short summaries of our faith. Just think of the Aramaic expression, preferred by John Main in his teachings on Christian meditation as *the* mantra *par excellence:* MARANATHA. "Come, Lord" is an entreaty, an appeal, but in reality also a profession of faith: "The Lord comes." He is coming. Yes, come, Lord Jesus, come!

The Creed or the great profession of faith that we recite or sing each Sunday after the Gospel reading and the homily is itself an extensive mantra. We benefit from saying it regularly: it is a prayer formula that serves to bring us home. Reciting this profession at the start of a meditation or a silent prayer, we free ourselves from the many cares with which we are unconsciously engaged. We empty ourselves of this plethora of minutiae and concentrate on the Three-in-One. We name the Father and Creator of all that exists, the Son as the revealing light personified, and the Spirit who in-dwells and hallows. The final phrases return us fully to the point where we stand, here and now in the Church, the forgiveness of sins, and the true life without end. Let the silent meditation begin.

To profess, whether or not we use standard formulations from the great tradition, is a very healthy exercise. With every profession I acknowledge Him for who He truly is. In so doing, a conscious relationship is created that unfailingly redounds to me. The greater the acknowledgment, the more humble is our sense of self. But underneath this correlation lies a paradox: the more humble we become, the greater our dignity. When I place myself under the gaze of God, the Creator, the Savior, He who completes all that exists, I recognize my smallness but realize at the same time that there is nothing I need to fear: I can only fall into his hand, a hand that carries everything and brings it to completion. I grow in faith and gratitude.

Paul states in one of his letters, "No one can say 'Jesus is Lord' except by the Holy Spirit" (1 Cor 12:3). This is an inspired insight and profession. We grow in our recognition of God to the extent that we give God's Spirit more room and freedom to act in us, and vice versa.

When Peter, in the heart of the Gospel according to Matthew, solemnly acknowledges Jesus with the words "You are the Messiah, the Son of the living God" (Matt 16:16), Jesus reacts with a double clarification. On the one hand, he points out to Peter that such an important recognition is not revealed "by flesh and blood." Such an insight can only be made known by "my Father in heaven." On the other hand, Jesus recognizes in analogous manner that Peter is the Rock "on which I will build my church" (Matt 16:17-18). Here we see with abundant clarity how one's profession of the other redounds to the subject who professes.

People who are inclined to narcissism cannot make a sincere profession. Similarly, those who remain stuck in a jealous comparison with others have great difficulty in recognizing and professing the greatness or the beauty of another person, let alone of God. Is it not true that the more qualities we are able to discern in another person, honestly and without jealousy, the greater we ourselves become and the wider our inner spaces continue to expand?

This kind of practice of professing our faith is the way of the "poor and humble," the *anawim* of the Bible, the way of Mary and her son Jesus. From them we learn to direct high, free, even sublime professions to Him who is everything to us. The rest is no longer a concern. "Cast your burden on the Lord, and he will sustain you" (Ps 55:22;

cf. 1 Pet 5:7). This is the grand about-turn that we may experience when we profess our faith. Slowly but surely.

See also: Adoration, Ejaculatory Prayers, Fear of the Lord, Gratitude, Mary, Poverty, Reciprocity, Spirit

PSALMODY

For centuries praying the psalms has been the great medium for people who want to live in close relationship with God.[1] Jewish scholars as well as devout "poor and humble servants of the Lord" (as they called themselves) have bundled the 150 psalms into a book of five parts.

In order to make this book into a lung of your life, quite a bit of work is necessary. The grand tradition prefers that the psalms be memorized and be prayed more from memory than from a written book. The book only serves as a support for the eyes and mind, but we really pray the psalms "by heart." If you want to do it well, the following five steps may be helpful.

1) Pick one translation and stick with it.

2) Commit about ten psalms to memory. We propose numbers 1, 4, 51, 62, 63, 67, 91, 113, 131, and 134. To learn them by heart is less difficult than you may think. Repeating them aloud several times a day is the start. If you learn a text in the morning, it will nourish you throughout the day. If you have copied a psalm, it is always within reach whenever memory fails. If you pray the same psalms every night, you will discover after a few weeks that you will effortlessly supply the words that follow upon what you started. By maintaining the order the whole series will be fixed in your memory. And as soon as the text is known by heart, it is available, consciously and unconsciously, in all circumstances.

3) Observe the tempo laid down by Benedict in his Rule: one psalm book a week. That means about twenty-five psalms a day, and usually that requires not much more than thirty minutes. Benedict, who lived in the sixth century, did not discover this tempo. It was already practiced by Pachomius in

1. More extensive treatments are provided in Fr. Standaert's books, *In de school van de Psalmen (In the School of the Psalms)* (Gent: Carmelitana, 1997), *Leven met de Psalmen (Living with the Psalms), Parts I* (Tielt: Lannoo, 2014), *II* (Tielt: Lannoo, 2014), and *III* (Tielt: Lannoo, 2016).

fourth-century Egypt (known then as "the angel's rule": twelve psalms in the morning and twelve in the evening, and doing this for seven days completes the psalter in a week).

It is still practiced in Jewish devotion to this day. A Jewish scheme, which we warmly recommend, goes like this: 1–29, 30–50, 51–72, 73–89, 90–106, 107–19, and 120–50. You can start on Sunday (first day of the week) or on Monday to end in celebration on Sunday with the final, jubilant series of 120–50.

Each day has its own atmosphere. Even if you cannot pray all of one series every day, your memory will know the menu for the day and the heart will know how to stay with the substance, with many words or only a few. The climate of every day is different and specific. The paradox is obvious: if you put in a bit of effort at the start you will see that ultimately the exercise will complete itself without effort, yes, almost spontaneously.

4) There are also psalms for certain occasions. For example, when you receive the news that somebody has passed away, it is a good time to focus with renewed concentration on the psalms. To pray the seven penitential psalms for the deceased, even in that person's name (the "I" of the psalm is then the person we commemorate), is a simple but very meaningful custom (Pss 6, 32, 38, 51, 102, 130, 143). In a way, these seven psalms constitute a little book within the larger whole. The same is true for the fifteen Psalms of Ascent (120–134) that we can pray in small groups of three during a midday pause; this takes less than fifteen minutes and refreshes the enthusiasm for the task at hand.

5) Once in a while, say on a Sunday, it is useful to read a commentary on a psalm. The associations lend breadth to the psalm and depth to the words that have become familiar. Sometimes you can simply lay two or three translations next to each other or read the references in the Bible's margins to see the psalm take on new life in a wider field of meaning. At the conclusion of such a study moment you may try to put to paper your own psalm prayer. Then you set out in your own words what God has revealed to you in the exercise and your own grateful response to Him.

Our life is destined to become a psalm, just as Mary's life became one great *Magnificat*. The movement that pervades the psalms is one of ascent: from lament to praise, from loneliness to community, from alienation and exile to the feast in the temple in Jerusalem. Those who continue to pray the psalms become poor, but in this poverty a worldwide engagement is revealed. The biblical "poor" intend what fundamentally connects all human beings and all peoples: to give concerted and humble praise to the one God of all.

Our psalmody is an ur-form, a sacrament, a life-changing practice that teaches our heart to think and feel like that of Jesus and God. Blessed are the persons who devote themselves wholeheartedly to this practice: they will be known and loved by God. The celebration has no end.

See also: *Anawim*, Feast, Gratitude, Jesus and the Jesus Prayer, Jubilee, Lament, Meditation, Name, Praise

Q

QUEST

Q for quest. No matter how, we find ourselves on a search, on a quest. In our earthly existence we continue to be pilgrims. A "vision of peace"—which is a possible etymology for "Jerusalem"—directs our steps. "Forgetting what lies behind and straining forward to what lies ahead," wrote Paul, "I press on toward the goal for the prize of the heavenly call of God in Christ Jesus" (Phil 3:12).

The concept of a quest means we are seekers who accept that we are after something that we still do not know and that, perhaps, is beyond our reach. In the Middle Ages the great quest was for the Grail: a chalice that once contained the blood that had flowed from Jesus' crucified body on Golgotha or the beaker he had used during the Last Supper. It is a symbolic search for that which is most precious and which lies at the origin of all that is holy in a given tradition.

Never give up searching. As the saying goes, "who searches, finds." The searcher will discover that she herself is being sought and found by an Other. According to the words of Christ to Blaise Pascal, "You would not look for me if you had not found me" (*Tu ne me chercherais pas si tu ne m'avais trouvé*), which also makes us think of the variant proposed by Jean Guitton: "You would not look for me if I had not found you" (*Tu ne me chercherais pas si je ne t'avais trouvé*).

"Our hearts find no peace until they rest in you," says Augustine at the beginning of his autobiographical work *Confessions*.[1] At the close of his greatest treatise on the Trinity, he prayed, "Grant that searching I may find you and that, when I have found you, I will continue to look for you."

The Bible contains a book that elaborates the quest: does the Song of Solomon not give dramatic and lyrical form to the deepest of all human quests? Immersion in that poetry frees our longing and pulls it along in a lasting quest until, freely, it can say to the Other: "Haste away my beloved, and be like a gazelle or a young stag upon the mountain of spices!" (Song 8:14).

See also: Peace, Pilgrimage, You as "You"

1. Saint Augustine, *Confessions*, trans. R. S. Pine-Coffin (Middlesex, England: Penguin, 1961, 1981), 21.

R

RECIPROCITY

The eye with which I see God is the same as the eye with which he sees me.
—Meister Eckhart

For the Lord *is righteous;*
he loves righteous deeds;
the upright shall behold his face. (Ps 11:7)

When you give alms, do it as if you received them yourself.
—Anonymous saying of the Desert Fathers (fifth century)

Reciprocity is a key. Where there is reciprocity, there is the Spirit. "Let him kiss me with the kisses of his mouth" (Song 1:2). Reciprocity is a requirement for the best kind of friendship, as well as for every spiritually driven life. At the apex of the ladder of spiritual experience there is no longer a distinction between seeing and being seen, knowing and being known, loving and being loved. Separating the active and the passive forms of the experience has become impossible.

We must continually strive to achieve these forms of reciprocity and to die to an existence of smug or one-sided knowing, possessing, controlling, or coveting. The desire for reciprocity is a vulnerable desire. It not only wants to know or to possess but at the same time it wants to be known, to be possessed. It does not grasp at the handshake but passionately extends the hand, open and totally giving. Every aspect of desire becomes an offering, the self becomes priest, altar, and gift.

"No one knows the Son except the Father, and no one knows the Father except the Son" (Matt 11:27). That knowledge is reciprocal and exclusive. The metaphor of "father" and "son" must give a little because, of course, in real-world relationships such a complete reciprocity between fathers and sons does not exist. But as God knows me, nobody knows me. This is true for Jesus and for everybody. But Jesus makes clear that God invites us to a reciprocal knowledge. God, vulnerable, opens himself up and allows himself to be known. This is nothing but an extreme and fully transparent, reciprocal knowing that goes hand in hand with the active presence of the Holy Spirit. We can never exhaust the contemplation of this mystery.

In the Old Testament, the teachings about wisdom, among others, show the way to this understanding. At first, wisdom is considered a quality to be striven for, a virtue to be pursued. But step-by-step we discover more: wisdom is Somebody, an instance in my own subjectivity. I sought for her as object and discovered that she is Subject, an alter ego within me, perhaps more even than my own subjectivity. Wonder of wonders. I am inhabited. We live inside each other, reciprocally, the Lord and I, in accordance with this surprising, yet solid pattern of Johannine mysticism. "Abide in me as I abide in you" (John 15:4).

Blessed is the person who in his or her spiritual journey has gained insight into this key necessity for reciprocity. At the top of the mountain there is an inexhaustible source, for reciprocity is never static. Life turns into bliss. We tumble from wonder to wonder. We die and are being born. The active movement within us ceases, and our passive self stands revealed like a jumping salmon defying the waterfall.

Paradoxically, as Ruusbroec frequently analyzed in his treatises, rest and work come down to the same thing. The Sabbath is the day of doing nothing, of keeping blissfully quiet, of pure wonderment at God's deed in which we stand and share. Because, as our theology teaches, God himself is reciprocity, and the revelation begins and ends there where He allows us reciprocally to share in his love for us. "Nobody knows the Father except the Son and anyone to whom the Son chooses to reveal him" (Matt 11:27).

Philosophers of friendship (starting with Plato, Aristotle, and the Pythagorean tradition) perceived some idea of this mystery. In the most perfect forms of friendship there is perfect reciprocity. We are not talking here of the temporary grouping of a clique or of plots, possibly even evil ones, that are sworn to under oath, but of the supreme demand to practice virtue together, in complete transparency and mutual knowledge. Any other reciprocity is not worthy of the name.

See also: Forgiveness, Friendship, Sabbath, Salmon or Mocking Gravity, Vulnerability, Wisdom

RESURRECTION

A spirituality of the Resurrection is based on the firm foundation of the apostles' testimonies of faith. They gave witness to what God had imparted to them. Their speech was rooted in God's word. And that word is always a transforming act. God taught them that Jesus, no matter how rejected, or that he was killed by people of his time, now *lives.* This sacrificed life is fully confirmed and ratified by God. Death does not have the last word on this existence. God himself taught the apostles this, and they became its fearless and joyous exponents.

Now what God signifies here in a powerful self-revelation, he did not just once, in passing, at *one* moment in history. Just as he fully revealed himself then, we may be confident that he is always doing.

This leads us to the following deep conviction and key insight: Wherever God is, there is a raising up and, in reverse, wherever we see any form of raising up and resurrection, we see something of God come into light. Just as Augustine had a fascination with the mystery of the Trinity and accordingly identified a trace of God wherever he found something tripartite under the sun, so let us track the God of the resurrection. Let's take a threefold path and figure out how the God of the resurrection gives us unmistakable signs in nature, in our human world, and in the symbolic world of liturgical ritual.

God in Nature

When the soul is listening
the cosmos speaks a tongue that lives;
it's a sing-song whispering
that sign and language is. (Guido Gezelle)

Do we still have the capacity for wonder? A worm becomes a beetle, a caterpillar spins itself into a cocoon and comes out a butterfly: what does all this tell us? Do we even get an inkling of the secret of the hibernation of so many mammals? Nothing that seems "natural" turns out, on closer inspection, to be self-evident. Cardinal Newman experienced every springtime as a miracle, a language through which God expresses his plentitude. On another occasion he asked his listeners to receive the great joy of Easter "like children who say to themselves: 'This is Spring!' or 'This is the sea!' " Admiration and wonder, in one breath. The authenticity of a child's heart!

In like manner, our simple rising in the morning may occasion a surprise in us. Rabbi Hirsh used to say to his disciples: "When a man awakens in the morning and realizes that God gave him back his soul and that he is a new creation, he should break out in song and praise God!"

Every morning is a miracle. It is striking how the Christian tradition so often uses the image of the rising sun when talking about the resurrection. We find this comparison already in Mark, the oldest of the Gospels (see 16:2: "when the sun had risen"). This is not just about an image. A language resounds in nature through which God expresses something from his heart. As told by Boris Pasternak, "The vegetable kingdom can easily be thought of as the nearest neighbor of the kingdom of death. Perhaps the mysteries of evolution and the riddles of life that so puzzle us are contained in the green of the earth, among the trees and the flowers of graveyards. Mary Magdalene did not recognize Jesus risen from the grave, 'supposing Him to be the gardener.' "[1]

A person who marveled quite a bit about this was Clement of Rome (first century). His long exposition about the resurrection starts with marveling at daily phenomena in nature. In them

> the Lord continually proves to us that there shall be a future resurrection, of which He has rendered the Lord Jesus Christ the first-fruits by raising Him from the dead. Let us contemplate, beloved, the resurrection which is at all times taking place. Day and night declare to us a resurrection. The night sinks to sleep, and the day arises; the day [again] departs, and the night comes on. Let us behold the fruits [of the earth], how the sowing of grain takes place. The sower goes forth, and casts it into the ground; and the seed being thus scattered, though dry and naked when it fell upon the earth, is gradually dissolved. Then out of its dissolution the mighty power of the providence of the Lord raises it up again, and from one seed many arise and bring forth fruit.[2]

1. Boris Pasternak, *Dr. Zhivago*, trans. Max Hayward and Manya Harari (New York: Pantheon, 1958), 493 [translator's note].

2. The First Epistle of Clement to the Corinthians, chap. XXIV, available at www.ewtn.com/library/patristc/anf1-1.htm (accessed November 11, 2016) [translator's note].

We recognize the territory because the parables of Jesus resound in Clement's examples. Jesus saw his own fate as this "grain of wheat [that unless it] falls into the earth and dies, [remains] just a single grain; but if it dies, it bears much fruit" (John 12:24). Paul also uses the metaphor of the seed when he reflects expansively on the resurrection for the Corinthians: "What is sown is perishable, what is raised is imperishable. . . . It is sown in weakness, it is raised in power" (1 Cor 15:42-43). This is the way God acts, in nature and in what we have to expect after our death. "God gives [the seed] a body as he has chosen, and to each kind of seed its own body" (1 Cor 15:38).

Let us pay attention and observe carefully how the most natural processes carry a message and refer to that mysterious abundance in which God reveals himself.

In Our Human World

Human beings are of a piece with nature. We also grow and blossom only to wither sooner or later. "As for mortals, their days are like grass," muses the psalmist, "they flourish like a flower of the field; for the wind passes over it, and it is gone" (Ps 103:15-16).[3] Also the so-called natural processes contain wonders. That a wound completely heals, that a fever leaves a person laid low by it for days, that a paralytic may be able to walk, read, and talk again, these are for me so many wonders.

Elderly people who are happy and radiate joy like daylight, despite their lesser or greater ills, are a pure gift, and we can only be moved in their presence. Some kind of "law of gravity" imposes itself on everything, yet to our surprise we find that here and there charm and grace escape that force, and that something gratuitous is possible under the sun. Here also, more is being said "when the soul is listening."

In our human world there are also particular forms of "death" and "life." We can kill somebody with our silence, with our neglect. Without lifting a hand we can destroy and rip people apart. *Homo homini lupus* (one person can be a wolf to the other) with hatred,

3. Cf. Isa 40:6-8, quoted in the Easter text, 1 Peter 1:24-25 and James 1:10-11. Apparently the early Christians were fascinated by the rich contrast of this text, which pits what is transitory against the enduring word of God, identified with the good news of the resurrection.

division, alienation, marginalization, etc. If we keep in mind the history of torture (which is still practiced in more than ninety countries today) we must recognize that there are no limits to the violence one human being can commit against another. We never see such horrible violence in the animal world. These days we use more technical language to describe it like "crimes against humanity," or "genocide," or "genocidal acts," or "ethnic cleansing."

Faith in the resurrection has everything to do with the abyss of evil. We can never adequately fathom that abyss, never fully describe evil. We fall short. But faith in the resurrection arises from the clear consciousness that good is stronger than violence, that unjustifiable evil, no matter how painful the experience, does not have the last word. Confronted with such senseless absurdity, over the course of history others have shown a different kind of human sense.

Perhaps the greatest enigma is how people come to such faith. But there are people who live that way, who demonstrate daily that love accomplishes more than death in all its forms. The greatest miracle under the sun is precisely that the freely given exists, that there is love that makes whole and that embraces what has been lost, that chooses what had been rejected, that forgives what had been found guilty beyond appeal, that unites what had seemingly been torn apart forever.

"We know that we have passed from death to life because we love one another" (1 John 3:14). Here love itself is resurrection, and resurrection is in the first place an act of love. "But we had to celebrate and rejoice, because this brother of yours was dead and has come to life; he was lost and has been found" (Luke 15:32). A godlike necessity comes through in the father's appeal to his oldest son. The reconciliation is expressed in terms of life and death.

There is no greater celebration among people than at the defeat of human evil; there is no more godlike moment here on earth than such a celebration of reconciliation. Accordingly, Luke the evangelist does not distinguish between the announcement of the resurrection and the announcement of the forgiveness of sins. For him the apostles are witnesses "that the Messiah is to suffer and to rise from the dead on the third day, and that repentance and *forgiveness of sins* is to be proclaimed in his name to all nations, beginning from Jerusalem" (Luke 24:46-48, emphasis added). Jesus' rising signifies that the world is reconciled in his Name. As the Messiah's suffering and death are announced, so also the good news is loudly proclaimed.

Whenever we are privileged to witness such a pivot, whether big or small—I am thinking of the joy of a Chilean priest upon the restoration of democracy in his country, or at the shared joy of African priests here in our abbey at the release of Nelson Mandela—the light of the Resurrection breaks through in our human history with renewed vigor.

Whenever we strive to bring a little more peace through justice here on earth and, in whatever form, change sadness into happiness, heal broken hearts, or assist the sick and the weak, we arrive directly at God, the God of the resurrection, and we are justified in believing that his Kingdom is at hand. This also means that we can only understand the full meaning of our faith in the Resurrection through acts of love, acts that are even capable of embracing extreme senselessness. As Saint Teresa of Calcutta said,

> When you go and visit the sick, you will encounter all sorts of misery. It may happen that you find a small child cradling the head of her dead mother. That is the moment when you must muster all your strength to console this child in her loss. We once found two babies next to the body of their father, who had died two days before. . . . God asks that we dedicate ourselves to take such suffering upon us . . . in order to prove that Christ is God.

Loving to the extreme reflects our belief in Christ, the Risen One, the Son of God made true. Because God is himself the love that is resurrection.

In the Symbolic World of Liturgical Ritual

Resurrection is celebrated. This happens most tellingly at Easter. Already in baptism we went through the process of resurrection from death to life, as Paul forcefully expressed: "For if we have died with Christ, we believe that we will also live with him" (Rom 6:8). Also, traditionally every Sunday is a remembrance of Christ's rising from the dead. Indeed, the first day of the week—"The day that the Lord has made" (Ps 118:24)—is "the day on which God created light and on which he raised our Savior from the dead" (Saint Justin, second century).

The celebration of the liturgy ties all the foregoing together: nature is recalled with inexhaustible symbols, and the whole human experience with its deepest longings for peace and happiness is included. Water, bread and wine, ashes, oil, fruits of the harvest, night and daybreak, light and dark, the dead wood of the cross and the tree of life, "everything speaks of Him." According to custom in parts of the East, every person who comes to revere the Cross on Good Friday receives a flower representing new life springing from old wood.

The Easter liturgy looks much like a play, a grand play where creation and human history, nature and culture, are placed into God's hands as one big offering. By playing that game, by as it were crawling into the received text and making every gesture our own, we ourselves become the words and deeds that we interpret, and we die to ourselves to be reborn in God's own world. In this way we anticipate the end and completion of time. The promise begins to be realized, the new and eternal life breaks through into our time, for a moment, completely here and now.

It happens when we really get into it, when we truly celebrate "with our whole heart, our whole soul, and all our strength." You could say that in the Easter liturgy we are twice invited to go the extreme and to push through to such "dying" and "rising." Because everything is focused on being crucified and buried with Christ in order to be raised with Him. Undeniably, this requires a way of celebrating that is quite literal, which can be difficult for us.

> A rabbi, whose grandfather had been a disciple of the Baal Shem, was asked to tell a story. "A story," he said, "must be told in such a way that it constitutes help in itself." And he told: "My grandfather was lame. Once they asked him to tell a story about his teacher. And he related how the holy Baal Shem used to hop and dance while he prayed. My grandfather rose as he spoke, and he was so swept away by his story that he himself began to hop and dance to show how the master had done. From that hour on he was cured of his lameness. That's the way to tell a story!"[4]

4. Martin Buber, *Tales of the Hasidim,* trans. Olga Marx (New York: Schocken Books, 1991), xvii–xviii.

Here we see literalness suddenly budding into new and restored life. That's the way to celebrate the liturgy! Each year adds a ring to the trunk of the tree; each year we become more rooted in God's own mystery, which is a resurrection mystery, an act of love "stronger than death."

Liturgy remains a surprising affair. Whoever sticks narrowly to the rules discovers in the end that he has to make up the real thing himself, but with only one rule, which is the rule of the gratuitous, the absence of all rules. Then the liturgy can again become God's play, a story in which the devout believer stays bonded with God in complete surrender, in a love till death.

The meaning of the Easter celebration consists in the personal experience of the story, in which the impossible turns out to be possible because it is God's story. At least, that is the objective, that it becomes for each one of us "flesh of our flesh" and "blood of our blood." Then we do not even have to talk about it anymore among ourselves because the lived experience is the only story.

> "The days are surely coming, says the LORD," so prophesied Jeremiah at the high point of all his visions of consolation, "when I will make a new covenant with the house of Israel and the house of Judah. . . . I will put my law within them, and I will write it on their hearts; and I will be their God, and they shall be my people. No longer shall they teach one another, or say to each other, 'Know the LORD,' for they shall all know me, from the least of them to the greatest, says the LORD; for I will forgive their iniquity, and remember their sin no more." (Jer 31:31-34)

See also: Feast, Forgiveness, God, Peace, Spirit

RETREAT

In the Catholic world, many priests, religious, and some lay people are in the custom of going off to an abbey once a year for at least five days for what is called a retreat. Some Protestants are rediscovering the formula. The women's community of Grandchamp near Neuchâtel in Switzerland, which is often regarded as the female counterpart to the brothers of Taizé, was born out of an initiative to organize retreats for lay people. Something similar has been put together in the last twenty-five years or so for Anglican clergy.

The schedule is quite intense: in addition to seeking seclusion, one studies the Scriptures, prays the psalms, practices silent meditation and adoration, and perhaps prays the rosary or the Jesus Prayer. Certain people may choose to get up during the night and keep a vigil, others may fast for a day. So, we are dealing here with one of the most concentrated forms of all the practices we have discussed so far. Frequently monks consider their whole life as a retreat.

Going on retreat has to do with coming clean with yourself. "When you come to the desert," taught a Desert Father, "you are like a glass of water into which sand was poured. As long as you stayed in the world, you continued stirring that glass. Now, in the desert, it is important not to disturb that water. What was an opaque brown liquid slowly becomes clear. The light can again shine through it from all sides, and at the bottom of the glass you begin to distinguish the individual grains of sand ever more clearly. They are your sins." Self-knowledge in the bright light of God's word is one of the most important fruits of a retreat.

Retreats can take many forms. Timewise, they can take up to thirty days. Saint Ignatius of Loyola devised a complete manual on how to spend such a long period. After him, the Jesuits also came up with a more concentrated form of eight days. The process is the same, albeit in a shorter timeframe. Those who are unable to live in seclusion for thirty days can do it at home, spread out over several months and with personal spiritual direction.

Every retreat contains the dynamic of our baptism: dying with Christ in order to be raised up with Christ and to live only in communion with God (see Rom 6:1-14). Thus, such a week generally shows many similarities with Holy Week, which is in fact a Christian's quintessential retreat within the whole liturgical year. In the readings of Holy Week we always cover the four songs of the Suffering Servant from Isaiah: the course of these four hymns relates as much to Jesus' journey as to the road traveled during a full-fledged retreat. Other than the Gospels themselves, one cannot think of a better menu than these four strong passages from Isaiah (see Isa 42; 49; 50; 52–53).

Every retreat begins with a regression: abandoning all forms of media, living simply, in a small space, with little or no possibility of distraction. It is important to be consistent; if not, you will flee from the retreat in a hurry. Phone, newspapers, radio, TV, email, text messages—free yourself from this spider's web of relationships. Breaking these habits may initially cause a certain disquiet or even pain, but the fruits will be all the greater for it.

Toward the end of the retreat it may be beneficial to plan for a gradual transition back to normal life. Some specific practices of the retreat can perhaps be maintained for a while so as to allow a step-by-step return to the old ways of acting. The masters from ancient traditions in Africa and Australia warn us that when people leave the cell of the initiation rite too fast their fervor can end up causing havoc in the community. A retreat has traits that are similar to an initiation, and it takes time to re-enter regular life.

In every retreat you learn to redefine your life's choice from the deepest root of your freedom. Usually a retreat ends with a new resolution, a clearly formulated engagement, expressed in the form of a prayer. Let us hope that we may freely live our calling and our mission in unconditional surrender.

See also: Fasting, Emptiness, *Lectio Divina*, Night Vigil, *Poustinia*, Sabbath

RITUALS

Il faut des rites (We need rituals).

—Antoine de Saint-Exupéry, *Le Petit Prince*

Rituals or rites are a *must*. It is the fox who teaches the Little Prince this lesson. If you want to approach and tame the other in suitable manner, meaning to create ties with the other, you have to prepare your heart. And that is done through rituals.

How can we continually give depth to life through the use of rituals? It requires a rediscovery. Anselm Grün shows in one of his books how creative we can be in expanding our rituals.[1] Life is full of transitions, we constantly turn a page and step into a new phase. The child starts middle school: how can you recognize the day with appropriate solemnity? A school year ends: how can you reflect this symbolically and handle it together with a proper ritual? Somebody comes home after a long stay at the hospital: how can you suitably enrich this homecoming, taking into account the taste and preferences of the person in question? Simple things sometimes are best for assuring a genial reception.

We should also be able quietly to pay attention to small, mindful rituals in our ordinary, daily life. Tucking a child into bed and entrusting it to the loneliness of night does not happen without an elementary ritual. From this we can learn how ritual can also give form to other ways of parting and confiding another to the unknown, like giving a kiss, reading a poem or a story, drawing a small cross on the forehead, or leaving a nightlight on. These are all symbols of closeness at the moment of distancing ourselves from the other.

How can Sunday have lasting significance if we do not interiorize its weekly presence with concrete rituals even in our living spaces? A white tablecloth for breakfast, a burning candle, a flower in a vase, freshly baked bread: not much more is needed to give each other the clear sense that today is Sunday, the day of the Lord, risen to life!

1. In Dutch translation: *Veilige Schuilplaats* (Tielt: Lannoo, 1997). The book does not appear to have been published in English. It is available in Spanish under the title *50 rituales para la vida* [translator's note].

The person who lives alone does not need rituals any less in order to live an alert and beautiful life. Picking a flower in the morning and putting it in a vase before the icon of the Blessed Mother, lighting a candle and an incense stick before the start of your Bible reading, listening to a particular piece of music during dinner on the anniversary of a relative's passing: there are so many modest rituals that can turn the outward life inward and transform it into a quiet and humble celebration every day.

Rituals can also be shaped by *not* doing certain things. From Jewish practice I learned to turn off the computer every Saturday after vespers until Sunday evening. To engage in business-like things on that day harms the special atmosphere that we wish to create. Abandoning some habits makes time and space for other things: reading, walking, visiting a person who is lonely, or enjoying someone's company. Because of Sunday's festive character, children can dress up in extra nice clothes and pick their outfits already the night before. Because it is a feast! And a feast requires rituals to break through the ordinary. Without a doubt, the heart needs the intermediation of the body and external accoutrements if it is to partake in the jubilation.

Who would deny that the quality of life in a school or organization instantly improves when somebody enriches it with symbols and rituals? Gratitude will fill people's hearts. In some sense we all share responsibility for this mindful shaping of life through rituals grand or small. The Church with its seven sacraments and its many liturgies (prayer vigil for the deceased, celebrations at pilgrimage sites, etc.) is masterful in dealing with rituals. Who is not grateful that we still have the Church for the performance of the last rites after the death of a loved one and thus ensuring a dignified farewell?

See also: Feasting, Heart, Jubilation, Mindfulness, Mourning, Sabbath, Sacrament, Visiting

S

SABBATH

The Sabbath is Jewish tradition's greatest gift to the world. By the institution of the Sabbath as an obligatory day of rest the world was given an opportunity to catch its breath, to reflect, and to appreciate anew the dignity of human life. Woe to the civilization that abolishes a structured Sabbath: nothing less than the destruction of the soul would be involved (according to Romano Guardini in a famous 1925 essay). The Sabbath gives us free time to rediscover and to celebrate our deepest identity. And vice versa, the person who honors the Sabbath receives a "supplement of soul" (*supplément d'âme*), as the Jewish thinker André Neher (d. 1988) put it.

The destruction of the second temple and the Diaspora occurring from 70 to 135 CE, led the Jewish people to attribute ever greater value to the Sabbath as a "temple in time." Consequently, Jews consider themselves to be "builders of time," in Abraham J. Heschel's felicitous phrase. The Sabbath is considered the greatest feast of the Jewish calendar. So, for example, one is allowed work on certain feast days, but on the Sabbath it is ruled out.

If we open the Bible we realize from page one how essential the Sabbath is. All of creation is accomplished within the time structure of a full week. On the last day, which is actually the first day for the newly created human being, God himself keeps Sabbath. What does He do on that day? We see in the texts that He is the subject of four verbs: God finished up the work he had done in the previous six days, he blessed and hallowed the seventh day, and then he kept the Sabbath.

This last term ("kept the Sabbath") is usually translated by an expression to the effect that God "rested," but in Hebrew "to rest" is another verb (*nuah*—see the name of the patriarch Noah). French translations of the Bible prefer the verb *chômer*, which means "to cease work" or "to abstain from work."

The law of Moses explains also that especially slave labor is prohibited on that day, even the animals are not allowed to work. In the second book of Moses, the Book of Exodus, we hear a fifth action (and a fifth verb) done by God: he "refreshes himself," "he takes a breath" (Exod 31:17). People and animals should also be refreshed on that day

(Exod 23:12). From this tradition comes the thought that we receive a "supplement of soul" when we hallow the Sabbath.

So on that holy day a special activity occurs, for God as well as for people. Thanks to a break from workday activities we can now focus on rediscovering the great acts of "blessing," "hallowing," "finishing," "resting," and "being refreshed," and give them ample space on that particular day.

Certain things are never done on the Sabbath, while other activities are preferably done on a Sabbath day. The Sabbath is a great day to study the Torah. The Sabbath is a great day to take a leisurely bath, to rest, to dress up, to go on a walk, to converse with children and friends, to sing psalms at home or in the synagogue. Certain pieces of equipment are not used on the Sabbath, and handling money is avoided.

These concrete points of heightened attention create a new space of freedom. We can become addicted to our computer, emails, and so many other gadgets and possessions, no matter how neutral or positive they may be. Putting a complete stop to their use for one day in the week allows you the opportunity to discover who you are and what you want. Cut down on certain habits and right away you discover new possibilities for other relationships that are often more immediate and not any less essential. It is certainly worth a try!

Jews already start celebrating the Sabbath on Friday evening. There is no problem at all with that, or in extending the Sabbath to late evening or the night of Saturday. The Sabbath belongs to the Lord, says the Bible (see Matt 12:8), and you don't want to shortchange him. So by all means, exaggerate in keeping the Sabbath, and do it for Him. A "normal" Sabbath always lasts longer than precisely twenty-four hours.

At the end of the Sabbath a liturgical ceremony takes place that is called *havdalah,* divorce, yes the same word as for a civil divorce! Because to celebrate the Sabbath is to receive a queen and to enter into matrimony with her. So the Sabbath is received in the home on Friday evening as a bride! People sing, *Lekha dodi, liqrah kala!* (Come, my dearest, welcome, my beloved). Every Jew has two wives: the human one and the Sabbath! The divorce, the *havdalah,* takes place late Saturday evening. Friday evening, however, is always a feast, even with an erotic touch. On that evening spouses are particularly affectionate with each other. It is said that in devout circles children are conceived during the night of Friday to Saturday.

People live from Sabbath to Sabbath. So as not to forget the good odor of the Sabbath during the work week, at the end of the *havdalah* liturgy an aromatic herb is distributed to the participants. Our nose has an excellent memory, some say it may even have the best memory of our whole constitution. So inhale the aroma real well, and remember the Sabbath, until it shows up again, next Friday!

The Sabbath is commenced by the mother, the wife. She lights two candles and thanks God, the Creator of light, who gave his people the command of the Sabbath. All the while she recites a specific blessing. Only she is allowed to do it. The week, time, and life are defined by precisely this opening gesture, performed by the wife. Thus every Jew knows who he is: his identity is conveyed through the ritual, performed by the mother of the household.

In Leviticus we read, "You shall each revere your mother and father, and you shall keep my Sabbaths" (Lev 19:3). Why first the mother and then the father? And why *revere* the mother and not just *love* her? Obviously, different answers are possible. To honor one's father was a given because he had traditional authority, but the mother? You must not only love your mother, you must also revere her. The fact that this command is followed immediately by the instruction to keep the Sabbath may have to do with the aforesaid: it is the mother who teaches you to keep the Sabbath. So if you revere your mother, you will keep the Sabbath. If you keep the Sabbath, you will live your life within a certain structure and you will keep the bond with the living God. "You shall be holy, for I the Lord your God am holy"—the verse that immediately precedes "revere your mother"!

"What would a world without Sabbath be?" wonders Abraham J. Heschel. "It would be a world that only knows itself, with a god who has degenerated into an object; a world cut off from God by an abyss impossible to bridge. A world without Sabbath would not know that eternity has a window that is opened to time."[1] "It would be horrible if Sunday ceased to exist," wrote Romano Guardini, for "without Sunday the soul is destroyed."

Let us listen to the Jewish thinker Abraham Joshua Heschel for a moment, for with the Sabbath we stand before something of tremen-

1. Abraham Joshua Heschel, *Les bâtisseurs du temps* (Paris, 1957), 116.

dous philosophical and religious importance. We may well conquer all of space, but what good does it do if we do not hallow time?

> We cannot solve the problem of time through the conquest of space, through either pyramids or fame. We can only solve the problem of time through sanctification of time. To men alone time is elusive; to men with God time is eternity in disguise. . . . We must conquer space in order to sanctify time. All week long we are called upon to sanctify life through employing things of space. On the Sabbath it is given us to share in the holiness that is the heart of time. Even when the soul is seared, even when no prayer can come out of tightened throats, the clean, silent rest of the Sabbath leads us to a realm of endless peace, or the beginning of an awareness of what eternity means. There are few ideas in the world of thought which contain so much spiritual power as the idea of the Sabbath. Eons hence, when of many of our cherished theories only shreds will remain, that cosmic tapestry will continue to shine. Eternity utters a day.[2]

See also: Emptiness, Feasting, *Poustinia*, Rituals, Sunday, Time and the Experience of Time, *Wu Wei*

2. Abraham Joshua Heschel, *The Sabbath: Its Meaning for Modern Man* (New York: Farrar, Strauss and Giroux, 2005), 101.

SACRAMENT

Everything is sacrament because "sacrament" is nothing but a practice in which God and human being encounter each other. Even "empty space" is a possible location and suitable place for this encounter.

During the Easter Vigil, the deacon sings in the *Exsultet* (the hymn to the Easter candle), "O truly blessed night when things of heaven are wed to those of earth and divine to the human." This night is sacrament.

If you follow your breath in silence, realize how you transition from exhaling to inhaling. It is pure gift, and focusing on it you pierce through to the sacramental moment of your innermost existence: everything is grace, a favor from God.

If you move your pinkie with mindfulness and wonder and realize how free you are in life you are touching one of the roots of sacramental life: that freedom is given to us, and the Giver lives inside the gift.

Sacraments are practices that work a transformation. So you may consider this whole book a treatise on sacraments. Transformation is a process. The goal is nothing less than sharing in the freedom of the Son, a playful dance in the glory of being children of God.

Ever since the Middle Ages the Latin Church has spoken of seven sacraments: seven here denotes completeness. These are seven selected forms than can accompany a person from birth till the portals of death. Even though they do not all have equal rank, they do have the same structure. In many manuals and catechisms we see how a central place is given to the Eucharist, the sacrament *par excellence.*

The church father Augustine (fourth century) recognized in principle only two sacraments: baptism and the Eucharist. On the basis of the latter, all of Christian life was thought to be one great sacrament. Immersed in the Christ of Easter through baptism, we live in Him, and our life is renewed with every celebration of the Eucharist.

Our whole existence must become one great thanksgiving, *eucharistia* in Greek. Theologians and poets like Olivier Clément and Patrice de la Tour du Pin write about "the eucharistic person" (*l'homme eucharistique*). That is the end goal of creation and the course of salvation. "Be *eucharistoi*," Paul says aptly in his letter to the Colossians (Col 3:15). Be "eucharistic." Be grateful. Be sacrament, in and through your whole being. "And whatever you do, in word or deed, do everything in the name of the Lord Jesus, giving thanks to God the Father through him" (Col 3:17).

In fact, there is only one ur-sacrament and that is the Word becoming flesh, Christ Jesus. His body, the Church, participates directly in this ur-sacrament. The Second Vatican Council called the Church itself "sacrament," a place of salvation "for the whole world." As soon as we understand the essence of sacramentality, many practices that we pursue with heart and soul acquire a special depth. Our art of living becomes spirituality in the fullest sense of the word: a place where God's Spirit blows and engenders new life, over and over again.

Blessed are they who lead their life in the brilliant consciousness that from now on everything offers an opportunity for encountering God and, thus, that everything becomes a potential sacrament.

See also: Breathing, Gratitude, Form and Formlessness, Spirit

SALMON, OR MOCKING GRAVITY

Salmon stand as a symbol for those who in our time want to live a truly spiritual life: swimming against the current or "mocking gravity," as the poetess says:

who by force of nature
must eleven rapids meet
and beat them with their tail
for, mocking gravity in the ascent,
the salmon must not fail. (Ida Gerhardt, from *Salmon*)

Here everything is grace and "force of nature." Happy are those who have felt the same impulse in their heart.

See also: Gratuitous

SERVING

I dreamt
that life was joy.
I awoke
and saw that life is service.
I served
and realized that service is joy. (Rabindranath Tagore)

Service belongs in the very center of an authentic art of living. According to the Rule of Benedict, reciprocal service is the hallmark of monastic life. "The brothers should serve one another" is the opening phrase of chapter 35. They should serve simply, consistently, and reciprocally.

In the Christian tradition, Jesus himself serves as the model. "I am among you as one who serves" (Luke 22:27) is Jesus' powerful expression of his fundamental attitude. In saying this, he supplies the answer to the question he had posed himself, "For who is greater: the one who is at the table or the one who serves?" (Luke 22:27). He, the master, tells the disciples he is firmly on the side of those who serve.

This is drawn out further in John's Gospel where Jesus gets up from the table, ties a towel around his waist, and washes the feet of his disciples, one after the other (see John 13:4-10). He performs the work of a servant, a slave. That's how low he goes, just to serve. After the long, practical catechesis in Mark in which a disciple is taught how to live his life, we hear Jesus say:

> You know that among the Gentiles those whom they recognize as their rulers lord it over them, and their great ones are tyrants over them. But it is not so among you; but whoever wishes to become great among you must be your servant, and whoever wishes to be first among you must be slave of all. For the Son of Man came not to be served but to serve, and to give his life as ransom for many. (Mark 10:42-45)

The Christian community must distinguish itself from the ways of the powerful and the peoples of this earth: the paradox is central to the group dynamic. The first one takes the place of the last, the leader serves.

With his philosophy of service Jesus recalls a long tradition that had left deep tracks in the Old Testament. To serve and to bear the sins of many are expressions borrowed from the fourth Suffering Servant Song in Isaiah. This unique figure, called "my servant" by the Lord himself, is typified by a strange paradox: he is at the same time strong and vulnerable. Fearlessly and uncompromisingly, he brings justice to the peoples with a mission that reaches well beyond the people of Israel.

At the same time, he has an eye for what is tender and injured: "a bruised reed he will not break, and a dimly burning wick he will not quench" (Isa 42:3). Nevertheless, he himself "will not grow faint or be crushed" (Isa 42: 4). He stands firm, triumphantly. Normally, when we allow ourselves to be vulnerable we lose our strength, and vice versa. This mature attitude appears to be the fruit of a life of much suffering.

The four songs of the Suffering Servant (Isa 42; 49; 50; 52-53) evoke, aside from Jeremiah, the figure of Moses, the man of God who is also repeatedly called "the servant of the Lord." In the final centuries before the Christian era a large group of devout people called themselves simply and proudly "the servants of the Lord." They sang it in jubilation, praised the Name, and experienced how their Lord and God looks down at the humble ones and poor folk in order to raise them up from the dust and to seat them with the potentates of his people (see Ps 113). His compassion is that large.

In his letters Paul calls himself not only "apostle" but also, and especially, "servant" and even "slave" of Jesus Christ. Looking up at Jesus, he recognizes his grandeur because Jesus agreed "to empty himself" and to take the form of a "slave" "to the point of death, even death on a cross" (Phil 2:7-8). From then on, Paul knows no other existence than life "in Christ." He wants nothing else but to share in mercy, tenderness, and compassion in Christ and to cultivate "the same mind . . . that was in Christ Jesus" (see Phil 2: 1-4). He transports himself as it were inside Jesus' submission so as to live his life in similar transparency.

To be a slave in Christ is liberation. While the outer person steadily dissolves, the inner one is renewed from day to day, born changed from glory to glory (see 2 Cor 3:18). The humiliated Christ was raised up high by God, and whoever becomes like Christ and shares in his suffering will also participate in his glory.

The Servant appears to be a central figure in the biblical and Christian understanding of community. No matter how much he is disdained, pushed to the margin, ridiculed, or condemned, in a mysterious way he pulls the whole body along to a point of glorious light. "Where I am, there will be my servant also. Whoever serves me, the Father will honor" (John 12:26). This new paradox is most precious. God honors the one who descends to the Servant in order to serve him! Strange, enchanting reciprocity!

How difficult it has become in our narcissistic culture to devote ourselves to service! People are out for recognition, respect, and affirmation. They are willing to serve, but never totally gratuitously. Every act of service quickly degenerates into a small area of monopoly. This servant puts a stamp on that area, wants to be recognized, and considers himself irreplaceable. As a result, he cannot accept assistance: he does it alone or he drops it. Nothing is really done together. Sometimes he may exert a hidden form of tyranny over the ones he serves. He makes the other dependent on *his* kind of service. His service works to enslave, not at all to liberate.

At the same time, how many people still want to be served? Self-service is the preferred option and it is considered humiliating to be served by another. A saying from the Desert Fathers teaches: "Whoever gives alms must do so as if he received them himself." Whoever offers a service must carry it out as if he were the beneficiary.

It is an art to serve gladly, gratuitously, and without seeking oneself, while able to improvise and to act creatively, never slovenly or submissively. The perspective must always embrace all of life. To serve life, *that* is truly a life of service—not one's own, neither that of the collective self of a particular group. "If the Church does not serve, she serves for nothing," in the words of bishop Jacques Gaillot. Woe to the shepherds who only feed themselves, said the prophet Ezekiel, who are only interested in the meat and the wool but let the sheep perish (see Ezek 34:2-10).

Mother Teresa of Calcutta perfectly sketches the centrality of service and how it assuredly leads to peace: "The fruit of Silence is prayer. The fruit of Prayer is faith. The fruit of Faith is love. The fruit of Love is service. The fruit of Service is peace."[1] At every stage unhealthy narcissism is shed as a superfluous garment.

1. Beliefnet's Inspirational Quotes, available at http://beliefnet.com (accessed November 16, 2016).

The Usefulness of What Is Useless—Service to Something of No Utility

Can we still discern the usefulness of something that is of no utility? For Chinese Taoists, this is a frequently recurring theme. Look at the tree that was saved. There it stands in all its glory. Why was that tree saved? Because it served no useful purpose. Its wood was too gnarled to be sawed into even planks for a cupboard or a door. It was unfit as firewood for the stove. People did not know what to do with it, so there it stands, brilliantly useless. But in its branches birds build their nests and under its ample crown cattle find shadow and shelter in blistering sun or driving rain.

So what kind of space do we still give to the child that cannot speak for itself, the very elderly, the man with an intellectual disability, and the woman who is mentally ill? In short, it may be that our planet will only continue on a healthy course if we dare to give space to people and things that ostensibly serve no utilitarian purpose at all.

See also: Emptiness, Humility, Mercy, Paradox, Reciprocity, Solidarity, Visiting, *Wu Wei*

SEXUALITY

Is it really possible to develop an art of living without dealing with sexuality? Sexuality is intrinsic to life. It is part and parcel of everyone's life story and must always be seen, oriented, assessed, and understood within that larger context. Sexuality is not a thing, neither is it a problem to be solved. Sexuality makes demands on the whole person within a history of values that we constantly interiorize and make our own.

At every stage of our personal growth, our upbringing, friendships, and bouts of loneliness impact our sexuality, suppress or question it, fill us with happiness or hurt. There is much in our sexuality that remains incomplete for extended periods of time and that requires further personal growth before it can be better integrated in our life and before it can be experienced in ever greater transparency.

There are no recipes. But you can set yourself a few rules: the sexual experience should never be reduced to a mostly mechanical event or be allowed to grow into an obsession or addiction. Between these extremes there is room for growth, for increasing self-knowledge, and for self-acceptance in our individuality and capacity for relationship.

Sexuality can assume the form of a life within my life: something that arouses my curiosity, occasionally assaults me or even overpowers me. This can be humiliating and fill a person with shame or deep discontent. A master taught me to accept sexuality as a form of revelation, a means of expression of our Creator. Astonished and grateful, we can then accept that life, beyond shame or spontaneous bashfulness.

Now, while your own sexuality may be a mystery that you discover with timidity and integrate over the course of many years, in the encounter with the other that mystery is more than doubled. It is true that in a relationship between two people one can easily become mired in a creepy game that is totally focused on the self. Yet a relationship can also forge the unconstrained surrender of two infinitely loving abysses. Let us never forget that in the Bible's imagery there is no loftier metaphor for the relationship between God and human being than that between man and woman.

The most intimate relations between man and woman serve as model for the relationship that God desires with his people, Christ with his bride, the Church. Reflect on this for a little while and you will sense the revelation of an uncommon depth: the freedom and reciprocity involved in the most intimate surrender from one to the other is rooted in God, who neither wants nor is anything else. Such insights elevate every sexual experience to the heights of true love, intimate affection, and the purest forms of tenderness.

A lifestyle that is sober and transparent, modest and chaste, creates an atmosphere in which sexual experience can be developed with tranquility and restraint. It is edifying to read in the Letter to the Ephesians: "But fornication and impurity of any kind . . . must not even be mentioned among you, as is proper among saints. Entirely out of place is obscene, silly, and vulgar talk; but instead, let there be thanksgiving" (Eph 5:3-4). A life of happiness and gratitude is nourished by self-control, which allows us to fast with the eyes as well as with our imagination. Undeniably, this will require us to do battle, especially today when graphic culture is often so provocative.

The realm of sexuality is often marked by suffering. There are experiences of hurt, disappointment, anxiety, frustration, shame, and, all too often, painful repetitions of an injured past. Also, people may have outsized illusions about the sexual life, fed by shows and performances of mythic proportions that stand in the way of any grown-up art of living. Levinas, the philosopher, maintained that even in the erotic experience the other remains other and cannot be reduced to the self.

The myth of love as fusion, which makes us believe that we can dissolve into the other, is no more than a mirage and inevitably leads to frustration. The thing that creates room for a relationship of true love is the artful practice of continually honoring the other in his or her otherness. To grow in this art requires patience, open dialogue, self-knowledge, and humility in treatment of the other. What is sown humbly in love produces the most beautiful fruit a whole life long.

See also: Chastity, Growing, Humility, Poverty, Reciprocity

SIMPLICITY

Kakua was the first person to leave Japan for China in order to study with the Buddhist masters. When after ten years he returned to his homeland, the emperor invited him to the court to preach what he had learned. The monk refused. The emperor insisted. Kakua came. He bowed deeply before the emperor and all his courtiers. Then he pulled a small reed flute from the folds of his garment. He brought the flute to his lips, blew for a moment, and one clear tone wafted into the silence. Then Kakua bowed again before the emperor and disappeared. Nobody ever found trace of him again.

Was he mocking the emperor? Was this the teaching, the core of all sutras? Kakua's testament: one pure sound, ineffably present, and suddenly gone. Forever. Simplicity. Simplicity is found at the end. Simplicity stands at the beginning. Between beginning and end there is nothing but beginning anew, "From beginning to beginning, in a beginning without end," in the words of Gregory of Nyssa. We continually grow poorer, and only in this way does simplicity increase.

We are led to simplicity more than it can be attained by force of will. We pray for simplicity: "Give me an undivided heart" (Ps 86:11). For as the rabbinic masters teach us, our hearts are double, dominated by at least two contradictory tendencies. So we pray with the psalm: "Give me an undivided heart to revere your name" (Ps 86:11). When we hallow his Name, God, the One, brings unity, reconciles, simplifies, creates that final limit of our existence, which is simplicity. When He becomes everything, we are one. As simple as that.

You steadily grow into simplicity by loss and catharsis, by letting go, like the shelling of a nut. The psalms show us the way. Here is Psalm 131:

> O Lord, my heart is not lifted up
> my eyes are not raised too high;
> I do not occupy myself with things
> too great and too marvelous for me.

Thrice you say "no," starting in the heart, then with the eyes, and then in your daily occupations. On the other side of that "no" you find tranquility, rest, and creative peace:

But I have calmed and quieted my soul,
Like a weaned child with its mother;
My soul is like the weaned child
That is with me.

The poet shows what simplicity is about through the image of an infant. Who would not understand? A child lying in the mother's lap, a nursing babe, sated and resting in pure abandonment. Hunger, thirst, fear, and displeasure are all gone. Life is radiant in simplicity, not just the child's life, but that of the whole community.

O Israel, hope in the LORD
from this time on and evermore.

When achieved, it appears that simplicity has no boundaries. Who is "Israel" in the psalm? The "man who sees God"? That is what the name *ish-ra'-El* suggests. Or the man made wholly straight, *rectissimus* (*yasjar-El*)? Made straight from the cunning, clever Jacob that he was before? After he wrestled with the angel, Jacob received a new name: "Israel." The encounter in the night straightened him out as never before. Though injured, now he is strong enough to go out and meet his brother. Simplification.

Hence, simplicity is appropriate for any collectivity that feels called to form a true community: "Save us, O LORD our God, and gather us from among the nations, that we may give thanks to your holy name and glory in your praise" (Ps 106:47). Any fractured existence begs to be made whole again. When, after a whirlwind of praise and thanksgiving, dispersion is brought to unity, we see the mark of a life that is complete. The Name is the power that assembles, also here. A prayer rises: "That they may be one"(John 17:11).

"And I, when I am lifted up from the earth, will draw all people to myself" (John 12:32). Simplicity is the hidden magnet from which we were separated at some point in time, but whose pull we re-experience within us after years of wandering. Our life becomes a pilgrimage: a *visio pacis* pulls us to each other. The pilgrims set out on their way, shoulder to shoulder. Nobody dominates anybody. Poor and happy we approach the gate of the holy of holies that inspires us with awe and great desire:

> For the sake of my relatives and friends
> I will say: "Peace be within you."
> For the sake of the house of the LORD our God,
> I will seek your good. (Ps 122:8-9)

Simply translated, in the language of Saint Francis this is called *pax et bonum* (peace and good). It is the ultimate goal of our journey. The feast of simplicity—God everything in all—has already started because one played the flute in the marketplace. We have recognized his song in our day—a word of peace for one and all.

See also: *Abba*, Beginning, Mindfulness, Peace, Pilgrimage

SLEEPING

I slept, but my heart was awake. (Song 5:2)

Sleep comes by itself. Surely it does not involve any kind of art on our part, or does it? The truth is that many people would have to admit that sleep does not come quickly. How many of us above forty don't take a little pill to help us go to sleep?

Regularly enjoying a deep sleep, all night long without interruption, is given only to a few. We have to face it: sleeping is not all that easy.

Sleep remains a source of wonderment. To live totally without sleep is just about impossible, even though there are yogis in India who try to do so, and some even succeed. Also in the Islamic tradition we find masters who have learned to live without lying down. On Mount Athos some monks prefer to hang in a cord at night rather than to lie down. On the other hand, Abba Poemen, the wise Desert Father (fifth century), taught that the three things we will never be able to do without are eating, sleeping, and clothing ourselves. Although, of course, we can all use some restraint.

Normally we experience sleep as a blessing, but sadly for some people sleep has become a hellish experience. Job complains that even in his sleep he feels tormented by terrible nightmares. His days are marked by pain and misery and his nights have turned into torture. In one of his writings Charles Péguy says that God does not love the person who does not sleep (*Je n'aime pas, dit Dieu, l'homme qui ne dort pas*). The night is a present from God, and whoever refuses this gift irritates the Creator.

Is there something we can do? Small children can be helped to fall asleep with a bit of gentle assistance. You can read them a story, say a blessing or a short prayer, hum a familiar melody, give them a last kiss before turning off the ceiling light and switching on the little nightlight. These kinds of rituals faithfully honored every evening, with or without variations, help our little ones to trust the approaching sleep and to yield to it. And what are we "big adults" other than erstwhile "little children"?

In any event, we can do something about the two transitions at the beginning and at the end of the night. I can do some reading:

something that leads to wisdom and breadth of mind. Then I can surrender to sleep in the same way. Over the years we discover that between waking and being fully asleep our mind gives up a measure of self-control. As a result the mind acquires a certain expansiveness, it becomes freer than usual and more open. The mind is at liberty to explore, and all kinds of associations become possible.

When an abbot gives a talk to his confrères, he sometimes notices one of the brothers dozing off. How can it be that brothers nod off while their abbot is speaking? Because they heard this refrain before? Because they are bored by it? Not so sure. The way to a deeper level of consciousness where we are free of self-control runs along the same path as the pathway of sleep. It sometimes happens that a brother, apparently asleep during the speech, afterward is able to repeat the abbot's whole discussion. While to all appearances he was "out of it," he certainly was alive to the depth and breadth of the talk's mental associations.

So, let us not allow just anything to enter our ears or to be imprinted on our retinas before we go to bed. With Compline, the Prayer at the End of the Day, the monks give us a tip. The three psalms (4, 91, and 134) and the Song of Simeon (*Nunc dimittis*): "Master, now you are dismissing your servant in peace"), followed by the *Salve Regina* predispose the heart to surrender to the grand picture: "And after this, our exile, show unto us the blessed fruit of thy womb, Jesus."[1] "For my eyes have seen your salvation. . . . A light for revelation to the Gentiles" (Luke 2: 30-32). "Lift up the light of your face on us, O Lord. . . . In peace I will lie down and fall asleep, for you alone, O Lord, make me dwell in safety" (Ps 4:81).[2]

Also getting up in the morning may be paired with well-chosen rituals. What do I murmur even before jumping out of bed? What do I repeat if I wake up for a moment in the middle of the night? An Our Father? A verse from a psalm, "Lord, open my lips, and my mouth will proclaim your praise." "Holy be your Name. Your kingdom come. Your will be done." Often it suffices just to repeat one expression, in wonder, in adoration, in quiet jubilation.

1. From *Salve Regina*, available at http://www.catholicchant.com/salveregina.html (accessed January 13, 2017).

2. This translation is from *The Revised Grail Psalms* (Collegeville, MN: Liturgical Press, 2012) [translator's note].

Waking up is just as mysterious as falling asleep and our consciousness still unshackled of its control mechanisms can freely associate in depth and in breadth, sometimes with great showers of creativity. Blessed is the person who can hold that moment for a while in all its breadth and gratefully experience its gathering fullness before stepping into the practicalities of the day.

Starting a new day usually follows a set pattern that fortunately does not require much thought: we wash up and brush our teeth on auto-pilot. In many spiritual traditions people are advised to lay out the night before the things that will be needed to begin the day, not just what shoes or socks you are going to wear but also the reading to start the day off with, the passage from Scripture that you want to reflect on. What you thought about the previous day will be reflected clearly and firmly on the clean slate of your heart in the morning. Doing *lectio divina* in the early morning is all the more fruitful when it is linked to a few rituals and customary practices like giving it some forethought prior to going to bed.

Sometimes we remember fragments of dreams in the moment of awakening. They provide us access to our subconscious. How is our deepest self doing? What do our dreams teach us? Libert Vander Kerken used to tell us that he kept a notebook near his bed. If he woke in the night he would immediately write down the dream and then go to sleep again. I am more than my common sense and my reasonable self-concept. That is what I discover, among other things, in these blissful moments between sleeping and being wide awake.

Consciousness is elastic. We can worry to excess and live a rather narrow, confined existence, or give free rein to our primary moods and disposition. Or we can train our consciousness and teach it to remain wide open, spacious, high and deep. In silent meditation we leave the primary layers, force them to be quiet, so that the greater consciousness can enter. As a Tao aphorism says, the big picture has no form. Similarly, the great consciousness has no limits. In the zone between sleep and being awake, a consciousness exists that is capable of much more than ordinary psychological understanding. Those who pay attention to it get to know themselves in a new way, in never-ceasing wonder.

Nighttime is meant for sleeping. This obvious truth is contradicted by monks because they split the night in two parts and have been doing so for centuries. One half of the night they sleep, the other half they remain awake. Some get up very early, others turn in early and get up in the middle of the night to pray for three or four hours. After that they allow themselves another couple of hours of sleep. But the old tradition holds that they never spend more than half the night in bed.

Breaking up sleep in the following way can also lead to fascinating discoveries: get up once or twice in the night for an hour or so and keep a vigil. If you wake up around 2:00 a.m., don't just turn over but get out of bed and kneel for a while, or spend thirty minutes on your prayer stool facing an icon. Calmly recite a couple of psalms. Spend some time in adoration, wordlessly. Allow the silence to get into your bones. "Give me an undivided heart to revere your name" (Ps 86:11). Repeat your favorite prayer, slowly and intently. Let the great consciousness enter: all forms and limits disappear.

The sleep that you give yourself afterward is of a different nature: the uncreated light that you admitted for a moment keeps burning within you, even if your eyes have closed again.

At times we are absolutely unable to get out of bed, even when it really is time to rise. Our willpower appears exhausted. The brain sees the situation clearly, but cannot get the will going. The heavy body stays prone. In a case like that, a complete deep exhalation can return our self-determination. It is worth trying! Breathing is important. Compared to breathing in, exhaling is by far the more important. The miracle is that it works every time even during the day. So it is beneficial when you have a spare moment, say sitting behind the wheel in the car or waiting for a train, to breathe out completely by pulling the stomach muscles all the way in, against the spine as it were. Some physicians recommend doing this at least once an hour. This breathing practice works on your nervous system in a manner that benefits your freedom, time and again.

See also: Breathing, Dreaming, *Lectio Divina*, Night Vigil, Psalmody, Simplicity

SMILING

To smile is a verb. To smile consciously is an art. Starting your day by smiling at yourself in the mirror is a delightful practice. You smile at yourself, at life, at a flower, at a child. "Whoever welcomes one such child in my name welcomes me, and whoever welcomes me welcomes not me but the one who sent me" (Mark 9:37). That pronouncement by Jesus must have taken his listeners by surprise—in his time children simply were of no account. Jesus views the child as a secret intermediary, just as he wants to be in his Father's name.

Elsewhere he says of "these little ones" that "in heaven their angels continually see the face of my Father in heaven" (Matt 18:10). Jesus discerns so much more than what we usually see: the face of a child, through the intermediation of its guardian angel, shows him the face of the invisible Father in heaven.

Angels smile. In the Western world, the most beautiful smile ever chiseled in stone is an angel's smile in the front portal of the cathedral in Reims, France. Children smile. An infant's first smile remains forever in the memory of mom or dad. That smile comes as a revelation, a message from the other side. Life vibrates in unfathomable depth because there is an opening up to a freedom that is tender, playful, intimate, ready for surrender and communion. The entire cosmos does not equal even one smile of the littlest child. As far as smiling is concerned, there is no distinction between children and angels.

Smiling has become difficult for many people. For some, it has become impossible. The face has hardened, the hundreds of small facial muscles have stiffened. The smile no longer happens: everything hurts, the mirror shows an odious grin, an extremely unpleasant grimace. The face has become a mask. Whoever wears it never takes it off again, not in public or in private. The mask and the face have become one. For this kind of person, to smile is a painful exercise.

Life chisels your face. Nobody is spared of suffering. You see dear ones die, friends go a different way, people treat you poorly. Different forms of jealousy, betrayal, and intentional enmity cross your path. Perhaps you experienced the horrors of war in your own body. So you do your best, you remain standing, you don't give up, but also you grit your teeth, you stick up for yourself, you don't budge, you defend yourself as best as you can. And where is the smile? Can a child, a clown, a bird, a yellow daffodil still relax your facial features and make you break out in a happy face? Or do you have to admit that a smile in the early morning causes more pain than pleasure? Cardinal Suenens once said that every person over fifty bears responsibility for the way his face looks.

Let's make smiling an intentional practice, and it will nourish us for the rest of our lives. A smile is the interface with the gratuitous, precisely that which is not ours. Nobody can smile and grit his teeth at the same time, literally and figuratively. To smile is a purposeful act of relaxation, a living paradox. If you are overly serious, the paradox does not work, actually no paradox will ever work.

The nice thing about a smile is that is a present that you receive yourself the moment you yield to it. The other person who receives your smile understands perfectly: this is pure blessing, pure gift. So when you smile, don't make it forced or the product of obstinate willpower: be ready to receive your smile at the same time, with childish abandon. Thus, to smile is really something grand, something mysterious, in all its simplicity.

In order to smile you have to take your customary seriousness with a grain of salt. But whenever you do, you win. As the Chinese saying goes, "If you can laugh at yourself, you will have fun your whole life."

The Buddhist monk Thich Nhat Hanh recommends that people who consciously apply themselves to their breathing also smile on the out-breath. Well worth a try! Many meditation masters say that in silent meditation you are actually practicing cosmetic surgery: you learn to let go of everything that is stiff and cramped in your face and to release all of that, even without intending it. As an integral part of this kind of practice, a smile is the royal road. Just do it. *Cheese.*

See also: Breathing, Love for One's Enemies, Paradox

SOLIDARITY

Humanity has to face choices. The train of economic and cultural globalization, with all its ferocious speed, appears difficult to control. Some doubt whether controlling it is still possible at all. The vehicle has become a monster that disregards the orders of its developer and continues obstinately on its course.

Only an enormous catastrophe or complete exhaustion will be capable of setting us on a different course.

What about the wisdom traditions, the Jewish, Christian, and Taoist-Buddhist masters from the East and the West, the wisdom of native Americans and of the Bantu tribes and the Pygmies, the ancient Vedas from India, yes, all sources of refined humanity collected throughout the ages? Will they be able to influence the blind course of *homo technicus* and *homo economicus* and direct them again toward a true compassionate humanity? Recent history offers no guarantee. Even to the contrary.

The best we can do is to remind each other that as a collectivity we are living extremely dangerously and that we need to venture upon alternative courses of action, going against the current. Continuing to do small, positive things within the framework of solidarity between East and West, North and South is part of the prophetic action of our day. In so doing we anticipate a hopeful future.

"Development is the new name for peace," wrote Pope Paul VI in his encyclical *Populorum Progressio* (1967). But how difficult it is to do this consequentially! "Sharing" is the key phrase, but how many governments in the North are prepared to give one percent, or even one-half of one percent, of their annual budgets to development? And how does that compare to what we are ready to spend on armaments?

How far does our solidarity go? The survival of our planet is only guaranteed if we do not exclude anybody. The new humanity can be seen in the amount of attention that is paid to those who are not usually counted: the intellectually disabled children, the incurably ill patients, the street urchins in the megacities, and all those who are left out because of race, social status, gender, caste, color, or disfiguration by illness. The communities of Jean Vanier and Mother Teresa of Calcutta show us the way. How remarkable is their universality! They show up everywhere: no system can prevent their infiltration! Universal solidarity of the poor is the lever of history.

In a prophetic vision, no middle way appears to exist: either you are part of the solution or you continue to be part of the problem. Blessed are they who resolutely opt for the solution: to make the world more human in solidarity.

See also: Forgiveness, Mercy, Peace, Poverty, Salmon or Mocking Gravity, Serving

SOURCE

No spirituality exists without a source. No life exists without a source of living water. No spiritual growth exists without a quest for the Source, a pilgrimage from oasis to oasis (Origen).

God is source. The Spirit is living water. There is a life within my life. There is an inexhaustible, always new source welling up at the bottom of my heart. "God is source" means God is "Act" (Louis Lavelle). An uninterrupted Deed, which supports everything that is, is completed in Him. We live by the grace of our partaking in that Act. Give yourself over to God, whispers the psalmist into the heart of the person praying before bedtime (Ps 4). By accepting this original freedom, new and invigorating life is created, "From beginning to beginning, in beginnings which have no end" (Gregory of Nyssa, fourth century).

We can lose sight of the Source. In Hebrew the words for "eye" and "source" are the same, designated by the same letter *"ain."* Of course, we can build our own vessels and cisterns. But standing water in vessels that will break into pieces at the first tremor provides only fragile support for the true life.

The Source is primal. The Source has neither beginning nor end. The Source is near, "more intimate than my innermost self" in the words of St. Augustine, or as Paul Claudel put it in an attempt to describe his experience of Christmas eve 1886, "an Other in me, more me than I myself" (*un Autre en moi, plus moi-même que moi*). "The water that I will give will become in them a spring of water gushing up to eternal life," said Jesus to the Samaritan woman (John 4:14). Jesus does not just siphon off some water from one basin to another. He announces the presence of a spring. Those who take his word to heart discover a source. The Source gushes up in them. "To eternal life!"

A culture of silence directs the heart to the original Act. That primal energy is all we need. The true art of living consists in not living by bread alone. The desert is humbling, says the Bible, and puts us on the path toward another source of life: the Word, yes, "Every word that comes from the mouth of the Lord" (Deut 8:3; see also how Jesus experiences the desert, Matt 4:4).

In the very last vision, on the last page of the Bible, the prophet of the book of Revelation sees water flowing. The Source of that water already gave life in the first garden, the Garden of Eden. The beginning and the end of Scripture are rooted where living water flows (cf. Ps 1).

See also: Beginning, Culture, God, Pilgrimage, Spirit, Wisdom

SPIRIT

How much Spirit do we allow into our lives, in all our doings? To make room for the Spirit means making room for nothing, for emptiness, for poverty, and in that emptiness making room for what is other than myself. Quiet people open their doors and windows for that other air in their lives. We breathe more freely in their presence.

But where do we learn to open ourselves up and to make ourselves vulnerable to the Spirit? "Give your blood," said a Desert Father, "and receive the Spirit." Give, let go, release, empty your hands so as to make room, to create true openness, for that fertilizing entity, the flowing Spring, the creative power capable of renewing all that is, gently and forcefully. The apostle Paul hears a deep groaning in all of creation and he recognizes it in his own heart: he calls it an "eager longing" as a "groaning in labor pains" in hopes of obtaining "the freedom and the glory of the children of God" (see Rom 8:21-26).

This happens *uuteweerts*, as Ruusbroec told us—not from the outside to the inside, but from inside, from our innermost self to the outside. The inside is where God resides, as Augustine testified: *deus interior intimo meo* (more inward than my inmost self).[1] *We* have to repent, to see the error of our ways, to live a modest, subdued life and make a journey inward, but *the Spirit* works the other way around, it wells up from the inside.

There is something important going on here. This is where it happens: the person who goes within has a mysterious encounter with the thrust of that which works from the inside out. She begins to perceive how past a point zero an inexhaustible force is constantly at work within her, which the bishop-martyr Ignatius of Antioch expressed in one of his testamentary letters as "Come to the Father." Dutch poet Ida Gerhardt speaks of an "urgent knocking," something

1. Augustine's expression has been translated into English in many ways. The translation used here is taken from Pope Benedict XVI, *Angelus*, December 11, 2011 (in which he also paraphrased it as "The Lord is closer to us than we are to ourselves"), available at https://w2.vatican.va/content/benedict-xvi/en/angelus/2011 (accessed December 9, 2016) [translator's note].

"concealed, approaching, " and in discerning it uncovers her calling as a poet. Indirectly, she reveals the essence of every vocation:

> In my fingertips it trembles
> concealed, approaching,
> the dark sound, the urgent knocking
> in the chambers of my heart:
> The water engages me. (Ida Gerhardt, from *the Diviner*)

Make it still. Make it empty. Make it poor. Do not pretend a thing. Wait and repeat in one form or another the ancient Aramaic heart cry of the first Christian communities: *Maranatha—the* watchword. For some, *the* mantra: "the Lord comes." Assuredly, he comes. He is coming already now, from within. Allow yourself to be surprised.

Ruah. The Spirit is life-breath, the Spirit is wind, the Spirit is angel. *Ruah,* this Hebrew word, covers three semantic fields.

As the breath's vital force, it gives life to humans and animals.

As the wind, it blows where it wants. It is and remains ungraspable, exists beyond and outside ourselves, broods over the ur-waters, and shakes the cedars and the oaks. "So it is with everyone who is born of the Spirit," explains Jesus to Nicodemus in their conversation in the night. Thus they are equally ungraspable and unpredictable. "You hear the sound of it, but you do not know where it comes from or where it goes" (John 3:8).

Finally, the Spirit also is angel: a distinct being that is in-between, an intermediary between God and human being, between the prophet and his Source. "Prophesy to the breath, prophesy, mortal." The *Ruah* is addressed by the prophet: "Come from the four winds, O breath, and prophesy upon these slain, that they may live" (Ezek 37:9). Just as the Spirit is the life force in the human being and the cosmic force that from the four winds blows over the valley raising up the fallen, so it is also the accessible interlocutor between God and his prophet Ezekiel. "I will put my Spirit within you" (Ezek 37:14). So it appears that a personal *Ruah* from God can be conveyed and become the foundational principle of new life, holy life.

"Receive the Holy Spirit" (John 20:22). That is what matters in the First and in the New Testament. Without emptiness, without silence, without poverty, without transformation from inside by awe for the Lord, we will never be able to receive the Spirit. Conversely, blessed is the person who in extreme distress has learned to call out to the Lord because "the spirit of glory, which is the Spirit of God, is resting on you" (1 Pet 4:14). For there is a poverty that is so pure that it never fails to attract God's Spirit. Jesus himself testifies to this and assures his disciples that in great distress they will come to experience it (see Mark 13:11: "Do not worry beforehand about what you are to say; but say whatever is given you at that time, for it is not you who speak, but the Holy Spirit"). "Blessed are those who mourn, for they will be comforted " (Matt 5:4). Yes, indeed, they will receive the Consoler, the Holy Spirit.

See also: Emptiness, Fear of the Lord, Meditation, Poverty, Source, Tears

STRATEGY

The spiritual way presupposes a method—that is self-evident. "Way" and "method" mean the same thing: "way" in English, *methodos* ("with way") in Greek. The obvious truth of this indicates that we should never start out on the way in random fashion, hit-or-miss, unsystematically. Without a modicum of strategy, the whole project is bound to fail.

Then the question becomes: How do I start? What should be my priority? What do I put right and center? From the rabbinical tradition we learn that the world rests on three pillars: (1) study of the Torah; (2) prayer or worship; and (3) good works. As the masters point out in their commentaries, the order is important. Start with study, the moment of insight, and the light. Only then switch to prayer. Finish with action, the ripe fruit of study and worship. Every classic catechism exhibits a similar structure: first comes the insight of faith, with the twelve articles of the Creed or a commentary on it, then faith is celebrated with the whole range of the sacraments, and finally there is a transition to concrete action on the basis of the Ten Commandments.

In Benedict's Rule we detect a similar concern for structuring the right priorities into the day and the rhythm of life. Benedict chooses the best time to devote to *lectio divina* (attention to God's word) in each season. That is a very clear priority in the daily schedule of every monk and the whole community. Elsewhere we read how the Divine Office (*opus divinum*) deserves absolute priority and that nothing must be allowed to supersede it. But at the same time we hear as a leitmotif of the Rule that the guest, the child, the elderly, the infirm, the youngest in the meeting, and anybody who in one way or another stands at the margin must receive prime attention.

Thus the Rule contains this remarkable paradox that a brother must handle priorities on three fronts at the same time. These three fronts correspond to the three pillars of the rabbis: study, prayer, and love of one's neighbor. In reality, it all has to do with God. Suppose you leave the prayer service to receive a guest. What is this other than leaving "God" in order to do God's will? This is the dynamic that Benedict built into his Rule. In the midst of all the choices before us, the absolute priority resounds: "Prefer nothing to the love of Christ" (RB 4:21).

Below I recount a parable that demonstrates how everybody can profit from keeping a close eye on the order that we have planned for our day, indeed for our entire life.[1] That order has consequences for everything else. Upon closer examination of the parable, it appears that respect for emptiness offers the best and greatest possibilities. How much emptiness do I preserve in all that I do? How much space is still available within each undertaking? How much silence is allowed to live among my words?

The Parable of the Mayonnaise Jar and the Coffee

The professor stood in front of his class to give a lecture on philosophy. He had a number of objects on the desk in front of him. Without saying a word, he started the class by lifting up an empty mayonnaise jar and began filling it with golf balls. When the jar was filled, the professor asked the students if the jar was full. They answered in the affirmative.

Then the professor took a box of beads and threw them into the jar. He lightly shook the jar and the beads rolled into the empty spaces between the golf balls. Again the professor asked if the jar was full. The students gave the same answer, "Yes, the jar was full."

Now the professor took a can of sand and poured the sand in the jar with the golf balls and the beads. Of course, the sand filled all the spaces between the golf balls and the beads. The professor asked if the jar was full now, and again the students answered, "Yes."

Then the professor took the two cups of coffee and poured their contents into the jar with the golf balls, the beads, and the sand. All the coffee disappeared into the jar; it filled up the space between the grains of sand. The students started laughing.

"Now," said the professor, "I want you to see this jar as your own life. This jar filled with golf balls, beads, sand, and coffee represents human life. The golf balls are the most important things in life: your family, your children, your faith, your health, and your favorite hobbies. Things that ensure that if there were nothing else in your life, it would still be very full. The beads are other things that are important:

1. The parable was given to me by a friend; I do not know its exact origin but the coffee, mayonnaise, and especially the golf balls hint at its cultural provenance. My thanks to whoever created it!

your work, your house, your car. The sand stands for all the little things you attach importance to. If you pour the sand first into the jar and fill it, there is no more room for the beads or the golf balls. The same thing is true in your own life. If you devote all your time and energy to the little things, you will never be able to get to the important things. Pay heed to the things that are important to you. For example, play with your children. Once in a while, take time off and have a physical exam. Take your partner out to eat. Do something fun, there is plenty of time left to clean or to fix this or that. First take care of your golf balls, the things that are really of greatest importance to you. Know your priorities. The rest is only sand."

One of the students raised his hand and asked what, then, the two cups of coffee represented. The professor smiled and said that was a very good question. "With them I wanted to indicate and affirm that, no matter how full your life may be, there is always time for a cup of coffee with a friend or someone close to you."

See also: Beginning, Emptiness, *Lectio Divina*, Meditation, Mindfulness

SUNDAY

Of all spiritual practices, hallowing the day of the Lord is one of the most fundamental. What is at stake here is nothing less than our identity. Simply put, it means that if we systematically neglect Sunday, we damage our essence, we kill our soul, as Romano Guardini once wrote in a letter to young people (1925).

The practice is thoroughly biblical, much older even than Christianity. Jesus did not come to eliminate any part of it. Indeed, the first Christians have always honored the Sabbath as a day of rest. Sunday was only made a Sabbath after the third century, and in this way Sundays received a double perspective.

In the centuries before Constantine the followers of Jesus observed the Sabbath on the last day of the week. On Sunday they went to work, after first having celebrated the resurrection, early in the morning. Sunday is the day of the rising, the day of the first light, the day on which the community gathers to celebrate Him who conquered death. Every Sunday is Easter.

The fact that we also rest on that day is the result of a later development, namely when Christianity became a state religion. But the fact that this day of rest is observed every week, now on Sundays and before that on Saturdays, is of vital importance for the meaning of the other six days, and thus for the meaning of the whole. The relationship between time and eternity is at stake, as well as the meaning of work and toil in human history.

In fact, we are faced with one of the greatest inventions of humankind. The institution came into existence in the sixth or fifth century before Christ. It is the gift of the Jewish people to all peoples, partly also thanks to the spread of Christianity. It is also a gift to every Jew, straight from God's attentive love. Deep wisdom lies hidden in this more than twenty-five-centuries-old practice. If we systematically overlooked it we would become dumb, dull-witted, yes, addicted, within the shortest time, that is, our humanity would be at peril.

So then, concretely, what does the characteristic Sunday obligation entail for us Christians? The new Code of Canon Law (1983) gives us an interesting characterization of what the day is and should be: "Sunday, on which by apostolic tradition the paschal mystery is celebrated, must be observed in the universal Church as the primordial holy day of obligation" (Can. 1246, para. 1). Here we learn at least three things: (1) On Sunday we celebrate Easter. Each and every Sunday is always the day on which we honor Christ's resurrection! (2) This is an old tradition going back to the time of the apostles. Indeed we can see it in the first writings preserved in the New Testament. We come together weekly to celebrate the resurrection early Sunday morning. (3) The "primordial holy day of obligation" is a translation of "*primordialis dies festus*" in the Latin text. A feast day, thus, and one of the first order. As a matter of fact, Sunday heads the list of all the holy days named in the canon, with the feast of the Nativity coming next.

The following canon then sets out what is expected: "On Sundays and other holy days of obligation, the faithful are obliged to participate in Mass. Moreover, they are to abstain from those works and affairs which hinder the worship to be rendered to God, the joy proper to the Lord's day, or the suitable relaxation of mind and body" (Can. 1247, para. 1). So, aside from the requirement to attend Mass on Sundays and holy days, which makes eminently good sense and is nothing new, we also learn that we have to abstain from work and anything else that hampers the worship service, joy, and the necessary relaxation of mind and body.

With its double negation (abstaining from what can be a hindrance) the formulation may sound a little surprising. We could put it the other way round: apply yourself to worship, to joy, and to relaxation, because they should be honored that day! So we note that we need to keep some space open in which these separate flowers can flourish: joy, true repose, and pure worship of God. Right away, this presupposes a whole art of living.

We may also wonder why the command expressly insists on relaxation (*relaxatio*) of mind and body as an indispensable part of Sunday. So many people often get into new things that are anything but relaxing; they can be even busier on vacation than when they are working.

Sunday must express joy, just as the prophet Isaiah in God's name urged his contemporaries to "call the Sabbath a delight and the holy day of the Lord honorable" (Isa 58:13). Jesus also emphasizes feasting as an inner necessity: "Let us eat and celebrate, for this son of mine was dead and is alive again; he was lost and is found!" (Luke 15:23-24). God's feast is bigger than our heart. When it is Sabbath for the

Jew and Sunday for the Christian, our whole demeanor has to show that it is a feast day for the Lord.

In addition, it is often said in Jewish practice that our own feelings and emotions must give way to the joy of the Lord, which must come first. We read in Nehemiah that the people of Israel were admonished to rejoice when listening to the Torah: "For the joy of the LORD is your strength" (Neh 8:10). A rabbi from the Talmudic era learned just prior to the Sabbath that two of his children had died of an illness. He kept the news from his wife so that they could celebrate the Sabbath together in joy, as is proper. Only when the Sabbath was over did he tell her what had happened to their children.

The festive character shows in many small signs and symbols: the clothes you wear, the flower in a vase, the white tablecloth, the lit candle, and, maybe, the pancakes for breakfast signify that a feast is being celebrated, for everybody and for the whole person, "mind and body" as the canon puts it. A poem by Ida Gerhardt says it perhaps more persuasively, in simplicity with precisely seven lines, beginning and ending with light:

> Sunday morning
> The light begins to travel through the house
> and touches all the things. We eat
> our early bread dipped in the sun.
> You've spread the white cloth
> and put grasses in a glass.
> This is the day when work is at rest.
> The palm of the hand is turned toward the light. (Ida Gerhardt, from *The Gardener*)

Litany of Names for Sunday

The meaning of Sunday is clear in the many names that the tradition has bestowed on that particular day. It would take no effort at all to put together a veritable litany of all the names and titles that have been given to Sunday throughout the ages. Each name reveals some aspect of the meaning of what is being celebrated. Pope John Paul II dedicated an apostolic letter to Sunday (*Dies Domini,* 1998) and he uses at least five different names for Sunday to provide the structure of the letter:

Dies Domini, The Celebration of the Creator's work.
Dies Christi, The Day of the Risen Lord and of the Gift of the Holy Spirit.
Dies Ecclesiae, The Eucharistic Assembly: Heart of Sunday.
Dies hominis, Day of Joy, Rest and Solidarity.
Dies dierum, the Primordial Feast, Revealing the Meaning of Time.[1]

Within the document itself we encounter at least three times as many names and characterizations of that one day! Here is a handful, and we can learn something from each one:

"The day of the Lord" and "the lord of all days " (Pseudo Eusebius of Alexandria, fourth century).
"Day of Resurrection," the weekly Easter.
"First day of the week," "the day of the creation of light" (cf. Gen 1:3: "Then God said: Let there be light").
"The eighth day," the day of the age to come, the *eschaton,* and eternal life.
"Day of the new creation."
"Day of the life-giving breath of the Spirit," "the weekly Pentecost" (see John 20:22-23).
"The day that the Lord has made," "Let us be glad and rejoice in it" (Ps 118:24; for the church fathers, Christ is that Day in person).
"Day of salvation," salvation from any kind of bondage.
"Day of the Word," when we enjoy the communal reading of Scripture. The same texts are heard and reflected on in all the churches of the world.
"Day of faith," when we profess our one faith together.
"Day of the breaking of bread."
"Day of mission," to go out and bear witness (every *missa* is *missio*).
"Day of joy."
"Day of God and day of man," sharing in each other's life and rest.
"Day of the new and eternal covenant" between Creator and creature.
"Day of solidarity," with a collection for the poor (see 1 Cor 16:2).

1. Apostolic letter of the Holy Father John Paul II to the Bishops, Clergy and Faithful of the Catholic Church on Keeping the Lord's Day Holy (*Dies Domini*), available at https://w.2vatican.va/content/john-paul-ii/en/apost_letters/1998 (accessed December 13, 2016) [translator's note].

"Day of rest."

"Day of the sun," the "sun of righteousness" or the "sun of justice" (Mal 4:2) and applied to Christ by Luke the Evangelist (Luke 1:78), by which the ancient pagan name is preserved but given Christian meaning by the church fathers.

From this multitude of names, let us not lose sight of these three: day of the Word, day of community, and day of relaxation. Can it truly be Sunday without real relaxation, without having a community experience and giving to others, without taking to heart the word of God selected for that day?

Cardinal Godfried Danneels once wrote ten rules of thumb for all who wish to make Sunday a true Sunday. The rules are straightforward, very recognizable, and each one is of vital importance. We adopt them here with pleasure:

1) Begin planning your Sunday during the week and start it on Saturday evening.
2) Wear different clothes, bring in a twig or a flower from the garden, put a candle on the table, give each other a Sunday kind of feeling.
3) Avoid all busyness, do everything twice as slowly: get up from bed slower, take it easy over breakfast, and talk more calmly with your husband, your wife, your child, your neighbor.
4) Don't criticize, but as often as possible say "yes."
5) Make time for your family, your friends, somebody who is ill.
6) Give a call to a person you forgot about the whole week, just to make him or her feel good.
7) Enjoy nature, music, a book. Visit a museum, an abbey, a town.
8) Participate in the social life of your neighborhood, your club, or your parish.
9) Be nice to people who have to work for you today and give you service.
10) Get together with your faith community in church. It is Sunday, after all!

See also: Emptiness, Feasting, *Poustinia,* Rituals, Sabbath, Time and the Experience of Time, *Wu Wei*

T

TEARS

Tears and repentance constitute the sure compass of the heart that seeks God and that wants to lead an authentic spiritual life. With "tears" the Fathers had far more in mind than constantly weeping eyes. The heart also "weeps." A crushed and broken heart can weep continually, and, through David, Scripture tells us explicitly that such a heart God will not spurn (see Ps 51). The fathers speak of a repentance that is comforting, healing, and even joyous.

These are strange paradoxes that do not mean much except for those who have experienced them. Wise Abba Poemen (fifth century) repeats in many of his aphorisms: "Weeping is the way the Scriptures and our Fathers give us, when they say 'Weep!' Truly, there is no other way than this."[1] For him repentance (*penthos*) is the gateway to all virtues, the hallmark of a proper mental outlook, the solid anchor for our hope of inheriting eternal life.

Through the concept of "tears" the Fathers are able to reach a very specific depth in the heart, much deeper than the many layers we can fathom within ourselves. Whoever lives in tears has abandoned any tendency to justify himself before God or his neighbors. He has given up any self-pity, any temptation to wallow in his own suffering. That very deep layer in the human heart is liberated, opened up, by persistent prayer of the psalms. It breaks us open and reforges us. Our clay is again made malleable in the hands of our Creator.

Humility and contrition prepare a fertile layer in the heart that is hospitable to God's grace. Every callousness, every form of anger or pent-up rage, even every expression of justified indignation is transformed by tears. Again we become capable of a lot more than that direct and often unfortunate vehemence of our reactions.

It is told how Abba Poemen once "found himself in rapture in the place under the cross where the Mother of God was standing." He had personified himself into the scene described by John the Evangelist. The disciple whom Jesus loved was also standing next to the Holy Mother. Apparently the Desert Father had identified with him and so became part of the tableau. About what he then experienced

1. *Sayings of the Desert Fathers* (Poemen 119), 184.

he could only say: "I wept much, and I wish I could weep like that forever." Here we sense a crying that is glorious, a crying that the abba wished would stay in his heart forever. Blessed are the weeping who just like Abba Poemen do not wish for anything more. "They will be comforted," says Jesus. They will receive the Paraclete, the Comforter, the Desert Fathers repeat in unison. The Holy Spirit rests, inalienably, on the broken heart. Break your heart. "Give blood and receive the Spirit," as Abba Longinus said.[2] Perhaps there is no better summary of the wisdom from the desert.

See also: Heart, Psalmody, Spirit, Weeping

2. *Sayings of the Desert Fathers* (Longinus 5), 123.

TIME AND THE EXPERIENCE OF TIME

Properly experiencing time is a marvel of mindfulness and freedom. For many people time has remained a god, as in ancient Greek mythology, and a terrible god at that. Cronos, as he is called there, devours his own children. Whoever serves this god must admit he does the same thing. Living under that god is relentless, filled with fear, driven by an inner tyranny capable of suffocating life. Time can kill.

Somebody once expressed his experience of time in the following way. Time, he said, is like a forest fire that destroys everything in its path. So what do you do? You can run fast but a strong wind is blowing, and how long can you keep on running like that? The best thing you can do is to make a little fire on the spot. Then when the big fire comes there is nothing left to feed it and it leaves you alone. We need to take our time with time, otherwise it devours us, no matter how fast we try to flee from it.

Desert Father Macarius taught: "Live as if you will die this very evening; and live as if you were to live another hundred years." Two perspectives on time. To implement them simultaneously creates space. The Desert Father taught in addition that we should distinguish between our physical and our psychic worlds. He said, "When you fast or keep night vigil or exhaust your donkey with heavy physical labor, remember you have a hundred years more to live!" Austerity is good and even indispensable, but never exaggerate: our donkey, brother body, has to last another hundred years. Let's treat it with respect and love.

However, when we deal with emotional or mental problems—anger, jealousy, a bout of depression, apathy—then, said Macarius, let's think that we may die this very evening and appear before the Judge. Imagine your final day with a sense of realism, and many fits of anger or despondency will immediately melt away. When I appear before God tonight, how important, really, are my feelings of jealousy or of being offended?

Living as if today is the only day of our life strengthens our focus on the here and now. But we know a whole choir of little voices within us will rise up and argue against. The movie of the past will be replayed before our eyes, and fears about the future will appear out of nowhere. Then we will realize that we are living our life without being free at all, and certainly not engaged in the present moment. So let us resolve to start each day as if it is the only day. This is not purely imaginary, even though it may appear to be so, but stark realism, even if the exercise requires the forceful engagement of our imagination.

"Day after day, may the Lord be blest. He bears our burdens; God is our savior" (Ps 68:20).[1] Remember that God never is elsewhere, never can be locked into a distant past or into an unseen future. God is always here and now. Every antithesis between time and eternity is resolved in God. To consciously think of this for a moment always feels good: to coincide with God is to coincide with a moment in which everything is synchronous, in which everything is present at the same time. Nothing is far removed, everything exists together in the one lap of our great God.

The communion of saints does not refer to a coming feast. Because God is God, a God of the living and not of the dead, He is already now "all in all." We simply don't see it yet. However, in meditation our spirit can rise to that wondrous perspective where nothing remains outside of God's omnipresence. Then time, which impatiently jumps forward as in a digital watch, falls totally still. Then the murderous compulsion of the experience of time is itself dead. An atom of pure silence reintroduces eternity. Gratitude reigns again, albeit for a moment, for awhile.

See also: Beginning, Gratitude, Feasting, Meditation, Mindfulness, Sabbath, Sunday

1. *The Revised Grail Psalms* (Collegeville, MN: Liturgical Press, 2012) [translator's note].

TSIMTSUM

This Hebrew expression comes from the verb *tsom*, which means "to fast." Tsimtsum is at the same time an intensive and a reflexive form of the verb *tsom*. In Jewish mystical literature, the Kabbalah, the term is used to denote God's creative act. In the beginning before God had created anything at all, there was only God. He occupied all space from beginning to end. There was nothing. Only God existed. A mystic like Meister Eckhart reflects on this and posits: even God did not exist because there was absolutely nothing and thus not anything, also not God. There was nothing and God was nothing. God only became God when something was allowed to exist outside of God. Now, however this may be, how was God able to create something outside himself?

In contrast with the then-current conception that God fabricated something, the mystics of the Middle Ages contended that God fasted on himself. He did tsimtsum. He performed a contraction, similar to the way the seas receded and the continents arose (to use another common metaphor). So the world does not exist outside of God but, rather, within the space that God opened within himself by momentarily emptying himself, by fasting.

Rabbi Jehuda Loew, the early eighteenth-century famous rabbi from Prague, thought this through in a remarkable fashion. In a warning to his contemporaries, he argued that it is all well and good for God to have a momentary contraction in order to create the world and human history, but if in his freedom man cannot manage to contract himself in awe before the Lord, then man himself will come to occupy that space entirely. Then, again, there will be "nothing," no God, no world, no thing! In the twentieth century, Jewish philosopher André Neher emphasized the pressing relevance of this insight for our generation.

Rabbinic tradition already held that God created the whole world only for fear of the Lord. It also said: God is omnipotent, but there is one thing he cannot bring about: fear of the Lord. That depends on the human being! Creation is, thus, an extremely precarious affair in which God and human being are bound to each other in a reciprocal relationship. If one of the two abdicates his responsibility toward the other, then everything collapses and soon there will be no more world, no God, no human being.

Hence, fasting on oneself is not just a matter for God, so that a world other than God can exist, but also we are meant to do a similar tsimtsum. If not, then we will perish under a totalitarian dream in which room for another than oneself is reduced to absolutely nothing. So here we see how practices like fasting and awe before the Lord are essential if we want to continue to honor the existence of the other.

The culture of abundance that surrounds us and that persists in imposing itself on just about every sector of society will, in the end, be incapable of saving itself, let alone saving something other than itself. The prophetic insight of the Maharal of Prague, Rabbi Jehudah Loew, hangs as a sword above our twenty-first century. The greatest threat is not terrorism by some underground groups like Al Qaeda or ISIS but, rather, the conceited totalitarian dream of those who like to call themselves the great powers. But is the kind of conversion that is required here still imaginable? We can only shake each other awake and continue to give warning, from the little ones to the powerful.

See also: Emptiness, Fasting, Fear of the Lord, Paradox, Reciprocity, Sabbath, Wisdom

U

UNAPPARENT VIRTUE

Your virtue should not be apparent. Hiding your virtue is quite an art. The Desert Fathers systematically demonstrated this. Some of them purposely fooled people in order to keep their highest virtues from being noticed. Almost all of them deflected indiscrete questions about their spiritual life. In this they followed in the footsteps of the Lord: "Do not let your left hand know what your right hand is doing." Jesus was talking about "treasures in heaven" where "neither moths nor rust" can consume them. What matters is to follow a number of practices not "in order to be seen by others" but by him who "sees in secret" and who "is in secret" (see Matt 6:1-20).

Abba Poemen once admitted that he purposefully took a nap when a brother came to find out whether or not the old man took a siesta in the afternoon. The gentle Abba Moses said: "The man who flees and lives in solitude is like a bunch of grapes ripened by the sun, but he who remains amongst men is like an unripe grape."[1] The following is also told about Abba Moses:

> The magistrate heard about Abba Moses one day and he went to Scetis to see him. They told the old man. He got up and fled to the marsh. Some people met him and said to him, "Old man, tell us where the cell of Abba Moses is." He said to them, "What do you want with him? He is a fool." So the magistrate went back to the church and said to the ministers, "I hear people talk about Abba Moses and I went to see him, but there was an old man going into Egypt who crossed our path and we asked him where Abba Moses' cell is, and he said to us, 'What do you want of him? He is a fool.'" When they heard this, the clergy were offended and said, "What kind of an old man was it who spoke like that about the holy man to you?" He said, "An old man wearing old clothes, a big black man." They said, "It was Abba Moses himself and it was in order not to meet you that he said that." The magistrate went away greatly edified.[2]

1. *Sayings of the Desert Fathers* (Moses 7), 140.
2. *Sayings of the Desert Fathers* (Moses 8), 140.

Here is another example:

> A brother said: "Many days ago I visited Abba Qoranis on mount Panahon. He imposed a heavy penance on me and ordered: 'Open your door only on Saturday and Sunday.' Afterwards I went to Abba Poemen and he released me of my penance and ordered me to keep my door open. He said: 'It is said that after the ostrich has laid her eggs in the desert, the hunters come, they follow the footprints, find the eggs, and take them away. Therefore, keep hidden the works you do for the Lord. Hide them, otherwise your efforts will be in vain. What man does in secret is dear to the Lord, because the inner exertion is pure and leads to victory. But if the soul surrenders to pride she will die. Fear of the Lord and discernment remove all stains.' "[3]

The same Abba Poemen was asked to interpret the verse in Ecclesiastes "a living dog is better than a dead lion" (Eccl 9:4). His answer proves once more the old man's powers of discernment and his systematic preference for what happens out of public view, for unapparent virtue: "A living dog is like a brother with a bad reputation. The brothers who see him say: 'He is bad.' However, in the eyes of the Lord the work that he does quietly is good, yes, even outstanding. A dead lion, on the other hand, is like a brother who enjoys a good reputation among all his brothers even though what he does between him and the Lord is 'dead' and utterly vain."[4]

What is most beautiful occurs at night, in silence, in solitude, hidden. The more silent and solitary one becomes, it was said in the Middle Ages, the more authentic one's life. With difficulty Abba Isaac got Abba Poemen to tell him where the latter has been in spirit during his silent meditation. When Abba Poemen finally relented, he said: "My thought was with Saint Mary, the Mother of God, as she wept by the cross of the Saviour. I wish I could always weep like that."[5]

3. Translated from the Dutch text in *Ethiopische Collectie*, 13:7 (Leuven: V. Arras, 1967) [translator's note].

4. Translated from the Dutch text in *Ethiopische Collectie*, 13:7 (Leuven: V. Arras, 1967) [translator's note].

5. *Sayings of the Desert Fathers* (Poemen 144), 187.

Abba Poemen said that Abba Moses asked Abba Zacharias, who was at the point of death, "What do you see?" He said, "Is it not better to hold my peace, Father?" And he said, "Yes, it is better to hold your peace, my child."[6] And Abba Zacharias died.

What is hidden, no matter how richly intuited by the other, remains unapparent, sealed unto death.

See also: Death, Emptiness, *Poustinia*

6. *Sayings of the Desert Fathers* (Zacharias 5), 68.

V

VISITING

To go visit somebody and to receive a visitor are two activities that presume a great deal of artfulness. The challenge can be enormous, with a vast panoply of possible situations: a sick child, an elderly uncle, a mother with dementia, a victim of a traffic accident, a widow shortly after the death of her husband, a cancer patient suspecting, but uncertain, that there is not much time left, a young mother after the birth of her first child, etc.

No theme is as present in world literature as that of the visit. Innumerable plays feature scenarios, comic or tragic, of visits that are or are not welcome. Not only friends but archenemies may be allowed to visit out of respect for social norms of hospitality, and a very ill person may realize that a certain visitor is only interested in what will be left after his passing.

The most beautiful as well as the most horrible things can happen during a visit. Words like "visit" and "visitation" have undertones that may denote judgment and perdition, or blessing and grace. When the Bible says of God that he "visits" (*paqad*) his people, only the context shows whether it will be to punish or to rescue. You always tremble a bit when you encounter that verb.

Benedict's Rule devotes a separate chapter to care of the sick brothers. The brother who goes to see his sick confrère realizes that he may encounter Christ in him. And conversely, the one confined to bed knows that the Lord is visiting in the person of the caregiver. In the successful visit, Christ encounters Christ. Benedict insists on this reciprocity not in spite of the differences between the two, but precisely because it reaches past all differences.

Sometimes the visitor wants to smooth over the disparities. When the patient begins to describe his pains and discomforts, the visitor starts talking about his own ailments (usually from the past!). The art consists in recognizing the other in his or her individuality and meeting him or her precisely there. Space for a true encounter only opens up when sufficient silence is allowed into the conversation and when people are truly listened to, without judgment, without comparison, without any kind of arrogance.

This art is difficult to master and these days many people are not even trying, although not so long ago it was considered a duty that should not be neglected. With narcissism in our culture riding high, the case for a visit is weakening on both sides. "Why should I go and visit?" the narcissist asks, unable to deal with awkward feelings and suppressed fears. "What good are all these visits to me?" complains the patient, "nobody understands me, nobody can even begin to feel what I have been through." So a good visit requires a lot of positive energy, not the least of the visitor, but also of the person being visited.

A successful visit always feels like something of a victory. To be able to experience reciprocity in and through the differences, that will always be the precious key. A quiet, unoccupied space between the participants is an indispensable requirement. Short, intense, vivid and comforting meetings occur when both sides could afterwards admit, "I no longer knew who was visiting whom! Who gave, who received? Who from whom?"

See also: Emptiness, Hospitality, Judge (Do Not), Listening, Reciprocity, Serving

VULNERABILITY

To allow ourselves to be vulnerable is a fundamental attitude that we need to pursue with persistence and that is as essential as our striving toward continual prayer.

To assume an attitude of vulnerability has nothing to do with being prickly or easily offended. The person who feels easily threatened or quickly loses his composure is obviously a vulnerable human being, but it is a puny ego that mainly figures in these forms of vulnerability.

The true or sublime vulnerability we are dealing with here starts when somebody detects suffering in others and allows it to enter in his own heart. Ethical vulnerability—which the Jewish philosopher Emmanuel Levinas constantly talks about—is one of the forms of this sublime vulnerability. In every relationship one discerns how the other comes first and how one can only be oneself in the reflection of the disarming face of the other. The face of the other evokes my responsibility, even before I can be myself. Vulnerable, I say, "Here I am" (see Abraham in Gen 22, or Isa 6:8).

At the apex of a mature vulnerability exists a paradox: the vulnerable person is able-bodied, ready to fight, but the reverse is also true. Pluck and courage do not render the strong individual insensitive or indifferent. In all his power, he preserves his total vulnerability toward the smallest and the weakest under the sun.

This is perhaps rendered nowhere as clearly as in the strange figure of the Suffering Servant in Second Isaiah (Isa 42–53). In the first of the four songs we read how the Spirit came over him and filled him with force: "he will bring justice to the nations" (Isa 42:1). But at the same time it is said that "a bruised reed he will not break" and "a dimly burning wick he will not quench" (Isa 42:3). His power does not make him indifferent to all that is tender and fragile. Furthermore, in that vulnerability in the presence of the weakest of the weak he himself does not become weak or feeble—the text expressly says, "He will not grow faint or be crushed" (Isa 42:4). On the contrary: "He will faithfully bring forth justice. He will not grow faint or be crushed until he has established justice in the earth; and the coastlands wait for his teaching" (Isa 42:3-4).

This is sublime vulnerability, portrayed in that exceptional figure of the Suffering Servant. Matthew the Evangelist saw the parallel with the coming of Jesus of Nazareth. In the midst of an exposition on Jesus' miracles he quotes the same verses from the prophet: Jesus as servant. Jesus goes around doing good deeds, affectively close to the people, heals and saves, without ever raising his voice in the streets (see Matt 12:17-21).

Still, this is strange: how is it possible to alleviate pain in silence, without raising your voice?

An Egyptian saying from the fifth century demonstrates how this ability is remarkably present in some people: "Abba Poemen said of Abba Nisterus that he was like the serpent of brass which Moses made for the healing of the people: he possessed all the virtues and without speaking, he healed everyone."[1] When Abba Poemen asked Abba Nisterus how he had acquired that virtue, observing that whenever a matter came up for discussion in the monastic community Abba Nisterus never spoke up and never intervened, he responded: "Forgive me, abba, but when I came for the first time to the monastery, I said to myself, 'You and the donkey are the same. The donkey is beaten but he does not speak, and when ill-treated he does not reply; now you must do the same, as the psalmist says, "I was like a beast towards thee; nevertheless, I am continually with thee"'" (Ps 73:22-23).[2]

Sublime vulnerability sent the small ego packing. The result is a boon for everyone, like the serpent that Moses held up in the desert. What could have been scary and deadly as a serpent became a communal remedy.

See also: Humility, Keeping Silent, Patience

1. *Sayings of the Desert Fathers* (Nisterus), 155.
2. *Sayings of the Desert Fathers* (Nisterus the Cenobite), 155–56.

W

WALKING

To walk is an art. We used to know how to do it, but we forgot. A little over ten years ago, I had an experience that shocked me. During a conference in Chicago I wanted to walk a bit along the shore of Lake Michigan. Immediately I was passed from all sides by people who were busily engaged in some activity: joggers, bicyclists on super-deluxe bikes with many gears, etc. As a simple wanderer enjoying the view of the water, the clouds, the skyline, I was all alone. Actually, I had to be careful not to be run over. Nobody smiled or said hello. No eye contact, nothing. Even in the lake somebody was exerting a lot of effort: a swimmer overtook me doing the crawl stroke in a fixed rhythm, while on the boardwalk somebody on a bicycle was actively coaching him. What a world, I thought. People have lost the ability of going on a simple walk. Everybody is busy with something and has to perform: always more, always better, always faster?

Yet the verb "to walk" features prominently in many schools of philosophy, in Buddhist exercises, in the life work of Jean-Jacques Rousseau, and in the core of Jewish spirituality (the *Halakha,* from the verb *halakh,* to walk). Just think of the precious verb *peripatein* that we find over and over in the New Testament to typify the true Christian walk of life: the walk with the Lord. See for example the beautiful *ambulate in dilectione:* "Be you, therefore, imitators of God, as very dear children, and walk in love" (Eph 5:1-2). Whoever walks in love imitates God.

We run, we race, we hike, we jog with discipline, but who still goes for a simple walk? What about the guy who lets out his dog at night: Could it be that it's the dog teaching him, yes, forcing him, to take a natural walk in the evening?

Intentional walking, carefree and mindful, is quite an art. Everybody would profit from doing this ritual for half an hour a day. What should we particularly pay attention to if we want to relearn the art? First, let us empty our head and be carefree, our mind uninhibited. Then, little by little, let us track our breath. Exhaling calmly and steadily deeper, without worrying about inhaling, which will come on its own. Our body has weight: intentional walking means transferring this weight from one leg to the other, firmly and fully planting the sole of each foot on the ground. The mind is free, open, the eyes are not fixed on anything in particular, the ears are more attentive than ever, the skin registers the coolness of the breeze, the nose picks up the smells in the air, scents of flowers, smoke, mould.

Giving and taking, inside and outside, silence and speaking, heaven and earth, back and forth, I and everything else, nearby and faraway, quick and slow: the walk accomplishes a reconciliation between many poles that are inherently part of our life and define it.

In every walk we can distinguish three stages: slowly getting going, adopting a steady rhythm, and then purposefully slowing down upon approaching the house. In the beginning, all of us will no doubt have to get out of the habit of looking at our watches: there is no goal to meet, no average to improve, no record to break. The proof is that after a walk I feel fitter, markedly less tired, freer in heart and mind, and am able to resume working with concentration.

It goes without saying that the art admits of all manner of variations because beside walking by yourself, you can walk with a friend, a child, a patient, an elderly person in a wheelchair. You can walk along the seashore or in the woods, a park, a city, a shopping area, etc.

Thich Nhat Hanh, the Buddhist monk, teaches people to "walk for peace." He once participated in a walk for peace in New York City. He and his brothers and sisters walked slowly and mindfully. Those who walk for peace do not march like an army. Thousands of people behind them were obliged to slow down and for the purpose of peace and reconciliation to take one step after the other in mindfulness. He recounts this story with a smile. Even when we organize a walk for peace, we race ahead as if we had to catch up with an imaginary enemy. This monk teaches us to use our feet mindfully, the whole person focused on the noble goal: peace on earth.

See also: Breathing, Dancing, Meditation, Mindfulness, Peace

WEEPING

After a monk has gathered himself in solitude and silence, he often feels the following question welling up, resounding in his inner sanctum with penetrating force: Friend, what is it that you came here to do? It is a serious question, even painfully so. Because it was precisely what Jesus told Judas in Gethsemane when he was about to be betrayed (see Matt 26:50). The one Judas would kiss was the one to be arrested, as it was customary for a disciple to greet his master with a kiss. So the armed men instantly recognized the master, and they led him away.

What is it that we came here to do in the desert, in the silence, in the solitude? To weep, was one of the most classic answers of the Desert Fathers. For "weeping is the way that Scripture and our Fathers have handed on to us," as Abba Poemen said in more than one of his aphorisms.[1]

Weeping has to do with contrition, with "a broken and contrite heart," as David put it so beautifully in Psalm 51 (v.19). Also in Psalm 34 we read, "The LORD is near to the brokenhearted, and saves the crushed in spirit" (v.18). Similarly, there is this: "Praise the LORD! . . . He heals the brokenhearted, and binds up their wounds" (Ps 147:1, 3).

For a monk "weeping" does not mean shedding a torrent of tears. It is about breaking with the inclination of self-justification. He is poor and utterly reconciled with his humble status. He knows his weakness and has learned to rely on God's help only. He even finds joy in this continual state of contrition. Abba Poemen said, "I wish I could always weep like that"[2] as, in rapture, he wept at the side of the Mother of God standing under the Cross. This expression, wishing always to be able to weep like that, testifies to a deep longing: the broken heart is not sad or depressed but, rather, intimately touched by grace and filled with divine consolation. Did Jesus not say in the opening lines of the Sermon on the Mount, "Blessed are those who mourn, for they will be comforted" (Matt 5:4)? The first monks said of this blessing that they will experience the in-dwelling of the Consoler, the Paraclete.

1. *Sayings of the Desert Fathers* (Poemen 209), 195.
2. *Sayings of the Desert Fathers* (Poemen 144), 187.

Let us go again in search of the truth hidden in the many proverbs of the wise Desert Fathers who repeat without end that happiness is found in continual weeping. The truly weeping heart is inhabited and can no longer be detracted by superficialities. The source wells up inside, incessant prayer continues: the heart beseeches and praises, laments and gives thanks. At the same time, the temptation to judge whoever or whatever, or to engage in negative comparisons, is chased away once and for all. The weeping heart is finally pure and free.

See also: Heart, Judge (Do Not), Lament, Praise, Psalmody, Source, Tears

WISDOM

Those who wish to apply themselves to wisdom may be guided by the following saying: "Wisdom is three things plus a fourth." Wisdom is encyclopedic knowledge. Wisdom is workmanship. Wisdom is being sensitive to the mystery of things. Wisdom is Someone.

Encyclopedic Knowledge

A wise person knows a lot and is interested in all manner of things. What is the structure of the universe? What do ants teach us? What explains the power of herbs? How do people relate to one another given the difference of their personalities? According to the Talmud, "If the Torah had not been given to Israel, we would have learned our sense of shame from cats, chastity from turtles, courtesy from roosters, and honesty from ants."

Wise is the person who has learned from cats and sparrows, and who has succeeded in being at home in more than one world or culture. Knowing many things includes the clear realization that one does not know everything. For the more you know, and the more in detail you know, the more you become impressed with your own limitations. You become more realistic: everything that is relative is really relative, only the absolute may be considered as such. True modesty is no longer out of reach. There is a hidden dynamic in this first track: remain a seeker, inquisitive and always open to what is other than yourself. Ignorance is sin. Much misplaced absolutism and fanaticism—not only in religious parlance—come from the lack of a broad cultural understanding.

Workmanship or Practical Art of Living

In Greek or in the Hebrew of the Bible a wise man is a man who has a sense for business and who knows his trade. Workmanship is wisdom. A good carpenter, a master blacksmith, and a skillful butcher are all "wise men." Whatever you do, to do it well, with the right posture, at the right time, completely at ease in whatever trade you practice, that also is wisdom.

A tale from Taoist China tells the story of a butcher who used the same knife for nineteen years without ever sharpening it. That knife still cuts as sharply as on the first day because the butcher knows the animals through and through and he always cuts into the space between the dense and hard parts of every animal. Herein lies his great wisdom.

The builders of the sanctuary in the desert, Bezalel and Oholiab, appointed by Moses, are wise men. The story notes how they possessed wisdom, understanding, and knowledge, the three virtues with which God, according to Proverbs, created the world (Prov 3:19-20). They built altars, carved pure lamp stands, wove fine vestments, prepared anointing oil, and they did all this with skill, understanding, and wisdom (see Exod 31:1-11).

Wise are they who know to conduct themselves properly in all their relationships, and who can control their tongue and even the thoughts in their heart. Desert Father Abba Poemen taught his disciple: "Teach your mouth to say that which you have in your heart," and "teach your heart to guard that which your tongue teaches."[1]

Wise men and women have learned to attune their heart with their mouth. In the liturgy their inner self is fully in accord with what they are reading, proclaiming, or singing. In open conversation with a spiritual director, they learn to give voice to their heart, with all its facets of light and shadow.

Where encyclopedic knowledge reaches far and wide, workmanship remains concrete, requires practice and persistence, and leads to true mastery, albeit of only one particular segment of reality. But those who have learned to do flower arrangements have acquired a quality that will pervade their whole life, just like the flower properly arranged in the vase fills a spacious room with harmonious beauty.

Sense for the Mystery of Things

The core of every thing
Is still and without end.
Only things can truly sing,
Our song is short, easy to rend. (Felix Timmermans)[2]

Wise are they who have a sense for the mystery of things. Whether their gaze is turned outward or inward, their eye has learned to stand still before what is unexplainable, simply to behold what is beautiful,

1. *Sayings of the Desert Fathers* (Poemen 63, 188), 175, 193.
2. Flemish writer and poet (1886–1947) [translator's note].

to recognize what is freely given, or to understand the tragic side of human existence. The sages do not destroy the mystery or break the silence with poems and proverbs but, rather, make them only more palpable, even greater, if possible. Questioning, sometimes with ironic detachment, they fathom what exceeds human intelligence yet falls within immediate experience.

They are familiar with abysses, large and small (see *Le plus petit abîme*, by Jean Sulivan).[3] This is how wise men and women develop a culture of wonder and an ability to live with paradox. They reach a limit where subject and object cease to stand in opposition to each other, where passive and active forms no longer compete but flow into each other, and where "foolishness" may be a fitting name for "wisdom." They do see the differences in customary opposites, but offer the possibility of a new insight: is everything not *one* and is God in his full transcendence also not immanently present in everything?

Everything starts with the ability to marvel at phenomena, sometimes very nearby, that are inexplicably beautiful or ghastly and deserve our attention for that very reason.

> The leech has two daughters;
> "Give, give," they cry.
> Three things are never satisfied;
> four never say, "Enough":
> Sheol, the barren womb,
> the earth ever thirsty for water,
> and the fire than never says, "Enough." (Prov 30:15-16)

In the same book of Wisdom, we also read:

> Sheol and Abaddon are never satisfied,
> and human eyes are never satisfied. (Prov 27:20)

This reminds us of a verse from the Song of Solomon:

> For love is strong as death,
> passion fierce as the grave.

3. Jean Sulivan is the pen-name of Joseph Lemarchand, French priest and writer (1913–1980). His book *Le plus petit abîme (The Smallest Possible Abyss)* was published in France by Gallimard in 1965 [translator's note].

> Its flashes are flashes of fire,
> a raging flame. (Song 8:6)

In the first of the three proverbs it is as if all the cosmic elements share in the mystery of insatiability, while the "barren womb" in the middle of the saying provides the human interface, with its own bottomless pain.

> Three things are too wonderful for me;
> four I do not understand:
> the way of an eagle in the sky,
> the way of a snake on a rock,
> the way of a ship on the high seas
> and the way of a man with a girl. (Prov 30:18-19)

Here again we have the mysterious tension between the vastness of the cosmos—the sky, the rock, the seas, the highest and the lowest—and the human heart. The latter especially, says the sage, remains "too wonderful for me," an indirect confession of the mystery of his own heart.

Wisdom Is Someone

Someone who looks for knowledge, understanding, and wisdom, who lives within the proper degree of awe before the Lord and thoughtful attention for what here and now is right, and who has a sense for the inexplicable mystery of all that can be seen or heard will, sooner or later, experience an inner shock. Step-by-step, in biblical testimony as well as by experience, wisdom becomes Someone. What originally appeared to be purely a quality now turns into an autonomous entity, a subject within our own subjectivity, an alter ego. Its many attributes are experienced as names of the One, as traces of the features of the Invisible.

Every Belgian child knows Guido Gezelle's poem about the swifts. The poet's point of departure is observation of and listening to the swallows gliding in the sky and swiftly skimming the church towers. But Gezelle sees and hears more: he discerns a calling and searching for Someone: "See, see, see . . . Who? Who?? Who???" Yes, "verily they serenade the One I do not see!"

This way of being mindful and wondering at certain phenomena or qualities in the world around us until one pushes through to Someone may surprise us from the standpoint of logic, but in fact is practiced in many traditions.

Gregory of Nyssa (fourth century), himself deeply steeped in Plato's thought, posited that virtue in its perfection is God himself. Applying ourselves to the virtues seems like climbing a mountain yet at the top, we find nothing other than God.

"Someone in me, more myself than me," was how Augustine phrased it, and his experience of a gathered inwardness has inspired saints and mystics throughout the ages. *Deus interior intimo meo, superior summo meo* (more inward than my innermost self and higher than my highest).[4] God is at the same time immanent to my innermost self and transcendent to my own spiritual transcendence. Paul Claudel's experience on Christmas Eve, 1886 was nothing other than the same undeniable breakthrough: *Quelqu'un d'autre en moi, plus moi-même que moi* (an Other in me, more me than I myself).

The Desert Fathers said that "fear of God" had to be the first point of focus for the monk if he wished to open the gate to the experience of the indwelling Holy Spirit. A quality leads to the Spirit in person. Benedict declares the same thing in his Rule. This studied practice leads him to the felicitous formulation that the brother assigned to the guest quarters should be "full of the fear of God" (RB 53:21); *cuius animam timor Domini possidet:* possessed, just like a city that is "occupied" or "possessed," by someone, an other than oneself.

Even in a philosopher like Jean Nabert (twentieth century) we observe a similar movement, however much he was guided by a severe critical attitude. "Whether God exists, I don't know," he wrote, "but with the word 'divine' I can call up very particular experiences: well-defined forms of goodness and forgiveness are undeniably 'divine.' " By reflecting on all phenomena that are recognized as "divine" in common experience, he drew the conclusion that the divine requires a divine Subject and that denying this Someone is untenable.

Also in the biblical Wisdom Literature we see that wisdom as virtue or as quality gradually assumes the features of a person next to or within the wisdom figure. Sometimes the transition is extremely subtle and still timid:

> For wisdom will come into your heart,
> and knowledge will be pleasant to your soul;

4. See Spirit, n. 1.

> prudence will watch over you;
> and understanding will guard you. (Prov 2:10-11)

Thus, wisdom will become a protective and guiding agency in the student's heart.

Elsewhere in the same book she appears as a lady who stands "at the crossroads" and cries out to passersby to listen to her teachings (Prov 8:2-3). She has a lot to offer! She mediates in the highest good: insight and life, yes, the favor of the Lord himself (Prov 8:35).

In various biblical poems Wisdom is thought of and described as moving in the immediate surroundings of God himself, as if she were God's assistant in the design and execution of his work when he created the universe (see Prov 8:22-31). At times she is the architect, at other times the young playful girl, close to God as well as "delighting in the human race" (Prov 8:31). This delight is possibly the source of the whole poem in Proverbs 8.

Because the wise one experienced her in her pure, penetrating, and most personal quality, he is able to exemplify Wisdom in all her relations—with God, with creation, and with the human person. He speaks in her name, in the first person, but in the very last verse confesses the joy he shares with her and she with him.

In this manner we push through to a wisdom that fully transcends the whole cosmos, no matter how imposing it may be, but that enjoys a personal relationship of pleasure and delight with God and with the human race.

"Wisdom is three things plus a fourth." Whoever mindfully practices the first three "things" will experience, sooner or later, the mysterious agency as "fourth" in him- or herself. What comes as "fourth" is no longer a "thing" but a subject in his or her own subjectivity. "It is no longer I who live, but it is Christ who lives in me" (Gal 2:20). Paul reaches that last measure of wisdom when he experiences life ever more radically rooted "in Christ" and no longer in himself. Then Christ becomes for him that wisdom personified, which is a paradox because in the eyes of the people she appears foolish and weak, all the while fully revealing God's power and God's wisdom.

See also: Conversation, Culture, Fear of the Lord, God, Paradox, Source, Wonder

WONDER

Wonder lies at the basis of any philosophical life, wrote Plato. In the first phase of wonder, we become aware how doors can open. The reality that faces us, life lived in our own experience, unexpectedly begins to reveal depths we never suspected. As Martinus Nijhoff, the Dutch writer and poet, once said, "Go ahead and read what is there. Yet, it is not what is there." In wonder, two things happen: we fully admit the reality that stares us in the face *and* we discover simultaneously how that reality escapes us, exceeds us, defeats us. There is always more, and it is different than we could surmise at first. Blessed are they who dare to wonder: they experience life as a source of flowing water.

Adopting wonder as a constant, basic attitude leads to a veritable art form. Only someone who is awakened sees forever new facets and different aspects of an icon, a flower arrangement, a landscape, an ocean. Like Hegel, she will admit upon seeing a waterfall: always the same and always different. So is the Holy Spirit. Wonder is a happening within the spirit of the Spirit.

Intentionally living in wonder presupposes the ability to become still, to withdraw, and to abandon old and rusted patterns, ossified habits, and nearly compulsive customs or behaviors. A culture of silence greatly promotes the facility for wonder so that we can continually discover the new and the unsuspected in the ordinary and the customary.

Desert Father Evagrius (d. 399) appears to have been the first person to place the experience of wonder at the highest level of the spiritual search. This thought, which he once shared in a letter to the Holy Sr. Melania in Jerusalem, received much attention in the later Syriac tradition, particularly by Isaac the Syrian (seventh century). Isaac regularly points to that beautiful limit of every prayer activity and contemplation when we tumble into a state of wonder that is boundless, yes, that knows no end. Words and images utterly fail to express all that the soul experiences in such a moment.

"Wonder of wonders," people may say when they observe or live through something that is unheard of or that is extremely complex. The expression is exceptionally apt here because the surpassing beauty of that state of wonder exceeds the capacity of all our faculties (intellect, memory, and will) to such an extent that we go from one wonder to another, in an infinite process of astonishment—a wonder without end that attempts in vain to respond to the inexhaustible original Life. The impossibility of the attempt is pure joy.

See also: Gratitude, Gratuitous, Growing, Jubilation, Paradox, Source

WU WEI

People only truly know where they live after they have traveled and lived elsewhere. If we don't mind spending a little time learning from the Chinese, we can give new impetus to the Sabbath rest, so celebrated in the Bible and in Jewish tradition, and in the fourth century converted by Christians into the day of rest on Sunday.

The invention of the wheel is based on the discovery of the silent hub in the wheel that does not turn with the rest. The wheel's own dynamic occurs when stillness and movement, turning and not turning, form a reciprocal reality. Stillness by itself and movement by itself fall completely outside the reality of the wheel. Only their mutual involvement defines the new discovery.

Chinese Taoist masters have reflected deeply on the functioning of the wheel, which is based on the still point in the heart of the turning circle. The relationship between, on the one hand, our usual busyness with all kinds of things and, on the other hand, a still, powerful "not doing" (*wu wei*) belongs to the most original considerations of Taoism. The most active, productive person is the one who is able to live life out of that still point of "not doing." The person who is busy all day and labors into the night, seven days a week, may believe that he accomplishes much but our Chinese masters severely doubt whether he actually has achieved anything at all.

Wu means "not," nothing, negative. *Wei* indicates doing, performing, working and figuring out, and also calculating or referring to. So the two characters together, *wu wei*, mean: "not doing (anything)" or "acting without calculation." The spontaneous life stands in opposition to the life that is intentional and purpose-driven. Instead of actively meddling or angrily disturbing the ordinary course of things, the wise person chooses to become still and one with the Tao, the Way, and to refrain from interfering.

Then everything happens *sponte sua*, as one used to say in Latin: spontaneously, "according to inborn necessity" (*volgens ingeschapen moeten*) in the phrase of the Dutch poetess Ida Gerhardt, or *velut naturaliter* as Benedict wrote in his Rule after a monk has climbed all the steps of the ladder of humility. In the words of Fong Yeoe-lan, what the Tao accomplishes is not consciously performed but is simply achieved spontaneously.

Here are some more Taoist sayings that further clarify what the Chinese have in mind with *wu wei*:

> Trees and mountains endure.
> Why?
> Because of "not doing." (Chinese proverb)

From the *Tao Te Ching*:[1]

> Practice not-doing,
> and everything will fall into place. (from chap. 3)
>
> The Master, by residing in the Tao,
> sets an example for all beings.
> Because he doesn't display himself,
> people can see his light.
> Because he has nothing to prove,
> people can trust his words.
> Because he doesn't know who he is,
> people recognize themselves in him.
> Because he has no goal in mind,
> everything he does succeeds. (from chap. 22)
>
> Therefore the Master
> acts without doing anything
> and teaches without saying anything.
> Things arise and she lets them come;
> things disappear and she lets them go.
> She has but doesn't possess,
> acts but doesn't expect.
> When her work is done, she forgets it.
> That is why it lasts forever. (from chap. 2)
>
> The Master stays behind;
> that is why she is ahead.

1. Lao Tsu, *Tao Te Ching*, trans. Stephen Mitchell (New York: HarperCollins Publishers, 1999).

> She is detached from all things;
> that is why she is one with them. (from chap. 7)
>
> The Tao never does anything
> yet through it all things are done. (from chap. 37)
>
> The great Tao flows everywhere.
> All things are born from it,
> yet it does not create them.
> It pours itself into its work,
> yet it makes no claim.
> It nourishes infinite worlds,
> yet it doesn't hold on to them.
> Since it is submerged with all things
> and hidden in their hearts,
> it can be called humble.
> Since all things vanish into it
> and it alone endures,
> it can be called great.
> It isn't aware of its greatness;
> thus it is truly great. (from chap. 34)

Periodically taking time off from work has little to do with *wu wei*. The Tao's "not doing" is present, vibrates, in all that we do and that we don't do. Many people in their formative years experience time as a bicycle pump: full/empty, full/empty. Panting from exertion, they carry on under severe pressure and rigid, chock-full schedules, often followed by periods of barren emptiness: sleeping till 11:00 a.m., surfing the TV channels, or chatting without end on their cell phones. Others vary their busy schedules with programs of recreational activities that are just as full: physical exercise, music lessons, dance recitals, etc. "Not doing" is nowhere to be found.

Jewish people close the Sabbath on Saturday night with a distinct service called *havdalah* (separation). Everybody receives a twig of sage, rosemary, or other fragrant herb. The point is not to forget the Sabbath's good aromas during the coming week. We live from Sabbath to Sabbath, and during the week a whiff of last Sabbath's perfume will linger in our memory. The celebration continues to quiver in us even while we do our everyday chores. Just as the Sabbath shares its fine perfume every day of the week, so *wu wei* needs to be part of all we do.

In the heart of every classically built monastery one usually finds a large, empty square. Enclosed on all four sides by cloister walks, it features an interior garden, often with a small pond or fountain at its center. The whole area serves no purpose. There is no work to be done there, no planting or seeding, not even meditating, let alone studying. All you can do is pass it, and you have no choice because church and refectory, community hall and library are separated by this central square.

Our abbey is built around this emptiness; it serves as a vital lung in the inner core of our house. How wonderful it is to move from one activity to another by being able to pass this zone of nothing. Everywhere in the house energy is being produced or used, but here nothing happens: zero energy. You pass it and you think of NOTHING. You sense right away how this nothingness rearranges you, calms you down, and enables you to receive new life in the next space you enter. It is a good question whether we would be able to carry on in the monastery as peacefully as we do without that emptiness.

Is there something like a still point or an empty, open space in the core of my existence? Do I recognize that it is deeper than my intentions, purer than my highest ideals, free of any mental association? Do I also experience the wonder of the wheel within me, or do I belong, unbeknownst to myself, to the many "primitive" civilizations that predate this discovery?

The still point is what Abbot Jerome Theisen, former Abbot Primate of the Order of Saint Benedict, called that key experience. He said it should never be absent from the monk's heart. It is as if a bubbling spring lies hidden in this cultivated stillness. On Sundays, the Christian Sabbath, you come and wash yourself in the clear waters of that spring. And during the week you always know where to go to be refreshed.

Let us listen one last time to a Chinese tale. The end happens on the "seventh day." But does something like this not happen every day, under our own eyes, in our own region?

> The king of the Southern Sea was called Speedy, the king of the Northern Sea was called Suddenly, while the king of the middle kingdom was called No Difference. One good day King Speedy and King Suddenly met in the land of King No Difference, who gladly received them both. Now Speedy and Suddenly wished

to repay their host for his gracious reception and they said to each other: "A person has seven openings to see, to hear, to eat, to breathe. No Difference has none. Let's drill these openings for him." They went to work and every day they made another opening. On the seventh day No Difference died. (Zhuang Zi)

See also: Emptiness, Sabbath, Source, Sunday

X

X

"X" stands for the unknown, the unnameable, that which is without form or manner. Meister Eckhart and Ruusbroec both appeared to have been fascinated by a mysterious excess that is beyond measure and that presupposes absolute indefiniteness. St. Bernard already said it two centuries before Eckhart: *modus orationis est sine modo* (the manner and measure of prayer is unlimited, without form). Because sooner or later, all forms will be consumed by fire.

With the fire image we reach even further back into history. We arrive at John Cassian (end of the fourth, beginning of the fifth century), who talks about the prayer of fire. When the soul offers thanks for what God already now has reserved for those who fear Him, prayer flares up in an all-consuming fire. Even memory cannot hold onto that moment in any shape or form. An ancient Greek proverb says the same thing: the definition (*oros*) or measure of prayer is unlimited, indefinite, indefinable (*aoristos*).

It remains a spiritual practice to expand limits again and again or to see the confines and the isolation of any system with greater clarity. Therefore, keep your desire open to that which is truly without limits. What we do not know about God is infinitely more than everything we think we know, even if we had the collective knowledge of everything that all peoples and all cultures have said about God. As the wise Nicolas Cusanus taught his contemporaries: "What we do not know infinitely surpasses everything all of us together could say or know about God."

Wonder and immense respect for the Mystery are able to truly unite all people, whereas comparative studies of their separate belief systems can only make us realize how irreconcilable these systems are. Precisely because of that incompatibility (see Raimon Panikkar), we would be well advised to stop expecting that such comparative exercises will solve everything. Growth is only assured when we apply ourselves, past words and concepts, to remaining in reverential relationship with that "X."

> The Tao that can be told
> is not the eternal Tao. (*Tao Te Ching*, chap. 1)

See also: Forms and Formlessness, Measure and Beyond Measure, Paradox, Wisdom, Wonder

Y

YES-AMEN

For the Son of God, Jesus Christ. . . was not "Yes and No"; but in him it is always "Yes." For in him every one of God's promises is a "Yes" (2 Cor 1:19-20).[1]

What engages our personal freedom deeper than to say "Yes" or "No"? This is why a pure "yes" or a radical "no" is difficult and rare. Some people contend they cannot say "no," which is often offered as a sort of excuse. If you recognize this trait in yourself, you should ask: "Well, am I able to truly say 'Yes'?" We all know that a double negative ("not no") is not the same thing as a forceful positive statement. A straightforward "yes" from the bottom of one's heart always has something grand about it. Jesus measures the depths of our heart when he says: "Let your word be 'Yes, Yes' or 'No, No'; anything more than this comes from the evil one" (Matt 5:37).

Paul, discussing his travel plans with his beloved Corinthians, asks, "Are we yes and no?" He certainly does not want his conduct to appear capricious, indecisive, let alone arbitrary. His only point of reference is Christ, who was one big "yes!" Further, when in the liturgy we affirm "Yes-Amen," we say that "yes" in Him, in Christ. He liberates us in our heart, it is He who animates our assent (see 2 Cor 1:20-21).

So we see how "yes" and "amen" coincide in one great assent. Every "amen" contains a profession of faith. When we say "amen" we assent and confirm that to which we assent. In Semitic languages "amen" actually means the same thing as "I believe" (*credo*). Our creed always starts with "amen," "I believe," and also ends that way. There we find the core of our freedom as created beings. By professing it, we tie ourselves to the self-revealing God, Father, Son, and Holy Spirit.

Nobody interprets this moment in the Gospels as pointedly as Mary when, in the annunciation, she is addressed by the angel Gabriel. Her "yes"—"Here am I, the servant of the Lord; let it be with me according to your word"—is of the purest quality and testifies to the greatest freedom found in all sacred texts. God created the whole

1. Translated from the author's Dutch text; it is necessary to understand the author's commentary that follows [translator's note].

world so that this could happen: somebody who can say "yes" to him, free as a virgin.

In the Bible, Amen stands for nothing less than a name of God and a name for Jesus. That is how exalted this word is, and how intensely it marks the relationship between God and human being.

The prophet Isaiah speaks of the God of the Amen, the God of faithfulness: the faithful God who confirms what he has promised in the covenant (Isa 65:19).

Finally, in the book of Revelation we hear Christ dictate to the angel of the church in Laodicea: "The words of the Amen, the faithful and true witness" (Rev 3:14). So here Christ calls himself Amen. He is the personification of the unbreakable bond of the divine promises through a freely professed amen.

"And let all the people say, 'Amen.' Alleluia!" (Ps 106:48). So ends the fourth book of Psalms. In these few words our whole destiny is summarized: in the Amen our assent and confirmation of God's will resounds, in the Alleluia we hear the ode of victory. Amen is the word of the night vigil in Gethsemane, Alleluia is the joyous cry of Easter morning. When we rock these two words to and fro in our heart and inwardly repeat them like a prayer formula, we share in Christ's Paschal experience. They contain the shortest summary of the whole book of one hundred and fifty Psalms. Whoever prays them, prays in the name of all the people. Christ and his body call out: Amen! Alleluia!

A Portuguese anchorite in the desert of Judah near Bethlehem once composed a short prayer and submitted it to her sisters: "Sim, Abba, Jesus, Amor" (Yes-Amen, Abba, Jesus, Love). It constitutes a recent Jesus prayer, based on the four divine names. The revelatory movement from Father to Son and Holy Spirit is easily recognized in the last three names. In the Yes-Amen we find at the same time the Marian moment of assent and the biblical confirmation of Christ as God's Amen in history.

It is well to carry these four words in our heart and to utter them softly as a short prayer, profession of faith, aspiration, and simultaneous beseeching and praising because by praying it God's love descends on us through Jesus, and we in turn can thank and praise him for his fatherly benevolence.

See also: Aspirations, Ejaculatory Prayer, Mary, Name, Profession of Faith, Reciprocity

YIN AND YANG

Yin and yang: let us be Chinese for a moment with the Chinese. Who knows, their wisdom may bring us a little closer to what, also for us, truly matters.

Yin and yang stand for two opposing and complementary energies. They relate to each other as shadow and light, earth and heaven, moon and sun. The former is soft, passive, receptive, female, and dark, while the latter is masculine, active, creative, hard, and clear. Both are required for the birth of the universe and its unfolding. Not only the whole cosmos but also we humans (health, physical balance, etc.) depend on the reciprocal interaction of yin and yang. Too much yang means excessive activity, while too little yin results in health problems.

The symbols for yin are the moon, water, clouds, the tiger, the tortoise, the color black, north, the chemical element lead, and even numbers. For yang they are the sun, fire, the dragon, the color red, south, the chemical element mercury, and uneven numbers.

In the classic *I Ching* or *Book of Changes,* yin and yang are graphically depicted as two short juxtaposed lines: yin is formed by a broken line of two equal lengths, with a small space in-between, while yang is an unbroken line of the same length as yin with its two parts. The whole of existence constantly changes according to the alternating arrangements of these two energy principles: each moment exists in a certain configuration of the two, at times with a preponderant yang, at other times with a predominant yin.

The canon lists sixty-four possible configurations of yin and yang lines, every configuration consisting of six lines (hexagrams). Within each configuration the strong and the weak sides of the current phase can be distinguished. The commentary never moralizes, but invites the reader to consider a proper management of the moment's energy possibilities. Sometimes emphasis may be placed on keeping distance, letting go, waiting and "not doing;" at other times sensitive and bold steps may be needed in order to achieve a new creative balance.

The circle with two fields representing the relationship between yin and yang is a well known symbol:

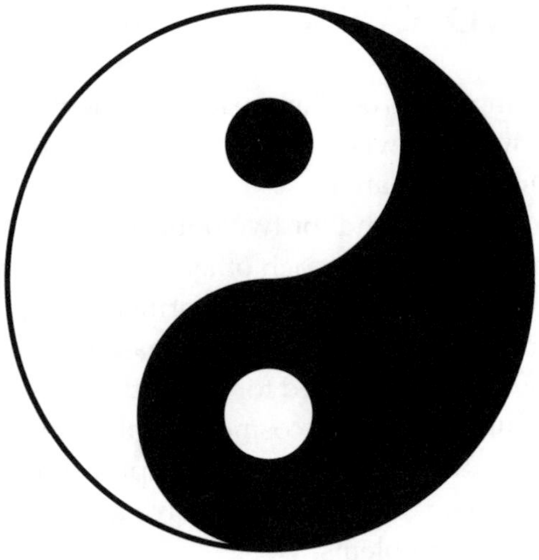

The round disk with its two fields of black and white, separated by a large S, shows a white dot in the heart of the black field and, conversely, a black dot in the white field. If you explore one field thoroughly, you find the reverse of that field in its center. If you move to one field's extremity, you tumble willy-nilly into the other. The totality of reality, symbolized by the circle, is divided dynamically in two opposite fields and colors. Nothing is only white or solely black. This is the core of the original wisdom of this Chinese view of the world.

This approach is not totally foreign to the West. Just think for a moment of Socrates and the question he posed to himself: Does the virtuous life consist in doing only what is right? Don't we see that a good runner is not just somebody who is able to run fast but one who, at times, slows down the pace? He is a good runner because he knows the right moment to switch between running fast and slow. But how about the virtuous life? Is the virtuous person the one who does the right thing some times and the wrong thing at other times? Or does he only do the right thing and never the wrong thing? Socrates left the question up in the air. The dialogue ends in an *aporia*, an impasse: his questions did not resolve the issue.

To appreciate the difference as well as the originality of this Eastern way of thinking, let us consider another image, one that is typically Western European and now increasingly familiar in the Far East: the soccer field. Soccer is the most exciting team game in human history. The game was created and took shape shortly after the onset of the industrial revolution in the West, and it reflects something of our culture.

The field is not a circle but a rectangle. It is not about the totality of reality but only a notch of it. The two teams must be clearly opposed to each other both in colors and in inner disposition—they should have nothing in common! For members of one team to be in cahoots with the other team is absolutely forbidden. If that should be observed, the game would be immediately cancelled and the score would be annulled. It's all based on pure violence, albeit channeled in carefully set out rules, for a clear oppositional (0/1) outcome. The inner dynamic of the game does not serve life, as does the Chinese drawing. At most, it serves (usually in a healthy way) to vent certain violent tendencies.

Yin and yang are present everywhere: there is a feminine aspect in men, and vice versa. In an analogous perception of the necessity of an inner complementarity, Roman thinkers have been preoccupied with concepts such as *anima* and *animus* (soul and spirit). So we in the West are not totally unprepared to make room for that oriental wisdom. Yet we have to admit that since the Enlightenment and the industrial revolution we have developed a remarkable one-sidedness, with disastrous consequences for the cosmos and the biosphere which are becoming clearer every day. So why not advance the cause of incorporating more Eastern wisdom into our Western thinking? The encounter between cultures and world religions requires sturdy and creative hospitality. It is precisely in the practice of that kind of hospitality that we can learn much from the yin-yang model for recognizing, and fully allowing, the other in me.

See also: Dialogue, Emptiness, Hospitality, Paradox, *Wu Wei*

YOU AS "YOU"

My heart seeks You,
To You it clings,
Your right hand upholds me. (Ps 63:8)

This is David's testimony in one of his psalms. The heart seeks with fervor that One, that You. Until it suddenly discovers that it is being held up by the Other. Until I suddenly discover that You supported me long before I searched for You. Sooner or later I realize that my search is animated by You, that my longing is rooted in your original desire. This understanding liberates me. In the end silence surrounds You, and there is nothing else.

In Mark we read how Jesus prayed in the Garden of Olives:

Abba, Father,
for you all things are possible;
remove this cup from me;
yet, not what I want,
but what you want. (Mark 14:36)

In four short phrases, the beginning and end address the same reality: Father and You. In-between these two extremes, the agony of personal freedom that is at stake, then the complete surrender. The Greek text does not even provide a verb in the last sentence; it simply ends in the pure profession of the Name of the Other ("but what You").

In the Gospel according to John, the prayer is translated in this original fashion: "Father, glorify your name" (John 12:28). The Son asks the Father to glorify his fatherly Name. Therein lies his salvation. That prayer is not expressly about himself. When the Father glorifies his Name, he also glorifies his Son: in the name "Father" the relationship to the son is understood. It is no longer necessary to mention the son's name.

Praying until that divine You prevails in its own radiance over one's whole existence, that is the limit but also the core of every prayer. The praying subject grows quiet and dies to himself or herself until only the Kingdom of God reigns over everything. "The LORD is King" is the opening phrase of various psalms. This reality exists from the very beginning until the very end. In prayer we realize how the One already encompasses the universe.

God is "You," but God is also "He." God even is "I." Our language uses three persons, as do all languages. In grammar "I" indicates the first person singular, while in actual experience we learn "I" last. A child who says "I" has come a long way in her development, past "you" and "he" until she arrives at herself, first expressed in the third person ("Jane wants this").

In Jewish mysticism we learn that God can be "You" as well as "He" and "I." Even more: in every you we should treat God as that Other; you becomes "You." At the same time, He is totally Himself, as the Latin masters knew very well when they talked about the *Ille* and the *Illeitas* of God.

God himself is transcendent, exalted above everything and everybody. And "God in me" refers to his immanence. He lives in me, more myself than I, or, in the phrase of St. Augustine, *deus interior intimo meo* (more inward than my innermost self).[1] And Augustine adds immediately, in a spontaneous movement to reflect the fullness of his experience of God: *et superior summo meo* (and more exalted than the highest in me). The two half sentences describe a double movement: from the outside to the inside and from the inside to above. All of Western mysticism finds its grammar in that one saying of the bishop of Hippo. Interiorization and sublimation. St. Bonaventure (thirteenth century) merges both movements as if in reality there were only one.

Now, in Jewish mysticism we also encounter the following paradox:

> We have to attempt to recognize the Creator in the traces of his presence, his works, and we should not try to reach him in the inner being of his glory. For He is infinitely close within his creatures and infinitely far away in his own being. We cannot grasp his glory, neither with our mind nor with our senses. But if we dispense with looking for him where He cannot be reached, we encounter Him immediately in the signs that He leaves of himself in all his works. (Bahya Ibn Paquda, eleventh century)

God himself, in the third person, in his *Illeitas*, is unreachable. God in his creatures, in the other and in ourselves, is extremely close: there

1. See Spirit, n. 1.

God is a "You" and an "I." In the face of every other person let us see, and honor, the mysterious and irreducible presence of the Other. This typically Jewish insight stands at the center of the whole philosophy of the Jewish thinker Emmanuel Levinas, and is infused with a highly ethical consciousness. When, in addition, we also make a practice of silence, we can experience how God continually, in everything, speaks: "I am who I am." He is the very being in things and, as the poet knows, "The things sing." *Being* sings. In me and in everything we hear confirmation of the original revelation: "I am." Who would not say with thanksgiving: "Your right hand upholds me"?

See also: Abba, God, Meditation, Name

Z

ZERO

For the last letter of the alphabet we choose a word that denotes the number "0." This number does not look all that different from the last letter in the Greek alphabet, O-mega. So we end up with Zero or Nought. How important is Zero in our life?

One of the most valuable insights for any spiritual life has to do with the proper expenditure of available energy. In "Night Vigil" and "Walking" we already saw that even though some energy is consumed in these activities, a new and different energy arises and accumulates. The notion of "zero" in relation to the use of energy may offer a useful perspective. Allow me to illustrate with an example that has been used before but that is also pertinent here.

In the center of the abbey where I live sits a courtyard surrounded by a hallway, the familiar cloister walk of Benedictine abbeys. That central space, more central than the church building or the dining hall, connects all the spaces where the monks' various activities take place: praying, working, meeting, studying, meditating, eating, and receiving guests. But nothing happens in that central space. It is a zone of zero energy.

How precious it is to have access to such a still space in the heart of life! Here we have the opportunity to return to inner calm, to regain our balance, simply by passing by that area in the center of the cloister walk. It is a chance to let off steam or to replenish, thanks to the silence and the absence of other energetic activity.

Moving from one activity to another, we are physically constrained to pass by that interior courtyard. The person who hastens too fast through the cloister walk or who starts talking loudly kills the hidden potential of the space. He or she remains the prisoner of whatever is excessively or superfluously rampant in his or her inner world and misses out on the great blessing of that zone with its zero energy.

The zero energy zone works equally at night. If you want to be assured of a good night's sleep, calm and carefree, after doing scholarly work or after intensive reading or a captivating TV program, then just walk the four sides of the cloister walk, thinking of nothing. Sleep will then arrive on its own. That at least is my experience.

What the abbey's architectural structure has accomplished over the ages and continues to provide to this day, we are called to realize in ourselves, with our available energy, with the shifts in our time and place. Nought is an abstraction, a limit, a border case. In actual reality there is always "something," and absolute "nothing" is not to be found anywhere. But if we wish to live a healthful life, then we must take time to do "nothing," to keep an open space for emptiness, for mindful breathing in complete silence, and to pull out of the spider web of thrilling and consuming relationships. Only then can we accomplish the inner rebalancing of our entire person in the great Zero.

Blessed are they who have a square inside themselves where "nothing" happens, a zone with zero energy, a nil that allows everything else to rotate freely. The zero is like the hub of every wheel. Without it we land in a rather harsh and rigid world, without even one wheel to propel us forward safely.

See also: Breathing, Emptiness, Keeping Silent, Meditation, Night Vigil, Sabbath, Sunday, Walking, *Wu Wei*

EPILOGUE

A Festival of Light

Spirituality has to do with applying oneself to practices that transform. But is that really sufficient?

What is sufficient? Life is sufficient. But life is also incomprehensible, it makes no sense. The superstructure of dogmatic systems that we have built up, sometimes over the course of many ages, is today best reduced to a minimum. "The Master is without ideas," as the Chinese Taoists remind us. The origin cannot be grasped, yet in our deepest being a source wells up and we discern an Act. The transformation that occurs when we apply ourselves to specific practices is one of steady interiorization of that original Act. As a result, an expanding sense of community is created. We become ever more "common," just as God is "common" in Ruusbroec's phrase.

In poverty and gratitude we breathe broadly and happily in solidarity with all that exists without pretense: a blade of grass, a sparrow, a child, a friend, a wisp of cloud in the sky, and a distant star. Death may knock at the door, it no longer scares us. A greater awe has already consumed that fear. To die is to give up one's spirit, to surrender one's breath completely—in a kiss, why not? The other side is a glowing Face, without features. Already now we walk in that light, and only what was light in our life will endure the crossing. The rest disappears into nothingness. The "light of Light" that visited us, and that ensured that we walked as "light in Light," shall lead us after death in what cannot be anything else but a festival of light.